THE
MOUNTAINEER

THE
MOUNTAINEER

AN EXPLORER'S GUIDE TO SUMMITING
THE MOUNTAIN OF THE LORD

CHRIS WEDIN

XULON PRESS

Xulon Press
2301 Lucien Way #415
Maitland, FL 32751
407.339.4217
www.xulonpress.com

Paperback ISBN-13: 978-1-6628-5323-4
Ebook ISBN-13: 978-1-6628-5324-1

To Andrew
A genuine mountaineer, 1969-2019

TABLE OF CONTENTS

Behold

Believe

Break

Belong

Burn

FOREWORD

I love this book so much! As I've pondered the words on the following pages, I've been struck by how the Lord always stretches and challenges us to climb ever higher in trusting and obeying Him. That remains a constant in how God works in our lives. What you're reading is not a "polished" view of mountaineering, but a real-life perspective of the journey.

I was very honored when Chris contacted me to ask if I would do a forward for this new book. Chris and I met for the first time in the Fall of 1991 at a missionary training center in Arkansas. Through the years, I've had the privilege to observe a life that is sold out to God and His call. The things that have impressed me the most about Chris are:

- **Character** – A life that doesn't just talk about the truth, but one who lives the truth.
- **Passion**–His genuine passion for God ignites passion in others. He's not satisfied with the status quo or with just getting by. As a real mountaineer, his intense desperation on the path to the summit is a way of life.
- **Heart**- Chris has a heart that pursues and hears from the Lord. He models a life that, in seeking and listening, has learned the gentle whisper of God in the very depth of his heart. This is a treasure far above anything that the world has to offer.

- **Perseverance**–With God's grace and enabling, the never-give-up attitude has marked his life.

For many years, I served as the assistant director of a large Christian missions ministry and a regional leader in our international mission. Along with teaching in many Discipleship Training Schools, that work gave me great joy and fulfillment. But God!! I chuckle when I write those words. He really knows how to stretch us. After 30 years in missions, God began to stir our hearts that change was coming. What do you do with that? It was as though we had reached a summit, yet the thing that burned the brightest in our hearts was the desire to always be in the center of God's will.

There was a higher summit that God was calling us to. My wife, Jan, and I spent an entire year walking our mission's property at 5:30 in the morning, crying out to God to show us His new calling. After a long 12 months, He spoke clearly to us. He called us to resign from everything we were doing and launch Streams of Mercy, a new ministry to orphans, widows, and the desperately poor and needy.

We knew it was God. At times the cost was more than we thought we could pay, but we stayed desperate for Him, and He stayed forever faithful! He walked with us up new and steeper mountain trails. He brought us to higher heights than we had ever been. We saw God's heart for orphans in new and powerful ways. We learned countless ways to become better mountaineers.

The greatest lessons are not learned the moment we finally reach the mountain's summit. With all of its grandeur and beauty, the summit is simply a capstone in the magnificent journey of getting there. Through his years of following the

Lord, Chris has developed a keen understanding of the keys to the journey of finding a deep relationship with the Lord. This book is where Chris reveals how the Lord LOVES to walk with us in our mountaineering journey. He doesn't wait until we get to the summit!

Grab your gear and your best spiritual climbing boots! Get ready to learn how to become a world-changing mountaineer. It will be an adventure that radically changes your life!

Wick Nease
Founder and Director,
Streams of Mercy

PREFACE

Here is a book about the exhilarating yet arduous adventure of seeking—and finding—God. It is a comparative analysis of the costs of comfort to the benefits of beauty. It will take you on a panoramic pathway with a view of the many struggles and difficulties faced when attempting to summit the mountain of the Lord. But if you consider what you read as you seek Him, you will find Him, and your soul will delight as with the richest of fare.

To illustrate these ideas, I will use many of my adventures—some of which were mild and others challenging. With these personal experiences, I will draw out some principles with which we can better understand what it means to climb the mountain of the Lord. Most of these stories have been directly copied from my personal journals, and in those instances, I've included the dates and locations of entry. I hope you can find meaning in all the angles from which I attempt to underline the Biblical values that lead to a deep devotion to God and others.

During this epoch journey, we will traverse Northwestern Pennsylvania along the Appalachian trail and search for a waterfall hidden in the Tennessee Smoky Mountains. We will camp in the wooded wonders of Kentucky's Red River Gorge and deer hunt in Missouri's Ozark mountains. As our adventure continues, we will snowboard in the Rockies of Colorado, backpack across the Wind River Range of southern Wyoming, and hike among the great Redwoods of Northern California.

Many of these expeditions take place in the mountains. But let it be clear that I am not a professional mountaineer, nor have I ever functioned at the level of exertion or risk that could compare with some of the world's greatest explorers. I do not mean to present myself as one of these elite, admirable adventurers, although I won't deny possessing a bit of healthy envy for their feats of ascent.

There are two important themes that must be understood to fully extract this text's value. The first is that of the mountain of the Lord, explained in Chapter One. The second is the temple of the Lord, introduced in Chapter One and further explored in Chapters 7-15. To assist you with these concepts, I've created a trail map that shows you the correlations between the Mountain, the section of the book you are reading, the chapter you are reading, and the aspects of the temple you are studying.

Insights on these two themes sprung forth from a bit of pondering over Hebrews 4:16 and a lot of subsequent digging. This verse says, "Therefore, let us approach the throne of grace with confidence that we may obtain mercy, and find grace to help us in our time of need." Have you ever wondered if this passage is literal? Can we actually approach His throne now? If so, what would that look like? Along with these thoughts, I embarked on a study of the throne of God and where it is that we must go to approach it.

Going before God's throne is another way of describing prayer. Prayer is a summation of such practices as "seeking the Lord," "fellowship with the Lord," "worshipping the Lord," and "intercession." All of these aspects of the pursuit of God are covered in the following pages, but not for the sake of providing you with information alone. The goal of these lessons is to understand the temple of the Lord and the mountain on which it sits, and then go to its summit and discover who is seated there.

You will discover specific conditions, or terms of engagement, in Scripture if you are to meet with God on His holy mountain. There are particular conditions made clear in Scripture for those who want to live a wildly fruitful and victorious life. These conditions will be met as we journey up the mountain, through the gate, into the court, past the altar, and into the very throne room of God.

Some of these conditions are prerequisites to even *trying* to seek God. For this reason, in chapters 2-6, I cover some critical and sometimes misunderstood topics like the authority and inerrancy of Scripture, discipline, obedience, works, and what it means to be "under the Law." Having a correct understanding of these crucial areas of doctrine is critical if we are to meet with God in such a way that profoundly changes us—and those around us.

Finally, it's essential to understand that Christianity is not, in its origins, an American or European religion, and its ideologies were not conveyed in modern terms but ancient ones. Christianity is intrinsically Hebrew, and much of what we learn from the Bible, we must learn through the grid of ancient Hebrew culture and paradigm. For this reason, it may be challenging for modern western readers to understand temples, altars, sacrifices, blood, and those things that went on in the earliest forms of worship.

Nevertheless, our God is the same today as He was then and can be found now as He was found then. Thankfully, He has left us a straightforward approach by which we can discover His fabulous presence and partnership in establishing His purposes in the world. I hope that you will embrace with all your heart the call of God to seek and find Him. Nowhere in life is there more upon which your soul can thrive than can be found in the presence of our Creator, who is enthroned upon the mountain.

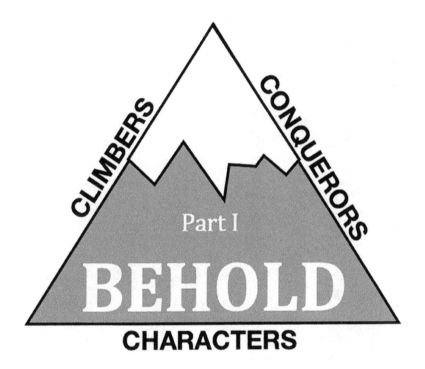

INTRODUCTION

In part one of *The Mountaineer*, we will survey the work ahead of us. Like adventurers just stepping into the foothills, we will behold the mountain from a distance and consider those who've gone before us. It is essential to understand that all summits *require* this survey, for the mountain has particular terms.

Consequently, we must see that all pursuits of God must be made on His terms. To understand His terms, we will answer questions such as, "What is the mountain of the Lord?" "What does it mean to summit or conquer?" "How can I condition myself to successfully summit every time I climb?" "What are the conditions I must meet?"

With these thoughts and questions in mind, I invite you to explore with me. Let's see how deeply a person can know the infinite God who made the mountains.

Literary Support

Once I saw the mountains angry,
And ranged in battle-front.
Against them stood a little man;
Aye he was not bigger than my finger.
I laughed, and spoke to one near me,
"Will he prevail?"
"Surely," replied this other;

"His grandfathers beat them many times."
Then did I see much virtue in grandfathers—
At least, for the little man
Who stood against the mountains.
—Stephen Crane, Once I saw the Mountains Angry

"Mountains delectable they now ascend,
Where shepherds be, which to them do commend
Alluring things, and things that cautious are
Pilgrims are steady kept by faith and fear."
—John Bunyan, The Pilgrim's Progress

"The mountains are calling, and I must go."
—John Muir

"I lift my eyes to the mountains—where does my help come
from?"
—Psalm 121:1

"I see the cloud, I step in
I want to see Your glory like Moses did
Flashes of light and rolls of thunder
But I'm not afraid, I'm not afraid"
— Kim Walker-Smith, Show Me Your Glory

Chapter I

CLIMBERS

The Mountain of the Lord

Imperative
We must seek and find the Lord, which is like
climbing and summiting a mountain.

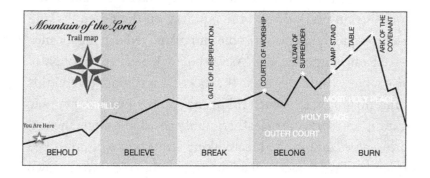

Snowboarding
January 2020
Boulder, Colorado

As I sipped my coffee, I watched the sunlight beaming ever more brightly against the masses of stone, which shot vertically from about midway up the mountainside. Like towering monoliths of Himalayan sea salt, a pink hue glowed from the stony surfaces with a warmth that could only be felt at this distance. The range seemed to grow smaller as it spread southward. Yet the mystery and adventure of exploration seemed to be beckoning me nearer.

Boxcar Coffee Roasters has a quaint, elegant atmosphere, an entrancing mountain view, and a good cup. But I took my last sip, put my Bible in my backpack, and got in the car.

Canyon boulevard cuts through the very hopping town of Boulder and up into the mountains. The walls of the Flatirons are angled sharply downward until they converge with the paved passageway. A river full of boulders is owed several hundred feet of respect for its millennia of work, carving the crooked canyon, by which I scaled upward toward Eldora Mountain.

Along the scenic route, high-altitude lakes lay against the foothills on one side and the highway on the other, making picturesque moments for some and distracted driving for me.

I hadn't forgotten how to snowboard. It had been a couple of years, but I could still make the moves. I was more careful this time; no jumps, no switch riding, no stunts—just the rhythmic cutting and spraying of feathery, fluffy powder. Among the towering pines and in the breathtaking atmosphere of unbridled splendor, I went back and forth through the cold thin air down the glowing slippery slopes.

People huddled at the very top of the mountain for food, beverages, and a moment to warm up, but inspiration was the most craved item on the menu. Gazers gathered on the deck, peering out over the distant ranges, which stretched forth in majestic white on a backdrop of blue. Sparkling snowcaps had ruffled coat tails decorated with innumerable conifers. Pale, puffy clouds converged above their silver-crowned peaks and mimicked a higher range. The sheer breadth of the sight drew longing out of my heart, and a hush of stillness descended deep into the valleys of my being. Nostalgia for eternity simmered in my soul, a distant belonging I had yet to fully grasp.

The Mountain of the Lord

It seems to me that mountains are supposed to be climbed. Particularly for the purpose of extracting those revitalizing moments of inspiration that can scarcely be absorbed elsewhere. Mountains can be observed from a distance and admired and will even strike awe in the beholder. But the mystery that lies upon them remains aloof; their fury and majesty can't be deeply known unless they are entered and ascended.

Mentioned more than 600 times throughout the Bible, mountains are profoundly important to the events, efforts, and emotions that link people with their Creator. Noah parked his ark on Ararat, Abraham laid his posterity on the altar at Moriah, Moses met with Fire on Sinai, Elijah whipped the prophets of Baal on Carmel, the City of David was built on Zion, and Jesus prayed until He sweated blood on Olivet.

Moses gave us some of the clearest understanding of the spiritual purpose of mountains. He was an avid explorer, among the original mountaineers, summiting Sinai. He took his leaders with him on one occasion, and they were breath taken by something far more significant than distant, snowcapped ranges. "They saw the God of Israel; and under His feet there appeared to be a pavement of sapphire, clear as the sky itself" (Exodus 24:10). Moses climbed up a little further at God's invitation (see Exodus 24:12), and there it was that God revealed Himself in what could only be described as a cloud of His glory, which looked like a "consuming fire" (Exodus 24:17).

King David was a first-class climber and offered a clear connection between scaling mountains and seeking the Lord. In Psalm 24:3, the king asked, "Who may ascend into the hill of the Lord? And who may stand in His holy place?" He also said, "Why do you look with envy, O mountains with many peaks, at the mountain which God has desired for His abode?" (Psalm 68:16). But, as literal as it was in David's time, could these holy ascensions be taken figuratively now? Must we be mountaineers to meet with our Maker? Must we be climbers to come near to our Creator?

"Going up" has had its spiritual implications for thousands of years, underscoring the innate human inclination toward discovery upon greater heights. Ezekiel prophesied,

> "For on My holy mountain, on the high mountain of Israel," declares the Lord God, "there the whole house of Israel, all of them, will serve Me in the land; there I will accept them and there I will seek your contributions and the choicest of your gifts, with all your holy things." (Ezekiel 20:40)

Jesus was a climber. He gravitated toward mountains, too. It says that "He went up on the mountainside by Himself to pray" (Matthew 14:23). On one occasion, He took some of His leaders with Him too, and they met Moses and Elijah on a mountain:

> Six days later, Jesus took with Him Peter and James and John his brother, and led them up on a high mountain by themselves. And He was transfigured before them; and His face shone like the sun, and His garments became as white as light. (Matthew 17:1-3)

Isaiah was also a climber. He knew that in the end times all people would become mountaineers if they wanted to know the Lord:

> Now it will come about that in the last days the mountain of the house of the Lord will be established as the chief of the mountains, and will be raised above the hills; and all the nations will stream to it. And many peoples will come and say, "Come let us go up to the mountain of the Lord, to the house of the God of Jacob; That He may teach us concerning His ways and that we may walk in His paths." (Isaiah 2:2-3)

Where must we go to meet with Christ, where His illuminated, awe-inspiring nature would bring calm in a tumultuous world? Where is the place in which His presence evokes that profound sense of belonging, approval, and purpose? Where is that place where His voice is heard, His healing is conferred, and His glory is all but visible? If the purpose of our existence is to know Him, for such is eternal life (see John 17:3), and if knowing Him is not entirely polarized to those academic endeavors of textual study and contemplation, but broadened into a spiritual knowledge impossible to confine with human words; then upon which hilltop is such learning facilitated?

Mountains, figuratively and literally, require effort to ascend. Navigating upward toward God will require much of the seeker but will be a worthy expedition. The pursuit of the place of God's presence is as parallel to scaling a mountain as any figurative and literal concepts can be. The reality is that nothing is more life-changing and awe-inspiring than meeting with God where He is enthroned. Incredible discovery and beauty lie ahead in this endeavor, though it presents a legitimate challenge, particularly if we are to move beyond deck-top, coffee sipping, armchair praying—with a mountain view.

Often, seeking the Lord is quite a challenge! In the pages of this book, we will explore the biblical connection between ascending literal mountains and seeking the Lord. You don't actually have to climb any of Earth's mountains to be a mountaineer by this book's description, but you will have to ascend the mountain of the Lord with all your heart—and find Him there.

For now, though, think about what comes right before you go away to seek the Lord. What challenges are there? Sometimes getting out of bed, being wholehearted, or pushing through distractions can deter us. But also think about the beauty and discovery that lie ahead: Seeking and finding God, the glory of God revealed in your prayer closet, new liberties, and freedom in your heart, the fire of God burning within you.

Our intention is not to meander in the foothills but to summit. What I mean by summit is that each time you seek the Lord, you would seek Him with all your heart, **and find Him** (See Jeremiah 29:13). When you "find the Lord," you will know it. It will be one of those times when you feel as if you are looking out over the world below from the invigorating vista of a lofty precipice.

God is a mentor. He wishes to meet with His apprentices individually for customized counsel and tailored transformation. The pursuit of God always begins at the individual level, spilling into the public. God is calling His people away to be fascinated with Him, His beauty, and His purposes. Yet He does not avail Himself to casual interest. On the contrary, the discovery of God is reserved for those who would seek Him with all matter of concentration and diligence.

Understand this: Jesus is never disinterested in you, but He is too *valuable* to be discovered by casual interest. Stare no more at the mountains from safe distances; it's time to get in, on, and up His holy mountain!

Enthroned in a Tent

Moses was a stellar outdoorsman with specialties in desert trekking and quail hunting. But he often went camping to meet with God. He climbed up the hill, pitched a tent, and got busy seeking the Lord. He eventually realized that God wanted there to be such a place where all Israel could meet with Him face to face as a man meets with his friend, so he built a bigger tent.

The original tent revivalist, Moses built something that would come to be known as the Tent of Meeting. This was a place specifically designated for prayer, worship, and listening to God; a place where he, Joshua, and others would experience "The Presence of the Lord" or *panim* in Hebrew (See Strong's 6440). Panim means "face" or "face to face," the implications being closeness, intimate conversation, friendship, listening, and communion with someone you care for deeply.

Winkie Pratney distinguishes being near to God in this way from seeing him fully, and states this:

> The expression speaking "face to face as a man talks
> with his friend" (Exod. 33:11) carries the image of
> frankness and intimacy and does not refer to any
> unveiled revelation of God (cf. 1 Tim. 6:16).

The tent of the Lord, or the Mosaic Tabernacle, would become a model for how men could seek and find the Lord. It would be a replica of the true Tabernacle in Heaven (see Hebrews 8:5), a place where God would annex his glorious throne (see Jeremiah 17:12) and share the wonder of His immense goodness with humanity; instructing, teaching, and commanding them in the place of his presence (see Exodus 25:22). The Lord said, "Let them construct a sanctuary for Me, that I may dwell among them. According to all that I am going to show you , as the pattern of the tabernacle and the pattern of all its furniture, just so you shall construct it." (Exodus 25:8-9). So Moses built it, and the Glory of the Lord came to rest between the wings of the cherubim above the Ark of the Covenant.

A.W. Tozer, in his classic, *The Pursuit of God*, stated:

> The interior journey of the soul from the wilds of sin into the enjoyed Presence of God is beautifully illustrated in the Old Testament tabernacle...The flame of the presence was the beating heart of the Levitical order. Without it all the appointments of the tabernacle were characters of some unknown language; they had no meaning for Israel or for us. The greatest fact of the tabernacle was that Jehovah was there; a Presence was waiting within the veil. Similarly the Presence of God is the central fact of Christianity. At the heart of the Christian message is God Himself waiting for His redeemed children to push in to conscious awareness of His Presence.

David drafted permanence to Moses' mobile design, and Solomon built it—on top of a hill. This, too, though a splendorous work of architecture, would be a replica of something unimaginably more glorious in Heaven. Nevertheless, the glory of the Lord filled the temple, and the people were in awe (see 2 Chronicles 7:1-3). God wanted the people to know that there was a place where He would be revealed to them.

Ezekiel's vision of this temple brought him to his knees, and God said, "Son of man, this is the place of My throne and the place of the soles of My feet, where I will dwell among the sons of Israel forever." (Ezekiel 43:7). Isaiah saw our king enthroned in His heavenly glory in the true tabernacle, and he cried out, "Woe is me, for I am ruined!" (Isaiah 6:5). A vision transported John into the same glorious court of the Throne of Elohim. His descriptions of this majestic place are betrayed by the limits of language and nevertheless strike awe and wonder in their readers (Revelation 4:2-11).

A cloud descended upon Moses' tent while he met with the Living God. Fire fell from Heaven and consumed the offering when Solomon prayed to dedicate the temple to the Lord. The Glory of the Lord filled the temple in Ezekiel's vision. Smoke filled the temple courts, and the place shook violently in Isaiah's vision. Flashes of lightning and peals of thunder came from the rainbow-encircled throne, which John beheld.

Seated on the throne was a Consuming Fire, the Living God, high and exalted above every power, ruler, and authority. It's no wonder these men of such similar visions fell to their knees and cried out for mercy. Yet, it begs the question, what is meant by the exhortation to approach *this* throne with confidence (Hebrews 4:16)?

Though seemingly a place of sheer terror, how is it that a Hebrew king would desire to be there and nowhere else? If such fright gripped the holy men who beheld this place of uncontested exaltedness, who would want to ever go there, especially in boldness, speaking with confidence? He says:

> One thing I have asked from the Lord, that I shall seek: that I may dwell in the house of the Lord all the days of my life, to behold the beauty of the Lord and to meditate in His temple. (Psalm 27:4)

What had the king experienced that gave him such an exclusive, single-pointed ambition to navigate only to this place? He says:

> How lovely are Your dwelling places, O Lord of hosts! My soul longed and even yearned for the courts of the Lord; my heart and flesh sing for joy to the living God. For a day in Your courts is better than a thousand outside. I would rather stand at the threshold of the house of my God than dwell in the tents of wickedness. (Psalm 84:1-2, 10)

This temple was on a mountain, the significance of which can not be overstated. It was *this* mountain they were to ascend and *this* temple they were to enter to discover the truest representation of beauty the eyes of humanity could possibly behold. It is this beauty that captivated the king and drew young Joshua to lay in the tent all day. This beauty caused joy and hope to well up in the prophets, and it is for access to this beauty that Christ came and suffered on our behalf.

In all the instructions and constructions, visions and visits, to both the replicas and the real, this temple has several prominent characteristics from which we must draw a particular meaning or symbolism. This is especially important if we are to understand what the Lord intended by so specifically guiding its design. Nothing He did in designing the temple is without purpose, and His primary goal is for His people to seek and find Him.

Some of these temple features are renamed in this book to reveal their purpose in our pursuit of God. They are The Gate of Desperation, The Court of Worship, The Altar of Surrender, The Golden Lamp Stand, The Table of His Presence, The Veil of His Body, The Altar of Prayer, and The Ark of the Covenant. When we ascend the hill of the Lord, we will encounter each of these facets of His temple.

If we are to move forward in the expedition, we must climb the mountain of the Lord and pitch our tent in pursuit of Him whose presence is to be found there. We must understand how and why we are advised to go confidently and boldly before the throne of Grace. In understanding the meaning of these elements of the temple and the throne room in Heaven, we can begin to understand how to approach God in the way He prescribed.

But let it be clear that mountain climbing is not for the ill-prepared or weak of heart. If you will summit the Mountain of the Lord, you must be determined, prepared, and fully committed. If it is to be a picture of "seeking the Lord," it must be understood that it is those who seek Him with "all their hearts" who find Him. It is upon those who earnestly seek Him that God bestows His reward. For this reason, the rest of this section is dedicated to helping you take on the right mindset about mountaineering.

Conclusion and Contemplation

Behold the Temple of the Lord and the Holy Mountain upon which it sits. Will you climb?

Prayer of Commitment

Father, I am eager to ascend Your holy hill! I want to find You and meet with You face to face as Moses did. I am looking up to the mountains, from where my help comes, and I am ready to climb. Help me to seek You in the way that You have prescribed. Amen.

Discussion Questions

1. Describe the correlation between seeking God and climbing up a mountain.
2. Could meeting with God be as breathtaking and profound as summiting a mountain? What should we expect to experience when we seek and find God?
3. Have you ever sought God casually? Explain. Have you ever exerted yourself to seek Him? Explain. Describe the difference between these two approaches to seeking God.
4. What does it mean to be a climber, in a spiritual sense?
5. What does the Hebrew word *panim* mean? Why is it important in the context of seeking the Lord? Where could Moses and the Israelites expect to experience *panim*?
6. Why did God want Moses to make a tabernacle? What were God's intentions for it?
7. What is the relationship between the Hebrew Temple where God was enthroned between the cherubim and what we could expect to see in Heaven?
8. Discuss Isaiah 2:2-3. Why do you think the "last days" temple in Isaiah's vision was located on top of the "highest of mountains?" Are we in these days now? Should we wait to "go up to the mountain of the Lord" until we know it is the last days, or should we start now?

9. If seeking God is like climbing a mountain, do you believe you have what it takes to *summit*? What do you think it means to *summit* in this context?

Chapter II

CONQUERORS
The Fruit and the Victory

Imperative
We must be more than conquerors,
summiting on behalf of others.

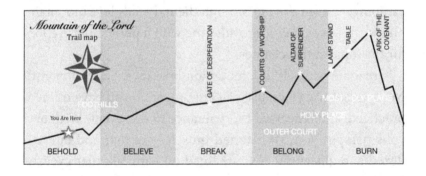

Mountain Bikes
April 2020
Barbourville, West Virginia

R osy cotton clouds lay in the valleys of the Eastern Kentucky
mountains. We traveled quietly down the freeway under a
star-speckled violet sky. Our journey east began in the black of
early morning, but as the day began to break upon the dawn, it
brought forth luminous folds of pink, orange, red, and purple.

The picturesque morning view enlivened deep sentiments in my soul. Soon, the wispy clouds, golden and glowing, stretched beyond the horizon, and a fingernail moon crept away into the increasingly blue canopy.

Asher and I were driving to West Virginia to buy a mountain bike. Later that day, we crunched over sticks and gravel, splashed across creeks, and burned up our legs, climbing to the tops of the mountainous trails. The "new-to-me" bike passed its first trail test and became the latest addition to the Wedin bike collection.

I got my first mountain bike in 1991 and competed in my first mountain bike race in 1996. I love everything that has to do with mountains and forests, whether hiking, snowboarding, camping, or even *driving* through them. I *really* love mountain biking, however, and it provides me with a perfect illustration for the topic of this chapter.

Imagine yourself in a mountain bike race. Scary thought? No. It is not scary because you are prepared: you have trained, practiced, and rehearsed every nuance of this event. With nervous perspiration, your toned muscles are taut and curved, flexed and glistening. You are lined up with 50 other cyclists looking out across a ½ mile of open meadow. A trailhead is at the other end of the grassy field, where the cluster will narrow into a single file scurry for the lead position.

What do you want out of the experience? Do you only wish not to crash or be injured? You certainly *don't* want to crash or be injured, but it wouldn't be enough to simply survive the race without a scratch. Do you want to be in last placc? Who wants to come in last in a race?

Most people can recall something in which they competed. Additionally, most people can remember when their team performed poorly or lost. For most people, this gives off a feeling of disappointment—even anger—right? It is innate to *want* to do well, win, or *conquer*. And we love it when we do just that.

Personal And Public

The Word of God says, "we are more than conquerors through Him that loved us" (Romans 8:37, KJV). But many of us feel as if we are barely survivors. It would be nice not to crash, but we do. It would be nice not to be *injured*, but we are. *Conqueror?* We often settle for *survivor*. Sometimes we feel like we can barely keep our heads above water. Yet we aren't called survivors. We aren't even called conquerors. We are called *MORE* than conquerors in Christ Jesus.

The Apostle describes in Romans 7:15-25 his struggle with sin and doing the very things he intends *not* to do. You've heard the phrase "conquering sin" or personal victory over temptation, trials, suffering, and the like—This could get you classified as a conqueror if you classify Christian maturity (which we don't).

To understand this identity given to us in Scripture, what does it mean to be *more* than conquerors? Try to think of the Christian life in two terms: personal victory and public victory. Where, as aforementioned, *personal victory* is your steadfast obedience and faithfulness in the face of trials, tribulations, and temptation, *public victory* would be your impact as you help others find that same depth in devotion.

For the summiting mountaineer, this means that we not only go all the way up the mountain of the Lord for our own sake, but we also go up for the sake of others. Only in this mindset can a person become *more* than a conqueror. You are seeking to find a place of God's presence so powerful that it grants you the power to walk victoriously and empowers you to help others do the same. That is a summit.

New Shoes

For our first foreign mission assignment as a married couple, Anne Marie and I went to a rural, mountainous area of Honduras. Our friends Charlie Hydes and Aaron G joined us, and we ventured up into the mountains led by our trusted missionary friend, Jim Taylor.

We loaded mules with supplies from the furthest point to which we could drive our vehicle and set off into the hills. The red, sandy clay beneath the wilderness carpet of vegetation shown forth from the many journeys of indigenous peoples and their livestock. This clay, powdery from a lack of rain, formed a broad pathway by which we graduated upward into the unknown territory.

Having carried us through the foothills, the trail narrowed and wound up sheer hillsides—along arid, dusty ridges. With sun-cooked faces and necks, we all wished we had Jim's broad, white cowboy hat. We plunged down stair-stepped rocks and roots into deep, shady valleys.

In one of these valleys, we walked for several hours through a very humid rainforest and took pictures of birds of paradise growing in the wild, watery biome. Strange-looking salamanders and tiny water creatures navigated the forest floor's trickling creeks. Loud bird calls and frog croaks rang rhythmically over us and sometimes made us duck our heads flinchingly.

Again we climbed upward, and it seemed like we would never reach the top. Finally, the foliage broke into an open mountain top where a family of coffee growers greeted us. They invited us into their one-room, thatched roof, dirt floor house and made us a cup of their homegrown coffee. The man pounded the coffee beans, breaking them into tiny pieces, and poured hot water through a cloth over the fresh grinds.

He then ran out into his field and cut down a long sugar cane stalk. Standing in each cup as a stir stick, the sugar cane was a delightful innovation. The black, sweet coffee swirled with the flavor of nuts, cherries, and floral essence. It was a pure expression of the kindness and hospitality of our hosts. After sipping away our delicious pour-overs, we prayed over the tender-hearted couple and then went up to the village.

That night we held a meeting and shared the gospel, then we slept on the benches in the church building. Invisible insects nipped at us through the night, and we worked to stay atop our foot-wide beds.

In the morning, children swarmed with giggles and games. Jim opened a large sack and handed each of us a pair of shoes; we were to find some feet that fit in them. Children took turns sitting on Anne Marie's lap as she slipped onto their feet the first pair they had ever worn.

Looks of bewilderment and delight lingered on the faces of the children as they took their first steps in their new shoes. Their mouths hung open. Looking down at their feet to see what they looked like, then up at us, they grinned with gratitude— still staring in delight. Like a slow-motion recess, new shoes traversed the churchyard toward proud parents and then back to us to deliver a teary-eyed "gracias."

We conducted a Bible study with the families that were gathered there. They had a lot of questions about God and faith, and we answered each of them. When we had everything together to leave and started down the trail, a man ran up to us and cried out, "I want to become a Christian!" So we stopped and spoke to him for a while, and then he prayed to receive Christ.

On the hike back down toward civilization, I pondered the comparison between equipping souls with truth and feet with shoes. Shoes protect the feet, adorn them with beauty, and make longer journeys possible. What can be given to someone through our prayers? Protection, growing inward beauty, and perseverance are meaningful blessings. We can bring these forth upon those we love and serve as we come before the Lord on their behalf. This is what it means to be "more than conquerors." For whom will you go up the mountain of the Lord?

Inward and Outward

Another way to look at what it means to be "more than conquerors," is in terms of fruit-bearing. You can think of this as "inward fruit," or fruit that produces a change in your own heart. The Apostle Paul wrote in his illustrious letter to the Galatians that we should have within us the "fruit of the Spirit" (Galatians 5:22-23). This is what *personal victory* looks like and how it comes about, that is, through the Holy Spirit.

So important was this inward fruit to the Apostle that he often prayed for the church in these terms:

> And this I pray, that your love may abound still more and more in real knowledge and all discernment, so that you may approve the things that are excellent, in order to be sincere and blameless until the day of Christ; having been filled with the fruit

of righteousness which comes through Jesus Christ, to the glory and praise of God. (Philippians 1:9-11)

Paul reaffirms that Jesus Christ is the source of inward fruit to the Philippians. Additionally, he underscores that love is to be the motive behind such abounding and fruitful growth. Love must be at the root of all our inward and outward development; otherwise, we fail.

To the church of the Colossians, Paul elaborates even more on the connection between living a fruitful life and being filled with wisdom, knowledge, and understanding:

> For this reason also since the day we heard of it, we have not ceased to pray for you and to ask that you may be filled with the knowledge of His will in all spiritual wisdom and understanding, so that you will walk in a manner worthy of the Lord, to please Him in all respects, bearing fruit in every good work and increasing in the knowledge of God; strengthened with all power, according to His glorious might, for the attaining of all steadfastness and patience; joyously giving thanks to the Father, who has qualified us to share in the inheritance of the saints in light. (Colossians 1:9-12)

With our own fruit tree bearing, we move on to "outward fruit," or fruit of the change in other peoples' hearts. Jesus commands us to bear this fruit. He said, "My Father is glorified by this, that you bear much fruit, and so prove to be My disciples" (John 15:8). He said we would be fruitful if His word abides in us and we abide in Him, but what does that look like in a person?

Rees Howells was more than a conqueror. He was an early 20th century Welsh minister whose ministry was characterized by his persistent and prevailing intercessory prayer and the revivals that seemed to follow him everywhere. If Rees was praying for something, it would happen—whether the healing of a sick person or the conversion of the lowliest sinner in the town. Such was his victory in prayer that many sought his prayers for their own personal needs.

But Howells was as much focused on preserving his integrity before the Lord as he was anything else. He once came under intense conviction for mishandling a single penny! Holiness and inward fruitfulness were one and the same for this man of faith. Perhaps one of the most outstanding examples of his outward victories is this excerpt from Howell's journal, as presented in Norman Grubb's biography entitled *Rees Howells, Intercessor*:

> The Sunday was October 10—my birthday—and as I preached in the morning, you could feel the Spirit coming on the congregation. In the evening, down He came. I shall never forget it.
>
> He came upon a young girl, Kufase by name, who had fasted for three days under conviction that she was not ready for the Lord's coming. As she prayed, she broke down crying; within five minutes the whole congregation were on their knees crying to God. Like lightning and thunder the power came down. I had never seen this, even in the Welsh revival. I had only heard about it with Finney and

others. Heaven had opened, and there was no room to contain the blessing.

I lost myself in the Spirit and prayed as much as they did. All I could say was, "He has come!" We went on until late in the night; we couldn't stop the meeting. What he told me before I went to Africa was actually taking place, and that within six weeks. You can never describe those meetings when the Holy Spirit comes down. I shall never forget the sound in the district that night—praying in every kraal, or native village community.

The next day He came again, and people were on their knees till six o'clock in the evening. This went on for six days and people began to confess their sins and come free as the Holy Spirit brought them through. They had forgiveness of sins, and met the Savior as only the Holy Spirit can reveal Him. Everyone who came near would go under the power of the Spirit. People stood up to give their testimonies, and it was nothing to see twenty-five on their feet at the same time.

At the end of the week nearly all were through. We had two revival meetings every day for fifteen months without a single break, and meetings all day on Fridays. Hundreds were converted—but we were looking for more—for the ten thousand, upon whom He had told us we had a claim.

Who doesn't want to have an impact like this? Many thought these stories only happened in the New Testament era, but God still desires to move in these ways, and He will when we focus on Him and His priorities. In the mountains, at the summit, lies that which brings forth such fruitfulness. Consider the victories ahead of you, behold the beauty of God's work through you in others, and ponder the effects of the majesty of God lived out in your daily life.

The Personal and Inward Priority

When ambition exceeds ability, a crash is imminent. During my first mountain bike race, I nosedived over a jagged, rocky hillside without using my brakes to stay in the lead. Although I survived that hill (barely), I was going way too fast. When down onto the smoother trail, I hit a jump, flew off into the trees, and crashed.

Similarly, personal victory, or inward fruit, should be commensurate in its growth alongside public victory or outward fruit. There is danger in projecting an outward fruitfulness while experiencing inward decay. We are called to both inward and outward fruitfulness. But here is a warning: Don't succumb to the pressures of men to perform for their praise by producing polished, plastic fruit. It won't last, and neither will you. You will crash. All Spirit-born, inward fruit produces the selfless motives inherent in producing lasting, outward fruit.

In the context of scaling mountains, it must be repeated that we are not simply trying to be conquerors. We would only climb the mountain for *our* benefit if we were. But the pursuit of God is always double in purpose: to change you so that you can help change others. Seeking God has in its fundamental values both the purpose of coming to know God and making Him known, of loving God and loving others.

The summit belongs to those who reach it on behalf of others. It belongs to those who've put to death their ambitions, their own need for success, and their love for achievement. The path to the summit is one of death to all lines of self-interest; it is a path to the graveyard of *your* vision for yourself.

In what is perhaps one of the most moving and powerful missionary stories of the contemporary church, Roland and Heidi Baker describe the tremendous difficulty they faced in their efforts to win Mozambique. Yet they have rescued hundreds of helpless children, fed thousands of starving people, and presented the gospel in the power of the Holy Spirit—healing the sick, casting out demons, and even raising the dead! In their book, *Always Enough*, Roland identifies this passage in Romans 8 as the driving force behind their perseverance and wildly fruitful ministry:

> We are asked how we can continue doing such tiring work. How do we put up with such poverty and stressful conditions? How can we deal with so many people and needs? How long can we do this? But we have nothing to gain by slowing down and trying to hold on to our lives. We give ourselves as a fragrant offering of love to Jesus, and in return, He gives us His supernatural life. We have to stand up and face some of the poorest people on earth, who suffer, starve, and die as most of us cannot imagine. Yet we confidently preach: "Who shall separate us from the love of Christ? Shall trouble or hardship or persecution or famine or nakedness or danger

or sword? As it is written, 'For your sake we face death all day long; we are considered as sheep to be slaughtered.' No, in all these things we are more than conquerors through him who loved us. For I am convinced that neither death nor life, neither the present nor the future, nor any powers, neither height nor depth, nor anything else in all creation, will be able to separate us from the love of God that is in Christ Jesus our Lord.'" (Romans 8:35-39)

Conquering the kingdom of darkness is not enough for one who would be more than a conqueror; such a person must also build the kingdom of God where evil once reigned. Therefore, to be *more* than conquerors, we must conquer our own challenges *and* go before the Lord to find the power, anointing, direction, and precision in our influence in the lives of others. This was evident in Reese Howell's life, it is evident right now in the Bakers' lives, and it can be evident in yours. On their way up the mountain, they found the strength to overcome their weaknesses, mature in the character of Christ, and become faithful servants of God. But they also found the power to rob hell and advance the gospel.

Are you willing to climb a mountain on behalf of others? This is precisely how Jesus, The Apostles, and the Early Church believers became so wildly fruitful, both inwardly and outwardly. These men went into areas of immense darkness and shined the light, winning the lost, healing the sick, casting out demons, and planting churches. Their focus? Others.

But, what did they do to be able to do these things amid persecution, hardship, and political oppression? Where did they summon the power to change inwardly and produce change outwardly? How were they able to scale the mountain of God and become more than conquerors? These are the questions we will answer in the following pages.

Conclusion and Contemplation

Behold the calling of the Lord to a life centered on others. Will you climb on behalf of others?

Prayer of Commitment

Father in Heaven, I want to become "More than a Conqueror." I want to be victorious personally and publicly. Lord, I want to bear fruit inwardly and outwardly for Your glory and show the world that I am Your disciple. I choose right now to make my life about loving and serving others. For whom would you have me come up your holy mountain? Please help me today to take the path to become more than a conqueror. Amen.

Discussion Questions

1. Why do people want to win? Have you ever celebrated your defeat? How badly do you want to win the "race marked out for you"?
2. What is the difference between surviving and conquering in the Christian life? What is the difference between being a conqueror and being more than a conqueror?
3. What are two types of spiritual fruit? What are the two types of victory? Why should one be a prerequisite to the other?

4. Describe your most prominent inward fruit of the Holy Spirit? Describe a time when you know that you bore "outward fruit" for the Holy Spirit. How did that feel?

5. Are we summiting the mountain of the Lord for our own benefit? How important is it that we make our pursuit of God about others as well as ourselves? How does that tie in to being *more* than a conqueror?

Chapter III

CHARACTERS
The Conditions of Success

Imperative
*We must have character for the sake of
our conscience and our credibility.*

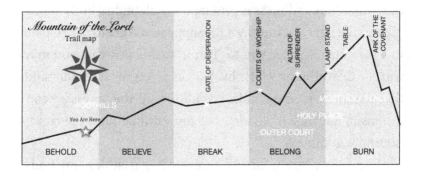

Mountain of the Lord
Trail map

GATE OF DESPERATION

COURTS OF WORSHIP

ALTAR OF SURRENDER

LAMP STAND

TABLE

ARK OF THE COVENANT

FOOTHILLS
You Are Here

MOST HOLY PLACE
HOLY PLACE
OUTER COURT

| BEHOLD | BELIEVE | BREAK | BELONG | BURN |

Spiritual Conditioning

When the pistol is fired into the air, hundreds of swim-capped competitors scramble across the sand and into the water. Soon, flailing arms and paddling feet go in and out, up and down, splashing and sometimes crashing onto the heads of other swimmers. A kick to the face or a smack on the thigh is expected and is just part of the battle in the triathlon swim. But

I'll take this treatment any day before being under-conditioned. If you're in this race, you better be prepared!

Most athletes can recall when they locked up with a cramp or pulled a muscle. These injuries don't usually happen because someone accidentally slapped you or kicked you. They happen because you weren't prepared. You didn't realize the importance of meeting the conditions your body would require if you were to complete the physical challenge ahead of you with any semblance of victory—and without injury.

Godliness is a summary term for the fruit of the Spirit: love, joy, peace, patience, kindness, goodness, faithfulness, gentleness, and self-control. Godliness is to imitate God's nature. The Apostle Paul tells his protégé, Timothy, that physical fitness has little value, but godliness is profitable for all things, both in this life and the next (1 Timothy 4:8). Suppose you are to participate in a race that requires you to "run in such a way that you may win" (1 Corinthians 9:24). In that case, you must understand that all serious racing requires conditioning, the necessary conditions in advance of victory. For the spiritual race, the conditioning is godliness.

Every time I train for and compete in a triathlon, my body indicates something for which I could have been better prepared. I remember learning about getting plenty of hydration in the days preceding the race. I've raced dehydrated, but I had to walk most of it. I remember learning about mineral supplements like salt, magnesium, and potassium. I've run while depleted and locked up or injured muscles. I remember learning about having a slow-build training plan and gradual progress long before the race in order to build proper muscle strength and endurance. I've crammed race prep into three weeks and been hunched over-exhausted, promising myself to never do this again. And then I did it again. And again.

Godliness

Every intentional success is built on specific conditions. If those conditions are not met, success is improbable, or it may be entirely accidental. Even something as simple as turning a radio on and hearing music or someone's voice has conditions. Much of what we are called to do and many of the promises of God are hinged on conditions.

On this thought, we must draw a distinction of enormous consequence between godliness (character) and righteousness by faith (justification). We cannot examine the conditions placed upon godliness if we do not understand this distinction.

When you draw near to the Lord and relish in the exquisiteness of His presence—offering worship, praise, and all your love—He will draw near to you. As a result, you will likely spend the remainder of your day with a welling up in your soul for all that which is the fruit of the Holy Spirit. This may better be called the "first-fruit" of the Holy Spirit because it is not until you have persevered through the fire of trials and tribulations, temptations, and tests that *His* fruit becomes *your* character (See Romans 5:4). This character is what is meant in the Scriptures by godliness.

Though an *unbelieving* man may have great character, he may not enter Heaven unless he is justified by faith. He may be humble, generous, patient, and compassionate, but he will not find eternal life on his own merit. Character without justification will not gain a person acceptance in Heaven. It is essential to understand, however, that neither will justification without character gain a person acceptance on earth. For the gospel to mean anything to an unbelieving world—that we can tread into Heaven on another Person's merit (that of Christ's)—they must see that we can tread through the earth on our own. For this reason, we must have both righteousness by faith and godliness by the practical application of that faith.

Many professing Christians believe that godliness is the same as righteousness given by faith. We are given righteousness before God on the basis of faith. This is not related to character; it is related to faith. This righteousness is an act of God's mercy and is for all who believe. It is a righteousness that is imputed or assigned by God to those who have faith that the work of Christ is sufficient for the forgiveness of sins. This righteousness gives people *access* to a relationship with God and, ultimately, Heaven.

You may come to God with nothing except failure, and if you have faith in Christ, you will be accepted by Him, welcomed into his presence, and forgiven of sin. The best example is the thief who hung on a cross beside Jesus. He confessed with his mouth and believed in his heart: "Jesus, remember me when You come in Your kingdom!" (Luke 23:42) But this is not godliness, and getting to Heaven is not the only goal of the believer. By faith, before God, I am as righteous as Jesus. In fact, I am clothed in His righteousness and given a place in Heaven by this standard alone (see Philippians 3:9). But that does not mean that I have lived or will live a godly life.

In his treatment of the difference between justification and personal holiness, J.C. Ryle states,

> He who supposes that Jesus Christ only lived and
> died and rose again in order to provide justification

and forgiveness of sins for his people, has yet much to learn. Whether he knows it or not, he is dishonoring our blessed Lord, and making Him only half a Savior. The Lord Jesus has undertaken everything that His people's souls require; not only to deliver them from the guilt of their sins by His atoning death, but from the dominion of their sins by placing in their hearts the Holy Spirit, not only to justify them, but also to sanctify them. He is, thus, not only their "righteousness," but their "sanctification" (1 Cor. 1:30).

We live in a world where we understand that there are conditions for nearly everything we do. Godliness is a condition placed upon us if we are to effectively know God, bear lasting fruit, and be zealous for doing good (see Titus 2:11-14). But due to the confusion mentioned above, a belief has crept into the hearts of many Christians that godliness will occur by default. Some people think that they will automatically become a godly person because they said yes to Jesus once. This is simply not true. Those who walk as Jesus did are those who truly know Him. The fruit of the Spirit is evident in those who abide in Jesus, who are filled with the Spirit of Jesus, and who have taken up their cross to follow Jesus.

It's important to remember that we have to move past thinking of only ourselves as we approach God. We must become fully victorious, both inwardly and outwardly, conquering our own challenges and conquering darkness that imprisons others. We must "forcefully advance" the Kingdom of Heaven (see Matthew 11:12) and build life where there once was only death. The characters of the kingdom have the character of the King. We are those characters if we belong to the kingdom of God.

The opposite of godliness is worldliness. Worldliness is the careless embrace of sin in a swath of disregard for the truth of God's word. Sin hardens hearts, and the last thing a person with a hard heart wants to do is climb God's mountain. Praying is as adverse to the ungodly man as the raking of fingernails across a chalkboard. If you're going to climb, you must want to be like Jesus.

When we climb the mountain of the Lord, we will be changed. Neither personal change, however, nor summiting are the ultimate goal. We must come down with what we found there. We must be able to carry the blessing of God's power and presence down the mountain to the people in whose lives God has placed us. Look how Moses came down the fiery mountain with the message of promise God had written for him:

> So I turned and came down the from the mountain while the mountain was burning with fire, and the two tablets of the covenant were in my two hands. (Deuteronomy 9:15)

To do this requires godliness, character, and deep commitment to holy living; otherwise, we may grieve the Holy Spirit, people will not trust us, and we will discredit the gospel.

Godly Christian living—which grows and spreads through the functions of the church in evangelism, discipleship, acts of compassion, and prayer—is the "race that is set before us" (Hebrews 12:1). But this "race" is not easy; no easier than carrying a cross with Jesus and denying ourselves daily (see Luke 9:23). This life of following Jesus, if lived in fruitful victory, is loaded with conditions. Ignoring them could mean being disqualified or injured and could have us walking in a race where we are supposed to be running. It might even lead us to quit. For this reason, the nautically oriented Apostle warns of living lackadaisically, compelling us to "fight the good fight," lest our faith should suffer "shipwreck" (1 Timothy 1:18-19).

Think of yourself paying your hard-earned money to sign up for a triathlon or a marathon *so that* you could get injured and come in last place. You wouldn't plan for that! When you prayed to repent and receive the Spirit of Christ into your heart, were you thinking about how quickly you could shipwreck your faith? Of course not! You were likely listening to encouraging words from friends or pastors about the journey of a relationship with God that, although challenging at times, would help you become the person He envisioned you to be. You imagined a relationship that would inspire you to run the race He marked out for you and win the prize of knowing Him deeply. You likely imagined at some point early on how you could help other people come to know Christ as you had and join the race with you. You dreamt of God's purpose for you and how you might impact the society around you and in the world. I know I did, and I still do!

Moral Responsibility

The dynamics of the Christian life are intentionally relational. Love is the zenith driver of action, and trust is the pinnacle dynamic of relationships. God isn't looking to mold clay to make inanimate pots. He intends to breathe life into his work and then relate to it. You are unique in that you are able to communicate, trust, love, enjoy and inspire in all your relationships.

This includes the relationship God helped you begin with Him. But like any relationship, growing in trust presents challenges, conditions, and the need to learn and adjust.

While God is sovereign and omnipotent, it would be over-stating His use of these attributes to suggest that a person's decisions are all made by God. He does not make the decision for you to be lazy. He does not make the decision for you to be rebellious. He does not make the decision for you to be self-absorbed, intoxicated, or immoral. These are not decisions that fall under His use of omnipotent power or His knowledge of future events. No, though God will *judge* such decisions, they are *made* by people. These are people to whom God has given a clear responsibility to live by the truth and maintain a clear conscience. Some people disown this responsibility in order to express their independence and liberation from God.

God gives men responsibility. He doesn't make the decision for you to pray; you do. He doesn't make the decision for you to help the poor; you make that decision. He doesn't decide you're going to fast and make you do it; you choose to fast. God doesn't make the decision for you to be a faithful husband, caring father, generous neighbor, or servant-hearted church member. You make those decisions, and He blesses your obedience in all of this. He will lead us to do these things by His Spirit, but we must follow. We must say yes. We must decide using the volitional capacity with which we are endowed. Ryle goes on to say,

> I maintain that believers are eminently and pecu-
> liarly responsible and under a special obligation
> to live holy lives. They are not, as others, dead and

blind and unrenewed. They are alive unto God and have light and knowledge and a new principle within them. Whose fault is it if they are not holy but their own?

Think of these responsibilities as "conditions" needed for you to run as if to win—to climb as if to summit. If you neglect your responsibility, you will lose. Imagine the number of people who have started races ill-prepared and quit or decided to climb a mountain and petered out. Unless you want that to be you, embrace your responsibility before God to live a godly life and honor Him in all your decisions. This will prepare and condition you to properly ascend the hill of the Lord.

Conclusion and Contemplation

Behold the conditions for having the character of the king. Will you take the responsibility to be godly?

Prayer of Commitment

Father in Heaven, I want to run the race You have marked out for me with perseverance, casting off the sin that so easily entangles me, with my eyes fixed on Jesus. I want to run like one who would win! I accept the call to be spiritually conditioned, fit, and ready for whatever You lead me to do. I accept my responsibility to make decisions that are in line with Your Word. I want to have a deep relationship with You on Your terms. Help me to do this, Lord! Amen.

Discussion Questions

1. Describe a time when you prepared for a competition and what was required.

2. Although the Christian life is compared to a race, it is, in all reality, a war. How is preparation for war similar to preparation for a race or a competition? How is it different?

3. Is it possible to lose a spiritual battle? Why does God want us to "fight the good fight" and "run as if to win?"

4. What is the cost of losing the spiritual battle we are fighting? What could happen if we ignore the conditions necessary for victory?

5. What is godliness? How is it like being spiritually fit or well-conditioned?

6. How does it affect people who don't know Christ to see "Christians" who are not godly? How does it affect the Gospel message?

7. What is moral responsibility? Who is responsible for your choices?

8. Do we have character because of God's sovereignty? Does God use His sovereignty to make our choices for us? What is the difference between God leading and God controlling us?

9. How does living a godly life help us succeed at summiting the mountain of the Lord?

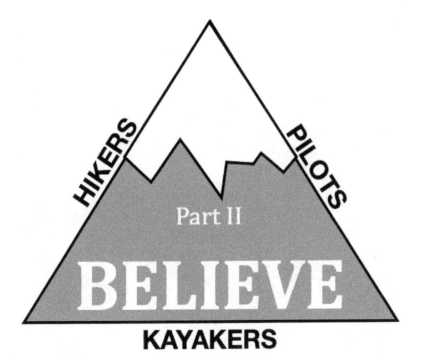

INTRODUCTION

S ummiting the mountain of the Lord relies on your belief in the truths He has set forth in His Word. These are prerequisites to seeking and finding Him. People avoid the truth because they don't believe it. Since God is truth, we will not find Him in falsehood or unbelief. If you seek God on your terms and doubt His, you are operating in falsehood, and you won't find Him. God's terms are written in His Word, but the Word must first be trusted, then "rightly-divided." Independence from God and His Word is rooted in arrogance, which is idolatry, which is falsehood. This behavior is markedly dangerous because if you seek God in falsehood, you might find *something* and call it God. Conversely, you may find *nothing* and stop believing.

Thus, in part two of *The Mountaineer*, we will see the importance of understanding and trusting the trail map as you hike, appreciating and appropriating the banks as you kayak, and finally adhering to the laws of love as you pilot your way up into the mountainous atmosphere.

Literary Support

The fog has risen from the sea and crowned
The dark, untrodden summits of the coast,
Where roams a voice, in canyons uttermost,
From midnight waters vibrant and profound.

High on each granite altar dies the sound,
Deep as the trampling of an armored host,
Lone as the lamentation of a ghost,
Sad as the diapason of the drowned.

The mountain seems no more a soulless thing,
But rather as a shape of ancient fear,
In darkness and the winds of Chaos born
Amid the lordless heavens' thundering—
A Presence crouched, enormous and austere,
Before whose feet the mighty waters mourn.
—George Sterling, *Night on the Mountain*

"Pay close attention to yourself and to your teaching; persevere in these things, for as you do this you will ensure salvation both for yourself and for those who hear you"
(1 Timothy 4:16).

"Mountains have a way of dealing with overconfidence."
—Herman Buhl

"Great things are done when men and mountains meet."
—William Blake

"Afflicted Saint, to Christ draw near,
Your Saviors gracious Promise hear;
His faithful Word you can believe:
that as your days your strength shall be."
— John Fawcett, 1740-1817, *Afflicted Saint to Christ
Draw Near*

"The farther one gets into the wilderness,
the greater is the attraction of its lonely freedom."
—Theodore Roosevelt

Chapter IV

HIKERS
Trust the Trail Map of God

Imperative
*We must believe in the Bible as God's inspired,
authoritative, and inerrant Word.*

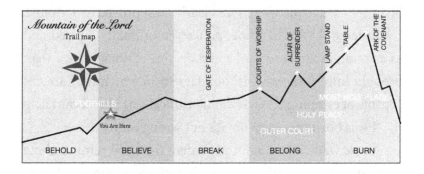

Trees and Reason
May 2019
Port Clinton, Pennsylvania

Fresh morning air surrounded us as we pushed up and coasted down the fluctuating landscape of North-Eastern Pennsylvania. The Appalachian trail was alive! Along the hillside to my left, a grove of blackberries sprawled out in the direction of the trail. Sixty-foot beams stretched limbless out of the ferny forest floor into the sky until they branched into millions of green leaves that seemed to be waving back at us. Here, I breathed deep the aroma of the blackberry blossoms, which rode eastward through the forest on a friendly breeze.

It was a perfect paradise to me and brought nearly indescribable satisfaction in the work of the Creator. My mind went to the first garden, where God walked with man in the cool of the day. I invited my Lord to walk beside me in this garden, and soon I sensed His presence all around me.

I asked Him how I could answer questions about controversial sins, ones that many people who believe in God didn't feel were wrong. Claims to physiological inclinations present from birth are used to justify actions clearly disapproved in Scripture. I wondered, "What if someone was emotionally injured and as a result, inclined toward a certain sin?" "What if they were brought into some spiritual bondage from which they are not capable of escaping?" What about justifications like, "I can't help it," "I was born this way," or "It's not wrong for *me*."

As we walked through the garden, the Lord reminded me again of the first garden, where He forbade Adam and Eve to eat from the Tree of the Knowledge of Good and Evil. The Holy Spirit began to stir my thoughts with His own: "Was the Tree good or evil?"

I contemplated. "It must have been good, because God created it."

Then in a moment of extreme clarity, a whisper echoed through the corridors of my mind, as if placed there by the gentle voice of the Holy Spirit:

"It doesn't matter if it was good *or* evil, I forbade it."

In the case of Adam and Eve, *this* was their mistake. They knew what God had said, but when they saw that the fruit *looked good*, they went with their opinion and sinned.

Whether or not we agree that something is right, wrong, good, or evil is irrelevant when God says "No" to it. All that matters is that we trust and obey the Word of God. People will say, "I will obey God, if I agree with Him on an issue." But God isn't interested in your opinion; He is interested in whether you believe Him. He is God. It is He to whom we must come humbly in search of mercy. He alone possesses infinite wisdom, knowledge, power, and authority. He is looking for trust-driven obedience that springs forth from faith without the reasoning of man. No exceptions. This is the least of which He deserves from us.

But when a person demands that God agree with their view, he or she will surely die. Is it not a mystery that any person should, in one breath, assert faith in God's existence, and in the next that God should change *His* commands to support *their* opinions?

But this is precisely what was expected of Adam and Eve by the serpent, which tempted them to reconsider what God had said. He begins his temptation by deconstructing God's directive and reconstructing it in his own terms:

> Now the serpent was more crafty than any beast of
> the field which the Lord God had made. And he said
> to the woman, "Indeed, has God said, 'You shall not
> eat fruit from any tree of the garden'?" (Genesis 3:1)

Adam seems paralyzed, immobilized by fear, muted. So, Eve responds. She does well in her first round of temptation, correcting the vile creature by accurately restating what God has said to them:

> The woman said to the serpent, "From the fruit of the trees of the garden we may eat; but from the fruit of the tree which is in the middle of the garden, God has said, 'You shall not eat from it or touch it, or you will die.'" (Genesis 3:2-3)

Adam raises not a word of agreement, no shield of resistance. He all but walks away. The serpent strikes. His venom sank deeply into the lifeblood of Eve's conscience. He directly challenges what God has said and asserts his own promises in a mixture of truth and deceit:

> The serpent said to the woman, "You will surely not die! For God knows that in the day you eat from it your eyes will be opened, and you will be like God, knowing good and evil." (Genesis 3:4-5)

Still able to resist the deceptive tantalization, Eve nevertheless gives way to the tempter and to the sight of what looked good to her:

> When the woman saw that the tree was good for food and that it was a delight to the eyes and that the tree was desirable to make one wise, she took from its fruit and ate. (Genesis 3:6)

Could Adam's silence have opened this door? Were sins of omission brewing in the foreground of the fall of man? Adam spoke not a word. He should have stepped up to protect his wife, but instead, he stood quietly, mouth presumably watering for the forbidden fruit in Eve's hand. He permitted his wife to eat it, hailing no return to reason, shouting no allegiance to God, crying out in no sounds of adversity whatsoever. Consequently, he found himself standing between unfettered friendship with Elohim in a paradise once free of evil; and his now fallen wife, who had abandoned the Creator in allegiance with the serpent:

> And she gave also to her husband with her, and ate.
> (Genesis 3:7)

Fill in the gaps here; put yourself in his position. Imagine this for a moment: Adam, standing before his fallen wife and the serpent, evaluating his next move. Eve looks at him longingly, Satan slyly. Pressure to conform builds in his chest. He doesn't want to abandon his wife, but he doesn't want to abandon his Creator. Pain wells up in his heart and begins to lead him. He questions what he heard directly from the Creator, and then he chooses—wrongly. He opens his hands to her—and eats.

Sin entered the world through one man's rebellion (Romans 5:12), a man who took his own evaluation of the tree and its fruit over God's command. He parted with the One beside whom he had just walked in friendship. Casting his allegiance upon adaptive, deceptive logic, he issued a firm and final dismissal of God's Word. In doing so, he trusted his own rationale. This was his grave mistake.

If you, like Adam, are inclined to trust your own reasoning, consider this: Rationalizing against the Infinite with finite rationality is infinitely irrational. It is perfectly wonderful to be curious, studious, and ambitious in our search for truth. Yet we must understand that we will not solve all of the mysteries of God's nature and purposes in this lifetime. Demands for an explanation prior to obedience will only be met with silence. This arrogance will always end in rebellion and will be followed by destruction.

The answers to humanity's moral questions will start with the tree. If a person obeys God even when what is forbidden "looks good," that person will have the kind of relationship God desires. That person will know God deeply and intimately, speaking with Him as a man speaks with his friend, face to face. That person will enjoy the wonder of walking with God in the cool of the day.

My 32-pound backpack squeaked and squawked with every step. Sticks, old leaves, and rocks crunched under my feet. I contemplated. "I will trust you even when I don't understand," I said.

The Ruler of Moral Law

We must believe the Bible. We must begin here to dismantle lies we've believed and tighten our interpretation and application of Scripture. No matter how much we learn, our need for answers and explanations will always be present. This doesn't suggest that we stop learning; it simply indicates that we will always have to trust God more deeply than our understanding can take us.

The ruler exists so that everyone's "inch" is the same length and everyone's 12 inches equal one foot. If everyone's rulers were slightly different, there would be no need for any rulers. The ruler for Christianity is the Bible, the inspired Word of God. Without this, we are left to interpret life and its challenges by our own reasoning, which simply does not work. A standard, or a measuring rod, so to speak, is needed and has been given and is the basis for all Christian beliefs.

This standard is the Bible, God's Holy Word, and it is without error; it is perfect—spoken by the mouth of God. There is nowhere we can go as Christians without this truth firmly rooted in our hearts, except to hell, prepared for the one who first questioned it.

There can be zero neutrality in one's stance on Scripture for very logical reasons. It is either entirely the work of men, or it is the inerrant, authoritative Word of God. Neutrality, as it relates to one's stance on Scripture, is THE reason people do not act according to it. The fact of inerrancy prevents a person from the subjective selection of what they deem to be "inspired" texts. Those who employ such a subjective approach to Scripture conveniently reject those texts that they find disagreeable and deem "uninspired." From this place, morality is quickly reduced to personal preference or opinion, and everyone rushes to do what is right in their own eyes.

The crisis over the authority and veracity of Scripture is one of the most significant battlegrounds in the history of Christianity, and it is only getting more intense. In his book *The Great Evangelical Disaster*, Dr. Francis A. Schaeffer drew a vital illustration to expose this devilish dilemma:

> Not far from where we live in Switzerland is a high ridge of rock with a valley on both sides. One time I was there when there was snow on the ground along that ridge. The snow was lying there unbroken, a seeming unity. However, that unity was an illusion, for it lay along a great divide; it lay along a watershed.

One portion of the snow when it melted would flow into one valley. The snow which lay close beside would flow into another valley when it melted.

What does this illustration have to do with the evangelical world today? I would suggest that it is a very accurate description of what is happening. Evangelicals today are facing a watershed concerning the nature of Biblical inspiration and authority. It is a watershed issue in very much the same sense as described in the illustration. Within evangelicalism there are a growing number who are modifying their views on the inerrancy of the Bible so that the full authority of Scripture is completely undercut. But it is happening in very subtle ways. Like the snow lying side-by-side on the ridge, the new views on biblical authority often seem at first glance not to be so very far from what evangelicals, until just recently, have always believed. But also, like the snow lying side-by-side on the ridge, the new views when followed consistently end up a thousand miles apart.

To summit the mountain of the Lord and not get lost or give up, this is the first truth that you must sure up. **You cannot scale the mountain of God without His trail map.** We have to trust the trail map of God! You cannot conquer the enemies of God's Word if you do not believe in God's Word as final and authoritative. Why? Because distorting and dismissing the Word of God is the primary tool the enemy uses against God's people. Just take, for example, the way that he tempted Jesus:

And he led Him to Jerusalem and had Him stand on
the pinnacle of the temple, and said to Him, "if You
are the Son of God, throw Yourself down from here;
for it is written, 'He will command His angels concerning You to guard You,' and 'On *their* hands they
will bear You up so that You will not strike Your foot
against a stone.'" (Luke 4:9-11)

We must accurately apply Scripture as a primary source
of our maturity and growth. Scripture must be the primary
weapon of our warfare; otherwise, as Schaeffer pointed out, we
may end up thousands of miles from where God wants us.

Sibling Revelry
April 2016

My very generous mom, henceforth referred to as "Grandma
Geyer," hosted a family reunion in the beautiful Smokey
Mountains of Southeastern Tennessee. In the spacious mountain top condo, my uncle Dave and brother-in-law Jerry turned
nearly every moment into something hilarious while we cooked,
played pool, and sat out on the deck overlooking the fog-filled
valleys.

Grandma Geyer brought a suitcase filled with her delicious
chocolate chip cookies, which she baked from scratch and then
froze. These were customized to accommodate certain aller-
gies and sensitivities that spanned the lot of us and became the
munch fodder between all activities.

One morning, my sister Dianne rallied my brother Andrew
and me, and we went for an adventuresome hike through the
mountains south of Gatlinburg. We believed if we followed a

particular trail out about 3-4 miles, we could find an impressive waterfall beautiful enough to make it a worthy 1/2 day's hike. So we packed a few sandwiches and a couple dozen of Grandma Geyer's cookies and headed into the woods.

Like our predecessors, we hoped to find something, and we did. The trail crossed valley creeks and scaled up and over progressively higher points along the mountain ridges. Along the way, we found that the newly produced foliage was a splendid backdrop against the forest floor of mayapples and yesteryear's fallen trees. Rounded stones with mossy tops garnished the walkway where many had traversed before us.

Along the trail, Andrew told us about parting with his delivery truck business and the girl he was interested in. As the conversation turned, so did the trail; and we grew closer together as we grew closer to our destination. Dianne spoke of her anticipation of retiring from military duty and focusing exclusively on her work as a physician. I shared about the challenges I faced at work and the blessings I was finding at home; and how God had been helping me understand the turns and twists that life seemed to inevitably include.

After a couple of hours of exploration, we arrived at a secret haven of beauty. An imposing bluff gave way to a voluminous spring rivulet, which fell about 40 feet into the ravine that sat between the ridges of the mountains. There, it pooled and swirled before descending further down the cascading hills.

We took dozens of pictures of ourselves and reveled our way back down the mountainside toward our vehicle. It struck me how a trail could provide the opportunity for brothers and a sister to discuss and discover the more beautiful things in life. The trail took us somewhere as it drew us closer together; it took us to places of depth and grandeur otherwise undiscoverable.

Trust on Trial

Years ago, on one of my missionary journeys, I stood on the balcony of my hotel room in Shanghai, looking down over the city. I saw hundreds and thousands of people milling about on the streets below. Cars whipped around corners, and bicyclists meandered through alleys. "So many people!" I thought. "How can we reach them all?" With these thoughts, a sinking feeling of defeat began to settle in my heart. "This battle is too great," I thought. Doubts arose, and I wondered if what I was doing was even worth it. "Is what I believe even true? Is the Bible even true?"

These thoughts flooded my mind just hours after seeing God do one of the most incredible miracles I've ever seen. Earlier that day, we were about to pass several thousand bibles under an x-ray machine where a guard sat analyzing all the baggage. Knowing that Bibles were on the top of the list of contraband, we prayed, then we put our bags on the conveyor belt in faith. Our prayers were immediately answered. The guard was pulled away into a conversation with another guard, and all our Bibles slipped safely past his watch! So we joyfully boarded the train for Shanghai.

After what I saw that morning, I *knew* what we believed was true and that God was blessing our efforts. And yet, like Elijah in the days following his Mount Carmel victories, I was experiencing significant doubts just after a major win. This was my first real struggle with this issue, but I prayed through it, found victory in the Holy Spirit, and God continued to bless our efforts.

After this challenging but victorious day, my team took a few days off. We looked at a map and picked a random city to visit in central China, where the landscape was well known for its beauty. A man greeted us at the bus station and offered to take us on a boat ride when we arrived. "You take boat ride?" He queried. We declined. He followed us to our hotel and continued to speak about the boat ride. "You take boat ride!" He demanded. We declined. He was outside the hotel the following day and offered us the boat ride again. "Today, you take boat ride?" He said with a crooked grin. We accepted.

It was a magical tour through central China's pointy, disconnected mountains. Men atop paddleboards cast nets into the river. Ancient architecture adorned the hillsides. Rice fields lay between the lofty hills, and workers sewed plugs of rice in them.

Then the captain unexpectedly parked the boat aside the banks, and our tour guide "Mike" came buzzing out toward our group. "Get off boat!" He said. "Go to village!" He pointed. His urgency alarmed me, but we consented. I told him, "you're coming with *me*." And he said, "Ok."

In the rural village, what amounted to a carnival, had come to town. 15 Americans, a full 16-inches taller than anyone there, crowded into the square. Also in the square was a corral full of oxen and about 100 villagers, staring in silence. I looked in amazement at the congregation of curiosity. So I said to Mike, translate *everything* I say, do not miss a word. "Ok," he complied. And I preached:

"There is a God who created the world and all that is in it, including each one of you. He loves you very much and wants you to know Him…".

I continued through the Bible with a short sermon that included our sin, the need for forgiveness, and the Savior—Jesus Christ. I concluded with a prayer, every Chinese eye open and watching me. Then to my surprise, a woman in the back held her hand up high for me to see.

I took Mike and a team member named Trevor Brunsink with me, and we went to see what she wanted. She invited us to her house. On the way there, the soft path oozed beneath our feet, and chickens jumped out of our way. Children followed us like we were friendly clowns, and mothers whispered to one another as we passed.

In her one-room house, she took a stick and dug a hole in the dirt floor. We all looked at each other and exchanged gazes of bewilderment as she stooped, digging. Then out of the ground, she produced a plastic bag. Shaking the dirt from the bag, she reached inside.

The Bible she pulled out of the bag, she said, belonged to her husband.

"My husband is in prison for preaching the same sermon you preached. I am am the only one who believes this message in my village. I often feel like giving up. I often feel hopeless. God sent you here to encourage me to continue to believe the words of this book," she said tearfully.

That random city in central China? *That* boat ride? *That* village? Rarely had I felt more centrally situated in the will of God than on that day, and doubts about his Word scurried away like that brood of frightened chickens along the village pathway.

In his autobiography, *Just As I Am*, Billy Graham described his struggle with this very issue early in his ministry. He said, "I had no doubts concerning the deity of Jesus Christ or the validity of the Gospel, but was the Bible completely true? If I was not exactly doubtful, I was certainly disturbed." It is fair to say that anyone serious about summiting the mountain of the Lord will cross this threshold at least once.

In a night of prayer in the darkened and wooded San Bernardino Mountains, 30-year-old Billy Graham fell to his knees in desperation for God to help him embrace the Bible as the living, powerful Word of God. He prayed,

> "Oh God! There are many things in this book I do not understand. There are many problems with it for which I have no solution. There are many seeming contradictions. There are some areas in it that do not seem to correlate with modern science. I can't answer some of the philosophical and psychological questions Chuck and others are raising."

As Reverend Graham waited on the Lord in this moment of tremendous importance to his future ministry, the Holy Spirit "freed" him to speak. He prayed this prayer and recalled the following experience:

> "Father, I am going to accept this as Thy Word—by faith! I'm going to allow faith to go beyond my intellectual questions and doubts, and I will believe this to be your inspired Word." When I got up from my knees at Forest Home that August night, my eyes stung with tears. I sensed the presence and power

of God as I had not sensed it in months. Not all my questions were answered, but a major bridge had been crossed. In my heart and mind, I knew a spiritual battle in my soul had been fought and won.

Billy Graham emerged from the trees a stronger, more victorious man. You must also fight and *win* this battle if you are to proceed anywhere near the prescription of Jesus for bearing fruit:

"If you abide in Me, and My words abide in you, ask whatever you wish, and it will be done for you. My Father is glorified by this, that you bear much fruit, and so prove to be My disciples." (John 15:7-8)

Why Trust the Bible

Every person on Earth should consider the Bible the singular authority in their life for knowing God and living in such a way as to honor Him. Why should you trust that the Bible is God's authoritative and inspired Word? **Because Jesus did.** Jesus' reliance upon Scripture to provide authority to his teaching was exhaustive. According to Harold Wilmington of Liberty University, of the verses in the Gospels in which He is speaking, Jesus refers to Scripture 180 times[1]. Jesus' teaching is taken directly from the following books of the Old Testament: Genesis, Exodus, Numbers, Deuteronomy, 1 Samuel, 1 Kings, 2 Chronicles, Psalms, Isaiah, Daniel, Hosea, and Jonah.

---

[1] Willmington, Harold, "Old Testament Passages Quoted by Jesus Christ" (2017). The Second Person File. 71. https://digitalcommons.liberty.edu/second_person/71

What would we have without Jesus? To discredit His use of Scripture dissolves the value of His message entirely. Who He claimed to be is rendered unfounded, His basis for morality is baseless, and His authoritative directives become the mildly attractive opinions of a questionable figure. We would not have any reason at all to believe that there is a heaven where we can one day go if we did not believe in Jesus. If we believe in Jesus, we must accept the basis of His teaching as he accepted it:

> "Do not think that I came to abolish the Law or the Prophets; I did not come to abolish but to fulfill. For truly I say to you, until Heaven and Earth pass away, not the smallest letter or stroke shall pass from the Law until all is accomplished." (Matthew 5:17-18)

> And the Scripture cannot be broken. (John 10:35)

> You are mistaken, not understanding the Scriptures nor the power of God. (Matthew 22:29)

> Then beginning with Moses and with all the prophets, He explained to them the things concerning Himself in all the Scriptures. (Luke 24:27)

> Now He said to them, "these are my words which I spoke to you while I was still with you, that all things which are written about Me in the Law of Moses and the Prophets and the Psalms must be fulfilled." Then He opened their minds to understand the Scriptures. (Luke 24:44-45)

It is clear where Jesus stood on the subject of the Authority of Scripture. But what about his followers who wrote about Him in what is collectively called the New Testament? According to George F. Pentecost, the Old Testament is cited or alluded to 885 times throughout the New Testament (including the above uses by Jesus Himself)[2]. The only books of the Old Testament not mentioned are Obadiah, Nahum, Zephaniah, and Esther. The book of Acts has 57 citations, the Letter to the Romans has 74, and the Letter to the Hebrews has 86! Thus, the veracity and authority of Old Testament Scripture became foundational to the veracity and authority of New Testament Scripture.

The writers of Scripture have pointed to other places in the Bible, indicating that these, also, are Scripture. Daniel verified the Book of Jeremiah as "the word of the Lord" (Daniel 9:1-2), Peter verified the letters of the Apostle Paul as Scripture (2 Peter 3:16), and the Apostle Paul affirmed the Gospel of Luke as Scripture (1 Timothy 5:18). If you thought the Book of Revelation was a bit extreme, note that there are 249 references to Scripture in this one book. That's an average of 11 per chapter! The Scriptures cannot be broken!

Paul states that "All scripture is inspired (*theopneustos*, or God-breathed) by God" (2 Timothy 3:16), and Peter stated that "no prophecy of Scripture is a matter of one's own interpretation, for no prophesy was ever made by an act of human will, but men moved by the Holy Spirit spoke from God" (2 Peter 1:20-21). These statements are not about how morally encouraging the Bible is but that, **since** the words of Scripture originated in the heart of God and were breathed by the mouth of God, they

---

[2] Pentecost, George F. "Quotation from the Old Testament in the New Testament" (2022). https://www.blueletterbible.org/study/pnt/pnt08.cfm

are inerrant. Inerrancy means there are no errors. "The law of the Lord is *perfect*" (Psalm 19:7).

Do you believe what Jesus believed about Scripture? Do you believe what Matthew, Mark, Luke, John, Paul, Peter, James, and Jude believed? Will you take a different stance than these men who walked with Jesus on the Earth? Will you disagree with them? You will have disowned them and disagreed with them if you abandon the Bible as the authoritative, inerrant Word of Almighty God.

Conclusively, if you removed the idea of the inerrancy and authority of Scripture—and its uses on this premise—from all of the New Testament, you would literally have nothing. None of it would make ANY sense whatsoever. You would not have a Savior, you would have no basis for morality, and you would have no expectation of what is to come. You would have nothing in which to place your faith and hope and no one in Heaven to worship for the immense gift of redemption and forgiveness (which you could not expect to be available to you). There would be no such persons as mountaineers, no mountain to climb, no God of Glory to behold, and no purpose for which to live—except for yourself.

What is the Bible?

"What exactly is the Bible?" Asks Derek W. H. Thomas. He expounds:

> On one level, it is a collection of approximately three-quarters of a million words in sixty-six books written in three distinct languages (Hebrew, Aramaic, and Greek) over a period of more than a thousand

years by some forty disparate authors in a variety of forms, including history, prophecy, sermons, letters, formal covenant treaties, travel narratives, poetry, parables, proverbs, architectural blueprints, apocalypses, Gospels, laws (moral, civil, and ceremonial), inventories, and much more.

Within these diverse literary genres, the Bible somewhat surprisingly gives a detailed account of the failures of those who ventured to know and follow the Lord. Such great men as Abraham, Moses, David, Solomon, Jonah, and Peter failed miserably at times, and the Bible clearly describes this. Many of the Kings of Israel and Judah were complete failures, and many of the early church followers fell away. Failure must be *understood* to be navigated or avoided, and the Bible is not shy to give many examples of what "not" to do.

Yet there are many beautiful stories of faithful men of God like Samuel, Daniel, Asa, Hezekiah, John the Baptist, John the Beloved, and the Apostle Paul. Many of these men gave their lives as martyrs for their love for God, and their examples of how they lived would inspire just about anyone from any faith.

The Reliability of the Bible
Manuscript Accuracy

Manuscript accuracy is the extent to which copies found in different places and from different eras match. As for the Bible, there are literally thousands, and they are consistent with one another almost perfectly, to a degree that surpasses any other material of antiquity. In his book, *Evidence That Demands a Verdict*, Josh McDowell extensively covers the reliability of Scripture from multiple angles.

> Although it was first written on perishable materials, and had to be copied and recopied for hundreds of years before the invention of the printing press, the Scriptures have never diminished in style or correctness, nor have they ever faced extinction. Compared with other ancient writings, the Bible has more manuscript evidence to support it than any ten pieces of classical literature combined.

Archaeological and Historical Accuracy

Doug Powell, author of the *Holman QuickSource Guide to Christian Apologetics,* found this:

> The accurate transmission of the text is, of course, irrelevant if the history it purports to preserve can be shown to be invented or contradicted by archaeological finds. Fortunately, there is no small amount of sites that have yielded and/or continue to yield finds relating the the ancient Hebrews. Like the new Testament, Many volumes have been dedicated to the cataloging of such finds.

Additionally, Powell says of the New Testament:

> Archaeology has repeatedly and consistently confirmed the New Testament. Much information about the Mediterranean world at that time that was found

only in the New Testament has now been corroborated by archaeological finds. Titles, names of local rulers, time periods, and landmarks that were once thought to be in error or even fictional are now considered to be fact.

McDowell also shows that Scripture is historically accurate when held against the annals of history from ancient civilizations like Egypt, Babylon, Greece, or the Roman Empire. Great detail on these subjects can be found in these authors' respective books and many other works on this topic.

Scientific Accuracy

Pastor John MacArthur gives a compelling synopsis of the Bible's firm footing in the world of science:

> The record of Scripture is accurate when it intersects with the fundamental findings of modern science. The first law of thermodynamics, which deals with the conservation of energy, is implied in passages such as Isaiah 40:26 and Ecclesiastes 1:10. The second law of thermodynamics indicates that, although energy cannot be destroyed, it is constantly going from a state of order to disorder. This law of entropy corresponds to the fact that creation is under a divine curse (Genesis 3), such that it groans (Romans 8:22) as it heads toward its ultimate ruin (2 Pet. 3:10-13) before being replaced with new heavens and the new Earth (Revelation 21-22). Findings from the science of hydrology are foreshadowed in places such as

Ecclesiastes 1:7, Isaiah 55:10, and Job 36:27-28. And calculations from modern astronomy, regarding the countless number of stars in the universe, are anticipated in Old Testament passages such as Genesis 22:17 and Jeremiah 33:22.

The book of Job is one of the oldest books in the Bible, written some thirty-five hundred years ago. Yet it has one of the clearest statements of the fact that the Earth is suspended in space. Job 26:7 says that God "hangs the earth on nothing." Other ancient religious books make ridiculous scientific claims, including the notion that the Earth rests on the backs of elephants. But when the Bible speaks, it does so in a way that corresponds to what scientific discoveries have found to be true about the universe.

With all of the inward and outward points of veracity considered, it is perhaps the most challenging thing for skeptics to dismiss the empirical data. That is, the testimonies of billions of people from nearly every nation on Earth whose lives have been guided, transformed, and illuminated by the inherent power in the Word of God. For *this* reason, it was penned into Scripture that it may be transformative in our hearts by the Holy Spirit. You can be among these, and may be already, if you will open the Bible and read it while asking the Counselor to guide you into all truth and help you to understand what you are reading.

Embracing Biblical Correction

Finally, I want to emphasize the importance of being in a body of believers who are deeply committed to the Bible. You will find that some battles are meant just for you to fight, and some are meant for the army of God to fight together.

God has placed the power and anointing of His Holy Spirit on the preaching of His Word, and you will flourish when you are continually absorbing His truths in this environment. Look for a church where the preachers use the Word of God to *make* their points, not just to *support* their points. Deep in your spirit will ring the confirmation and clarity of God's truths, and your commitment to his Word will grow.

If your congregation is too large or watered down to include biblical practices of accountability and correction, you are probably on the wrong side of the watershed. The Apostle Paul points out four key uses of Scripture to his disciple, Timothy:

> All Scripture is inspired by God and profitable for teaching, for reproof, for correction, and for training in righteousness; so that the man of God may be adequate, equipped for every good work. (2 Timothy 3:16-17)

Teaching and training seem like relatively benign activities until you realize that the purpose is to be equipped for battle! Rebuking and correcting come into play when members of the body are out of alignment. In the spirit of gentleness, these acts of love will bring that person back into alignment, giving health to the whole body (See Galatians 6:1).

With these thoughts in mind, we will move into the following two chapters of Part II, "Believe," where we will dial down some of our ideas and beliefs that may need fine-tuning. It is first essential to be committed to the Word of God as our guide and source of truth in life and then to extend that commitment into the *proper* interpretation of the Scriptures.

Conclusion and Contemplation

Believe the Bible is God's inerrant and authoritative Word, delivered through God's mouth to those who penned it. Will you believe His Word?

Prayer of Commitment

Father in Heaven, thank You for Your Word. I trust that You have spoken through the authors of Scripture by Your Holy Spirit, and I commit myself to know You and obeying You through the study of Your Word. I set aside my questions for now and realize that no matter how many facts I have, I will always need faith to know You. I choose to constantly stay in tune with Your will as expressed in Scripture and maintain a deep relationship with You on the terms outlined in Your Word. Please help me to grow in my knowledge and application of the Bible. Amen.

Discussion Questions

1. What would happen if everyone's ruler was a different length? Could we work together to build something that required precise measurements?

2. Why is one "objective" and "authoritative" moral law important?
3. How does the Bible function like a trail map for those summiting the mountain of the Lord?
4. Should we expect to understand everything about the Bible? How does trust factor into this?
5. Why is finite rationality inadequate and inconclusive in determining moral standards?
6. Where did Scripture originate?
7. What is inerrancy? What makes the Bible inerrant?
8. Will we always feel satisfied with our level of understanding on every issue? What should we do when we don't understand what we've experienced, felt, or observed, or when the Bible doesn't answer us clearly?
9. Discuss Billy Graham's struggle with the Bible. How did embracing "God's trail map" affect the fruitfulness, inwardly and outwardly, of Billy Graham's life?

Chapter V

KAYAKERS

Follow the Banks of the River

Imperative
We must produce discipline as a fruit of the
Holy Spirit if we wish to summit.

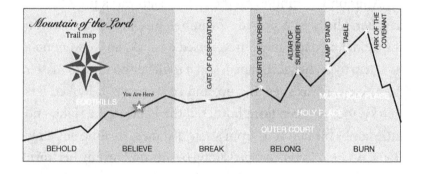

The Salt River
April 2021
Louisville, Kentucky

I hoped we could avoid toppling the kayak. A glassy reflection beautified the surface of the otherwise muddied waters—a murky river pretended to be clean. It wasn't salt that seemed prominent in the Salt River, but dirt as it cut through the lowland fields of central Kentucky toward the much broader Ohio.

73

The water cut away at the soil that comprised the steadily edited river banks. Once majestic and lively trees were toppled after their roots were exposed by the mischievous erosion. They had grown too close to the edge. These fallen heroes of the forest became waterlogged villains, and they prodded ghoulish arms up and out of the slow-moving squalor. Spider webs sprinkled with dew, were stretched between their greyed, leafless fingers.

I was sure there were hundreds of snakes, maybe even alligators, under the surface. But only a few turtles made an appearance. The mystery ate my courage. Toothed fishes with foot-long snouts appeared in my imagination and swam beneath the kayak, waiting for me to lean the wrong way.

After only 4 minutes on the river, Asiah was a professional kayaker. She was to provide swimmer support for a triathlon the following day but had never used a kayak. So we went on a float trip to get her acclimated, and it took her no time to master.

The river was speeding up, and so were we. It looked less murky, too. A sheep farm bordered the bank to the right, and little lambs bleated at us from a safe distance, stealing our affections. A Great Pyrenees sped along beside us, barking his warnings to keep away from his wooly family. He was indeed bred to protect these lambs, and he meant to do an excellent job of it. I remembered our beloved Pyrenees, "Buddy," and wondered if they were distant relatives. I missed him, his bark, and his protective diligence.

Ducks waddled with ducklings in line behind them. The scene was so adorable that Asiah "cooed" and "awed" at the sight. Soon, our anxiety over the strange waters changed to laughter, and the sun crept up onto our arms from behind the tree line.

Rapids. "Which way should we go?" As we approached the point of no return, the thought repeated itself in my head. A small stone island stood slightly to the right of the center. "Go left," I said, thinking the wider passage would be safer. We ground to a halt.

"We should have gone right," Asiah said, now an expert.

I faked a smile at her, squinting.

Scooting, by thrusting our weight in the downstream direction, dislodged us, and we began to float again. The water was clearer now and cleaner, we suspected.

Downstream a bit further, we harbored at a rock island centered in the waterway and broke out the cooler. Sandwiches, granola bars, and iced drinks refreshed us, and Asiah put on her swim goggles. "I'm going to swim a while," she said and slipped into the waist-deep current.

Mussels abandoned their oval homes, lined with rose-colored mother of pearl, and left them lying wide open on the gravelly shore. Asiah discovered them as treasures and stowed a few in the kayak. One was still home, and she pried it open to see its occupant. It was slimy and white and an entertaining spectacle.

In the kayak again, we floated slowly under a bridge. Seventy-five feet above us, automobiles buzzed along a rural highway. Ahead, we could see some intimidating rapids, ones that looked like a waterfall. We braced ourselves and discussed our success strategy. Asiah was now steering in the rear of the kayak, and I was calling out the maneuvers. Like pros, we rowed through the rapids in complete control, and our confidence escalated, gradually replacing our fears.

The Salt River received a tributary at a t-shaped junction, and the currents formed a swirling pool. Leaves and bubbles road the merry-go-round and enticed us out of the kayak again.

Now transparent and less intimidating, the water's cool temperature banished the burning of the sun. We swam around in the pool, dog paddling and diving under to see what would perhaps swim by.

Asiah took the kayak out by herself for a while and paddled up the tributary, giving no sign of novice inhibitions. Rays of light glimmered through the trees, whose branched reached out over the waters, then reflected up to create a collision of colors and sparkles. We had reached beauty at the cost of an intimidating entrance. Khaki stones piled up alongside the rippling waters until they met with its edge. Submerged, they became slippery and green and covered the river's bed.

She picked me up, and we coasted over to the primary route downstream. Rapids formed again, but we were experts now, laughing our way down until we came to rest on the top of a rock garden. The current turned us sideways, and we squealed with humorous horror as we approached the likelihood of toppling over. Somehow we managed to make it out of the dilemma but floated backwards down the rest of the rapids.

A calm, clear passage led straight downstream to the end of our adventure. The water was deeper there, and so were kinships.

The Greatest Discipline

This experience reminds me of my daily voyage to meet with God. The carnal mind is at enmity with God. War breaks loose when you decide to ascend the hill of the Lord; your flesh cries out against you and works to minimize your efforts. Like setting out in a kayak above murky waters, you consider turning back, abandoning the cause. The primary difference between the ghoulish deterrents of the Salt River and those imposed against our pursuit of God is that *these* enemies are not imaginary; they are real! A real war has been declared against you to prohibit your discovery and pursuit of God. However, at the cost of your comfort, you can navigate through it and reach deeper kinship with the Lord.

The very idea of expending serious effort can be unappealing, especially to the carnal mind. Many of us slip back into carnal thinking, motivated by comfort, ease, and the wants of our bodies. Our flesh imagines—correctly—the death that awaits it, and deters us. Jesus said, "It is the Spirit who gives life, the flesh profits nothing. The words that I have spoken to you are spirit and are life." (John 6:63). Again, He says, "Keep watching and praying that you may not enter into temptation; the spirit is willing, but the flesh is weak" (Matthew 26:41).

But the disciplined mind stays the course, which is why discipline is central to success for all mountaineers. Climbing always requires effort, focus, and perseverance. Falling requires no effort. Discipline, therefore, is fundamental, but that word strikes terror in many people's hearts.

When you think of discipline, you may envision eastern asceticism or western authoritarian intolerance. These extremes, which may reflect discipline, do so to the demise of their adherents. The discipline the Holy Spirit produces, however, is a wholesome fruit and it nourishes the spirit of man.

What does a disciplined Christian life look like? The primary discipline of the Christian life is to abide in Christ with His Word abiding in you. It is the essential action by which Christians may be "led by the Spirit of God" and show themselves to be the "sons of God" (Romans 8:14). Abiding in Christ is the summation of all other disciplines. It is the state of abiding in Christ by which believers may constantly access the grace of God in its *poikilos* or many diverse colors (1 Peter 4:10). This manifold grace is critical so that we are not trying to complete with human effort what began in the Spirit (see Galatians 3:2). This is the goal—all else leads here.

In this place of abiding, one may have communication with the Father, friendship with the Savior, and partnership with the Spirit. By abiding in Christ, we become what we were intended to be, completing all He prepared in advance for us to do.

Our purpose in this text is to abandon any of the following mindsets: that our duty to Christ was done for us, our devotion is an act of His sovereignty, or our discipline is an unnecessary picture of religiosity or legalism. It is to emphasize that as followers, we must not turn away. We are responsible for our actions and our inactions; we are those to whom He directed His words, "If anyone loves Me, he will keep My word, and My Father will love him, and We will come to him and make Our abode with him" (John 14:23).

However, Christian discipline is not a stage on which to show one's mastery of internal government. It is no more than a path we choose to arrive nearer to God. Richard Foster noted, in *Celebration of Discipline*, "The disciplines allow us to place ourselves before God so that He can transform us." Collaboration is evident in the Savior's call to discipleship, our part is to follow, and His part is to transform the inward places of our lives.

Spiritual discipline is the activity engaged in by conscious choice that both mortifies the flesh and facilitates spiritual growth. Discipline is focused effort with a specific end in mind. It is calculated planning followed by committed performance. Spiritual discipline has often been described as the banks of a river. The banks don't limit the water; they give it direction and momentum. But if the banks are weak, they erode and make a murky graveyard of fallen trees, once fruitful.

Wheels
August 2016
Louisville, Ky

It was summer in Shelby Park, and that means Cyclouvia! Cyclouvia is a festival of man-powered wheels during which a mirthful circle of cyclists throng the two miles of barricaded streets. Whizzing through the corridor of vendors in their pop-up tents, they pass a different folk or jazz band on every corner. The neighborhood associations collaborate with the city to provide open streets for cyclists, skaters, scooters, and just about every other type of non-motorized summer sensation-seeker.

Anne Marie, Asher, Asiah, and I always join the festivities and peruse the lackadaisical flow of wheeled neighbors as we all breathe deep the smell of beer and brats in the warm, sunny, Sunday-afternoon air. We have occasionally paused amidst the bicycle river to internalize the unique sounds and aromas only summertime can make so wonderfully alive. For me, it is sheer bliss, like a lazy river. A profound joy and exhilaration in the entire spirit of what it means to be a community deeply set in the heart of Louisville.

Do you think that if lazy rivers existed when Jesus was around, he would have said, "take up your tube and float with me"? Somehow, I think we have come to believe that the Christian life should be like a lazy river. Some seem to think, "All the work was done on the cross, now we can just drift along by faith until we go to heaven." Ease: our goal for life. Comfort: our gauge for success.

Cyclouvia is one of my favorite events in Louisville. Trust me, I love times of rest and relaxation like anyone else. In fact, we are invited to come to Jesus and find rest where His yoke is easy (Matthew 11:28-30). However, neither a lazy afternoon nor a lazy river is a good parallel to his expectations for discipleship.

Disciples are Disciplined

If Jesus didn't mean for us to be disciplined in our approach to following Him, He might have called us *laziples* or *easiples*. Admittedly, that's very cheesy, but we are called *disciples* because Jesus expects us to be disciplined in our learning, growing, and working for the causes of knowing Him and making Him known. He wants us to see that a lack of discipline in the Christian life is a lack of Lordship in the Christian heart.

When it comes to subjects like discipline, works, obedience, etc., we tend to have a lot of little adages to justify our exemption. We say that works are religious or that discipline is legalism, and we skip away in some sort of "freedom." Some people call this grace, but this grace is "grace we bestow on ourselves...grace without discipleship," as Dietrich Bonhoeffer put it. It is not the grace that comes from God the Father and Christ Jesus our Savior (see Titus 1:4), about which the Apostle Paul wrote to Titus:

> For the grace of God has appeared bringing salvation
> to all men, instructing us to deny ungodliness and
> worldly desires and to live sensibly, righteously, and
> godly in the present age. (Titus 2:11-12)

Biblical Christianity has among its core values effort and discipline: "And He was saying to them all, 'If anyone wishes to come after Me, he must deny himself, and take up his cross daily and follow Me'" (Luke 9:23). Again, if you are undisciplined, you are not under the Lordship of Jesus, and you are not following Jesus. You are back-sliding.

If you are not *devoted* to Jesus, you do not *belong* to Jesus. You belong to yourself and have reclaimed a once surrendered will. You might recognize Him as Lord, but like the devil, you rebel against Him to pursue your own agenda. But as you draw near God, you will be infected with a love for His purposes, plans, and principles. You will want with fervor and zeal to carry out all that He has for you to do; you will be willing to lay your life down for your heavenly King. You will recognize Him as Lord and gladly do all He has commanded. But you must draw near to Him to have such vision. By the grace of Christ bestowed upon the humble, you must access the strength that invigorates your work alongside the Master Craftsman (Proverbs 8:30-31).

Find me a mountaineer in the world who climbs to the summits of Earth's most splendid mountains, and I will show you a disciplined person! Find me a man or woman of God who has highly impacted this world for Christ, who has been to the summit of the mountain of the Lord, who has known the Lord and loved him deeply, and I will show you someone disciplined!

The Disciplines of War

As mentioned earlier in this chapter, the pursuit of God takes place amidst a real war with real enemies. You are in this battle, either as one securing victory or as one succumbing to defeat. There are seven fundamental battle disciplines that the

Apostle Paul gives us in the sixth chapter of his letter to the Ephesians. These verses are not often considered a treatise on spiritual discipline, but what is war without a strategy, if not injury, slavery, and death? Unless you are prepared to carry around an actual shield and wear a real helmet, you might want to think of this passage as symbolic of a more profound truth. That deeper truth is the discipline represented by each component of the soldier's garb.

The Belt of Truth (Ephesians 6:14) is the discipline of study. It is the pursuit of, and the possession of, Biblical truth, but it is not only the study of the Word of God (2 Timothy 2:15). It is also the rigorous use of the mind in studying the lives and messages of the people of faith who have gone before us. "Remember those who led you, who spoke the word of God to you; and considering the result of their conduct, imitate their faith" (Hebrews 13:7).

One of the most inspirational means by which to study is to read the biographies of great saints. This will broaden your scope of understanding and challenge you to live to a higher standard. We must study if we intend to understand the terms of the mountain, the terms of the struggle against the forces of evil that opposes us, and the truths that would empower us into victory. Many failures might have been successes with just a bit more truth on which to lean in times of battle.

The Breastplate of Righteousness (Ephesians 6:14) is the discipline of holiness. This means you must consider what is required to live a life of holiness and then apply yourself to it with all your heart. You will be quickly removed from the battlefield if you fail to see the value of holiness in a spiritual war. Wild beasts roam the mountains and wish to prohibit your advancement. They only need you to send up a flare by making provision for the flesh (Romans 13:14), and they will be upon you in an instant.

Holiness is the framework of character by which we walk as Jesus did, abide in Jesus, and live according to His commands. Holiness, much like godliness, is centered on holy living. It is the degree to which we are separated from evil. It is driven by the call to "come out" from the world and "be separate" (2 Corinthians 6:17). It is critical to the mountaineer because "without holiness, no one will see the Lord (Hebrews 12:14).

Gospel readiness (Ephesians 6:15) is the discipline of evangelism. Paul describes this readiness in terms of having put on your shoes so that you can be firmly prepared (*hetoimasia*) as a result of, or in light of, the gospel of peace. These shoes help you prepare and improve the foundation upon which you stand. "How beautiful are the feet of those who bring good news of good things" (Romans 10:15).

Evangelism as a regular practice in all the goings and comings of a believer is a clear mark of two things: One, that you believe the gospel. Two, that you are filled with the Holy Spirit. Sharing your faith with others keeps your awareness of your need for God's power and wisdom very sharp. The Apostle Paul prayed for Philemon "that the communication of thy faith may become effectual by acknowledging every good thing which is in you in Christ Jesus" (Philemon 1:6, KJV). Evangelism will play an essential role in the partnership you will form with the Holy Spirit in the furnace of intercession discussed later in the book.

The Shield of Faith (Ephesians 6:16) is the discipline of belief. What are you believing God to do right now? If nothing, you are likely not engaged in the work He has called you to do. Trusting God for your own needs is a great place to start, but *great* faith is built as you believe for God to move in the lives of others. By walking in this faith, your prayers are enlivened, your purpose in life clarified, and your fruitfulness made bountiful.

Always ask God what He would have you *believe* for Him to do. Always know what this is, and always trust Him to do it. As you walk in this kind of faith, the value of what you believe He will do becomes greater and greater, and you will want God to protect both yourself and the object of your faith. This kind of faith will be a shield that guards you against the enemy's traps, assaults, and threats.

The Helmet of Salvation (Ephesians 6:17) is the discipline of the mind. Your mind is like a stage upon which the many scenarios of life are enacted. Some of these are driven by fear, some by greed, some by lust, and some by pride. You must evaluate every thought that comes across the stage of your mind, some of which engage your imagination with illustrations of doom or fantasy. Thoughts eventually drive action, and if the thoughts are evil, the actions that follow will bring destruction.

It is important to realize, however, that Jesus didn't just save us from something evil; he saved us for something extraordinary. God wants to fill your head with His ideas, plans, and purposes. He wants to unleash divine intelligence between your ears and have you thinking in terms of eternity, not just this life. The helmet of salvation protects you *so that* your mind can be useful to the Lord.

The Sword of the Spirit (Ephesians 6:17) is the discipline of the Word of God. This is your use and implementation of God's Word in your life and ministry. The Word of God is pictured as a sword because it is your most potent weapon against the deceptive aggression of the enemy. Without the Word, you will not have the mind of Christ, you will not have the bread of life, and you will not have the truth that sets you free. The discipline of the Word, like many aspects of our faith, is both inward in its impact and outward.

The outward impact of the Word of God should be in the form of your message, doctrine, and example of godliness. The Sword of the Spirit should be used as a machete in prayer and an instrument of surgery in preaching. Never lacerate the people of God, but carefully conduct the division of soul and spirit, bone and marrow as you rightly divide the Word of truth. But in prayer, swing the sword like you are forging a pathway through the jungle. Tear down strongholds (2 Corinthians 10:3-5), loose the chains of injustice (Isaiah 58:6), and destroy the works of the devil (1 John 3:8).

Praying in the Spirit on all occasions (Ephesians 6:18) is the final discipline necessary to summit the mountain of the Lord. It may be tempting to read this Scripture as "Pray in the Spirit" and miss the "on all occasions." This would nullify the point entirely because it makes little difference to the devil if you "prayed in the Spirit" once. The hordes of hell are driven away from your endeavors by Spirit-led prayer, but then they come back to see if you've stopped praying. Every turn, every moment, and every change of circumstances must be accompanied by Spirit-led prayer.

This may seem like a lot of work. That is precisely because it *is* a lot of work, but that's why we are called disciples. We have abandoned all notions of casual pursuit. We have committed ourselves to a rigorous, unswerving, life-long chase after the Lord—no matter the cost—because He is worthy.

Devotion and Discipline

One of the fatal miscalculations of doctrine is that discipline is equivalent to legalism. Yes, some legalistic people are disciplined. Anyone can be disciplined in their own power. People of different religions may be disciplined, but that does not mean that discipline has no place in Christianity. Discipline is one of the defining attributes of the Holy Spirit. (Galatians 5:23, 2 Timothy 1:7)

To correct the miscalculations between legalism and Holy Spirit inspired discipline, we can position them as an equation:

Spiritual Discipline minus Spiritual Devotion
Equals Spiritual Death

Because obedience to Scripture requires *discipline*, we cannot replace it. Because love for Christ requires *devotion*, we cannot remove it. Because following Christ always yields an abundance of life, we cannot arrive at *death*. Our equation must read like this:

Spiritual Discipline plus Spiritual Devotion
equals Spiritual Depth

Spiritual devotion is intimacy with God driven by a covenant of love. A covenant of love is a binding promise to abandon all others and love exclusively. Much like a marriage, our covenant with God is entirely exclusive.

You don't know someone unless you are close to them. Reading about them is not enough. Meeting them once is not enough. Devotion takes a person beyond a love for the "idea" of God to a place where they love the person of God; His voice, His friendship, His character, and nature.

In his book, *The Essentials of Prayer*, E.M. Bounds describes devotion like this:

> The root of devotion is to devote to a sacred use. So that devotion in its true sense has to do with religious worship. It stands intimately connected with true prayer. Devotion is the particular frame of mind found in one entirely devoted to God. It is the spirit of reverence, of awe, of godly fear.

Thus, to be devoted is to be consecrated, set apart, holy unto God. It is to aim one-hundred percent of one's affections directly at the person of Jesus Christ and the knowledge of God through Him. Without this critical element, our pursuit of God is bronzed into nothing above human effort posing as divine communion; our discipline is rendered fruitless for the purposes of eternity.

Love Works

Can you wholeheartedly say, "I love works!"? If you cannot, it is because you have been fed to believe that works are bad. You have been preached Ephesians 2:9 without being preached Ephesians 2:10. Paul says this,

> (9) Not as a result of works, so that no one may boast. (10) For we are His workmanship created in Christ Jesus for good works, which God

prepared beforehand so that we would walk in them. (Ephesians 2:9-10)

The problem with leaving out verse 10 is that an understanding is generated that works are just what people do who are trying to be saved by their good deeds or even please God in their own strength. The answer, however, is not to disown works—obviously. The solution to this dilemma is to disown *your* strength and depend on the Lord's strength. "Cursed is the man who trusts in mankind, and makes flesh his strength, and whose heart turns away from the Lord" (Jeremiah 17:5).

But works are so important that you may not really know Him if you're not motivated to do something for Christ. Not knowing Christ will have a severe impact on your eternity! Saving faith always produces activity that advances the gospel. James makes this clear when he writes, "What use is it, my brethren, if someone says he has faith but he has no works? Can that faith save him? Even so faith, if it has no works, is dead, being by itself." (James 2:14, 17).

Jesus said, "We must work the works of Him who sent Me as long as it is day; night is coming when no one can work" (John 9:4). Notice He said, **"We must work...."**

Paul said, "Fire itself will test the quality of each man's work. If any man's work which he has built on it remains, he will receive a reward. If any man's work is burned up, he will suffer loss; but he himself will be saved, yet so as through fire" (1 Corinthians 3:13-15).

Hebrews says, "For God is not unjust so as to forget your work and the love which you have shown toward His name, in having ministered and in still ministering to the saints" (Hebrews 6:10).

When it comes to seeking God and finding Him, it is essential that you are coming in from the harvest field—and planning to go back out to it. Remember, summiting the mountain of the Lord can never be a selfish pursuit or one in which only *you* benefit. To really summit, we must go in obedience to the two greatest commands: Love God, and love others. When you are working diligently for the Lord, you identify specific focal points for your prayer times before the Lord.

If your works are motivated by love, you can love works. Otherwise, they are a waste of energy and won't glorify God. Don't stop working; repent and change your motives. Ask God to pour His love out in your heart through the Holy Spirit, and then get busy.

Good works are broken down into two categories, both of which are acts of obedience to the Word of Christ. Yes, this requires effort, focus, determination, and the power of the Holy Spirit, but all believers are equipped to do what God has prepared for them to do from the beginning of time.

The first category is the work of personal character, or becoming like Christ. You can't do this without Christ, and He *won't* do it without you. He is not interested in sovereignly making you holy. He wants you to participate in the difficulty so that you can share in the reward.

The second category is that of your love expressed toward others. This can be in word, deed, or simply spending time with someone out of compassion. For this, Jesus gives us a great place to start in Matthew 25 with the parable of the sheep and the goats.

Doing these things does not mean you are under the law. It means that you are above the law! To be under the law is to be obligated to execute a task list performed in your own strength. To be above the law means that you are compelled to obey Christ because you are in a covenant of love with Him, and it is how you can most highly honor His Word. To be above the law also means that the law is fulfilled by faith in Christ. This leads to obedience to Him through His powerful Spirit: "For it is God who is at work in you, both to will and to work for His good pleasure" (Philippians 2:13). Finally, being above the law means that you are literally building your life on top of the solid rock of His Word by putting into practice what He has taught (See Luke 6:47-48). If you are "standing" on the promises of God by faith in the work of Christ and the power of the Holy Spirit, you are above the law!

It's time to say it: "I love works!" Good works, that is, the ones created in advance for me to do, the works that bring glory to the Father and a reward to the worker.

Conclusion and Contemplation

Believe that discipline is your duty as a good soldier of Christ. Will you live wisely, carefully, and in the Spirit of discipline?

Prayer of Commitment

Father in Heaven, I want to be more disciplined. Help me break old habits and establish new patterns to recognize your Lordship in my life. Help me do this because I love You and want more than anything to know You. I ask you to expose my excuses for not seeking You with all my heart, to expose my excuses for not obeying Your Word, and expose my excuses for placing ease and comfort above faithfulness and diligence in my pursuit of you.

Enable me to do this by your strength in me, through Your Holy Spirit. Amen.

Discussion Questions

1. What is spiritual discipline? Why is it important?
2. What is the difference between Ephesians 2:9 and 2:10? Do you love works? Why or why not?
3. Read James 2:14-17. What is faith without works? Can you be saved if your faith does not produce outward fruit, or works?
4. What is the most significant discipline of the Christian life? Why is this discipline central to all other disciplines?
5. Are Christians in a war or on a cruise? Is a lazy river a good picture of the Christian life?
6. How does Ephesians 6:10-18 relate to discipline?
7. What is legalism? Why is it dangerous to think of discipline as a form of legalism?
8. What is devotion? What is the role of devotion in Christian discipline? What do you get if you have discipline without devotion?
9. Can you be under the Lordship of Jesus and not be disciplined? Why or why not?

Chapter VI

PILOTS

Obey the Laws of Flight

Imperative
We must become obedient to the Word
of God if we wish to summit.

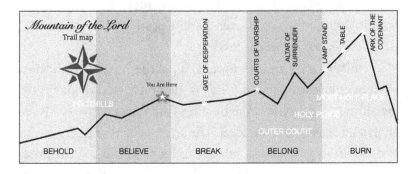

Altitude and Attitude

I grew up around airplanes. My dad is a pilot, and we often flew Cessnas, Grummans, and an occasional bi-plane. One Saturday morning, when I was about eleven, my dad took me out for breakfast at Shoney's and then for a ride in the bi-plane. We did a bunch of loops and rolls, and when we landed, I couldn't walk straight. Dad laughed and patted me on the back. As nauseous as I was, I still love that memory, and it brings up an important illustration.

The Antonov AN-225 is an airplane. It's not what you imagined just now—not even close. According to Christopher McFadden, who authored an article about this monster of aerospace, the AN-225 is the largest airplane currently in use in the world. At 275 feet long and with a wingspan of 290 feet, it is a flying football field! The AN-225 can carry a payload of up to 250 tons and weighs 285 tons when empty. It can fly at over 500 miles an hour and has a maximum take-off weight of over 600 tons! That's a big airplane.

Imagine if it was your job to fly it. How careful would you be? Can you think of the consequences of crashing it in a populated area? Of course, you would die, but so would countless others if 1,200,000 pounds of airplane, fuel, and cargo came crashing out of the sky at over 500 miles an hour!

Focus is critical to success.

Airplanes have an instrument called the Attitude Indicator. Most people know what *altitude* is, demonstrated in planes by the altimeter. *Altitude* is the height of an object above sea level or, in some cases, ground level. The *attitude* of aircraft, however, is all about its orientation relative to Earth's horizon. The nose might be angled too far down if the attitude is off, resulting in a crash. If the nose is angled too much above the horizon, the plane could stall, also potentially resulting in a crash.

Attitude is critical to success.

The Apostle Paul wrote about attitudes to the Philippians:

> "Have this attitude in yourselves which was also in
> Christ Jesus, who, although He existed in the form
> of God, did not regard equality with God, a thing
> to be grasped, but emptied himself, taking the form
> of a bond-servant, and being made in the likeness

of men. Being found in appearance as a man, He humbled himself by becoming obedient to the point of death, even death on a cross." (Philippians 2:5-8)

Obedience, to the point of death, began with attitude. Humble yourself. Empty yourself of all vain ambitions. Jesus IS God, yet He didn't regard equality with God. You are NOT God. Therefore, you definitely should not regard equality with God in evaluating your life and liberties. Become a servant. Become obedient. These are the attitudes that will keep you from crashing. This attitude shows you are friends with Jesus, "you are my friends if you do what I command" (John 15:14). This is the attitude of the most fruitful disciples of Jesus on Earth.

Obedient to Lists of Rules

"Obedient? But we aren't under the law," some may say.

"Your not suggesting we have some list of rules, are you?" Someone once said to me.

But the Bible *has* lists of rules. Why, though? If, as some suggest, we are not under obligation to obey them, why does the Bible have *lists of rules*? Jesus gave us lists of rules, Paul gave us lists of rules, Peter gave us lists of rules, James gave us lists of rules, and John gave us lists of rules. Should you toss your Bible out the window with its lists of rules?

Why even read the Bible if you don't intend to obey its lists of rules? Obedience, or doing what the Bible says, is what James meant when he challenged his readers to become "doers of the Word" (James 1:22). Let's embrace reality: We are commanded to obey Scripture. So the question is not one of "whether" to obey but of "how" to obey Christ. We should not ignore the many directives in the Bible, but perhaps the kind of obedience Jesus desires flows from the ability to see beyond the list into something much more profound.

It *certainly is* in how one sees the lists of rules. If one sees them in the singular perspective of obligation to "do," one will miss the point and grow weary under the burden of legalism. Yes, we must *do*, but this *doing* is to flow from our purpose in *being* like Christ. Being like Christ is the end goal, but mere adherence to the list will not achieve this. We must adhere to Scripture with the end in mind of conformity to the character of Christ. With this proper attitude, *doing* leads to *being*, and *being* flows from *doing*.

If the Spirit of God lives in you, you will not be controlled by the sinful nature (Romans 8:9). If you *do not* want to be like Christ, you will *not want* to obey His Word. Those living in constant disobedience must ask God if they have the Spirit of Christ in them. This might describe you, in which case, I urge you to keep reading. In the chapters ahead, I will walk you through the manner in which you can be as certainly filled with the Holy Spirit as you are with air in your lungs.

If you *do* want to be like Christ, you will see the adventure that lies ahead, not just the obligation. If I want to summit a mountain, there is an obligation to climb; but I will not see it as an obligation. Instead, I will see the adventure *within* the activities required to reach the top, challenging as they may be. Becoming like Christ is the reward of the mountaineer.

Lists of Character Qualities

Paul was immersed in a life-quest to become like Christ. In his letters to the churches, Paul was as much describing observations *of* Christ as he was delineating obligations *to* Christ. The Scriptures are the living Logos, declaring the nature and character of Immanuel, God with us. The goal of the Holy Spirit as He spoke through the apostles and prophets was to declare the beauty of Christ and illuminate the path upon which we might tread in our purpose to become like Christ.

Let's take, for example, this list he gives us from 1 Thessalonians 5:14-25, taken from the NIV Bible. Try to see this as a "to be" list rather than a "to do" list, and you will find what you need to avoid the death sentence of legalistic obedience:

- *Warn those who are idle (Christ was busy with the Father's work)*
- *Encourage the timid (Christ brought peace to the fearful)*
- *Help the weak (Christ loved and helped the helpless)*
- *Be patient with everyone (Christ was very patient, especially with Peter!)*
- *Make sure that nobody pays back wrong for wrong (Christ did not retaliate)*
- *Always try to be kind to each other and to everyone else (Christ was kind)*
- *Be joyful always (Christ was joyful and wanted to share his joy)*
- *Pray continually (Christ set the example in prayer)*
- *Give thanks in all circumstances, for this is God's will for you in Christ Jesus (Christ gave thanks)*
- *Do not put out the Spirits fire (Christ was full of the Holy Spirit)*
- *Do not treat prophecies with contempt (Christ honored prophecy)*
- *Test everything (Christ tested the teachers of the law)*

- *Hold on to the good (Christ found good in every circumstance)*
- *Avoid every kind of evil (Christ had nothing to do with evil)*
- *Pray for us (Christ ever lives to intercede for us)*

Every command of Scripture is a means by which we may see the person of Jesus. As we engage His beauty—described in His word—we will find ourselves loving Him with all our heart, soul, mind, and strength; and loving others as ourselves. Thus we must see the character of Christ in the Word of Christ to abide in Christ and become like Christ. Consider this: If I have embraced the words of John that "the one who says he abides in Him ought himself to walk in the same manner as He walked" (1 John 2:6), and with a deep ambition to be like Christ and love others I carefully align my behavior to Scripture, taking each failure as an indication of further need for heart change, am I legalistic? Absolutely not!

Repentance

But let me be clear, becoming like Christ is not optional for Christians. We ought to *want* this with deep, earnest desire. But in all reality, we are *commanded* to make this our primary objective. In fact, before the foundations of the world, we were "predestined to become conformed to the image" of Christ (Romans 8:29). We were destined to be under His Lordship, impacted by His presence, and changed by His Spirit. If we belong to Christ, we are under the Lordship of Christ. This means He is our Ruler, and we are His subjects.

There is no such thing as "grace" that allows Christians to do as they wish. Such tolerance is issued from one's own conscience to one's own sinful nature. This thing which some have mistakenly called grace, is a wolf in sheep's clothing; it is self-absolving anti-christ humanistic atheism; it is the flesh crying out for "provision." If this mindset is what keeps you happy, abandon it immediately, throw yourself at the feet of Jesus and plead for His mercy.

To align one's self with the nature and character of God in all thought, word, and action is the basis of repentance. Such alignments are clearly put forth on the pages of the Bible by men who "moved by the Holy Spirit spoke from God" (2 Peter 1:21). This preliminary discipline is to be entirely motivated by a love for Christ, not by human strength apart from Christ. This is to become habitual in the elementary days and months of a person who has been born again, and it is to become so second nature that the individual can move on to maturity.

> Therefore leaving the elementary teaching about the
> Christ, let us press on to maturity, not laying again
> a foundation of repentance from dead works and of
> faith toward God, of instruction about washings and
> laying on of hands, and the resurrection of the dead
> and eternal judgement. (Hebrews 6:1-2)

Some people, however, are still staggering around like drunken fools, touting in a tirade of immaturity, "freedom from the law." Christ frees us from the law, no doubt, but in these whitewashed tombs, neither heart-change, repentance, nor a desire to be like Christ has ever occurred. These are unconverted, unrepentant, and unfaithful people who engage in precisely the same lifestyle choices as the world from which they were supposedly delivered.

Some may say (of their spiritual depravity), "I guess God wanted to teach me something," blaming the consequences of *their* sin on some misconstrued distortion of *God's* sovereignty. Yes, God wanted to teach them obedience, but they rebelled against Him, and now He is teaching them repentance again. How many times will they lay this foundation? This was precisely the predicament of the Israelites throughout much of the Old Testament history; they rebelled against God with stiff necks and stubborn hearts, forgetting what His word said and embracing the inclinations of their own hearts.

If these "sons of disobedience" were the kinds of pilots that they are Christians, they might all be in Hell, having crashed their planes because they thought obedience to the principles of flight was optional. In Hell, they will surely cry out, "What are you trying to teach me now, oh Flight Instructor?" Silence.

What did the Savior mean when He categorized as goats those who neglected to do as He commanded? In even the most straightforward ways, they were ignorant of His heart to love those around them whom the world had rejected—those Christ deemed "the least of my brothers." These were some of the most basic affiliations to Christ's nature and character, and they ignored them. How did He handle this? He said, "depart from Me, accursed ones, into the eternal fire which has been prepared for the devil and his angels" (Matthew 25:41). Again, we ought to *want* to be like Christ, for who is there better to imitate than Him? But want or not, we are under the severe consequence of eternal fire if we *neglect* to be like Him.

Legalism and Relativism

One of the most significant doctrinal mistakes is generalizing obedience to Scripture as being "under the law." It is of supreme importance that you understand there is a chasm between the two of immeasurable breadth. Spirit-empowered obedience to the Word of God is a fundamental *requirement* for every person who would venture to be a disciple of Jesus. Denying this is to subscribe to antinomian heresies and purchase Hell at the price of neglect. Rejecting obedience to the Word of God under the pretense of legalism is the same thing as rejecting the authority of the Word of God under the pretense of relativism.

Relativism might seem like a modern idea advocated by "liberated" people who have raised their intellect to the stratospheres of the gods. But this faulty ideology leads to a point at which *man's wickedness becomes exceedingly great, such that every inclination of the thoughts of his heart is only evil all the time.* (See Genesis 6:5). So relativism happens to be the reason God sent the flood in Noah's time—nothing new, then.

Relativism is essentially the abandonment of Christ as King in exchange for pseudo-liberty. The relativistic mind has no intention of doing what Christ has commanded, but rather, it does whatever it desires. Israel is again our example of this; millennia ago, when they *"had no king and each man did what is right in his own eyes"* (Judges 17:6, KJV). Having no king is not possible in the Kingdom of God because in the Kingdom, Christ *is* King, and we are His servants.

Thus, in the absence of absolute truth, or objective truth, men consider their opinions as equal to God's commands and as viable alternatives. People will say things like, "what's right

for me is right for me and what's right for you is right for you."
That only works for you until what is "right" for someone *else*
is to harm *you*. Most people don't realize that they are sub-
consciously subscribing to relativism as a means to justify
living according to the desires of their flesh. Doing whatever
your flesh leads you to do is dangerous living, especially for
Christians. Paul told the disciples Colossae it was "because of
these things the wrath of God will come upon the sons of disobedience" (Colossians 3:6).

The Nature of The Law

The primary differences between those under the law and
those who are faithful servants of Christ aren't all that difficult
to ascertain from Scripture. But these, which I will discuss, are
not the reasons people don't obey. Disobedience to the Word
of God occurs because the hearts of people are rebellious. Deep
down, they don't *want* God, they want their independence, and
they believe they will do well enough in it. A vile and degenerate
rebellion can appear hideous to the more refined parts of society,
so it is often covered with a sort of quasi-virtuous adherence
to the constructs of Biblical values, minus any change of heart.

Nevertheless, being under the law is a real thing. There are
Christians who are, sadly, "under the law." But being under the
law is not equivalent to being obedient to Scripture; these two
are diametrically opposed to one another.

Legalism, or "being under the law," has at its roots several
distinctions. First, it can be defined as *a selfish motivation to imitate biblical values by human strength without a change of heart
or a relationship with Christ*. Legalistic people are focused on
outward behavior over inward character. Legalism is behavioral

modification without spiritual sanctification. This is the reason Jesus called these imitators "whitewashed tombs" (Matthew 23:27-28).

Secondly, it is important to note that since legalism is the religious mechanism for establishing *false* spirituality and piety, it wholly depends on man's willpower. Legalism is characterized by those who "help themselves." Contrary to popular humanistic thinking, however, God does not "help those who help themselves." He "helps those who throw themselves" at His feet and cry out to Him as the singular source of heart change.

Humility is the primary driver of spiritual transformation, and no one ever matures beyond the need for it. How arrogant and independent it is to think that we help ourselves. We can do *nothing* apart from Him. We can offer Him nothing with which to work but our very lives in total surrender at His feet.

Legalism, on the contrary, is void of any deep-rooted intentions to know God intimately and honor Him in His Majesty. Thus it will be driven by pride rather than humility, and the praise of man is its full reward (see Matthew 6:5).

This willpower-driven self-righteousness is the essence of legalism. Despite all the "good" behavior, the person is still wretched before the perfect holiness of God and in desperate need of a Savior. Still, they can't see this because they are so proud of having fasted twice a week and having given 10% (see Luke 18:12).

This religious fervor will never produce lasting fruit since legalism is driven more by willpower than the Holy Spirit. This mechanism skirts around the Holy Spirit *because* it is rooted in the pride of life, and the Holy Spirit will not interact with that falsehood. This was the fault of the Galatians and the cause of the Apostle Paul's stern rebuke (see Galatians 3:3).

Thirdly, not only is this person *devoid* of intimacy with God, but they actively *avoid* intimacy with God. Locked in the functions of the flesh, the law-bound person will not venture through the corridors of humility that are prerequisites to knowing God intimately. Such people may pray, but they will pray to themselves and about themselves (see Luke 18:9-11). These folks do not go away justified before God, though in their eyes, they have achieved much because they were "praying."

Fourthly, this person has not experienced a heart change. They likely have not been born again, are not children of God, and do not belong to God (see John 3:3-5).

Lastly, these people have a form of godliness but deny the power of God (2 Timothy 3:5). Don't be mistaken; this doesn't mean they deny there *is* the "power of God," this means that they deny the Holy Spirit his rightful role as Governor and Guide of our lives, whereby we are filled to all the fullness of God and endued with His power for the purposes of the gospel. In essence, legalistic people are unyielded, un-surrendered, unbroken, and unavailable to God. Ironically, this is the same heart condition of the hyper-grace antinomian liberalist who thinks that God's love is such that there are no rules.

If you do not have constant fellowship with the Holy Spirit—having His power "coursing through your veins," you will not be able to obey Scripture except by your own human strength. If you succeed by your own strength, you will deny that the power of the Holy Spirit even exists; and you will have become a Pharisee. It was for this reason that Jesus explained the Pharisees were in error because they knew neither the Scriptures nor the power of God (see Matthew 22:29).

The Law of Christ

Paul describes the "law of sin and death," as that which is "of no value against fleshly indulgence" (Colossians 2:23); and distinguishes it from "the law of the Spirit of life," by which we are empowered to live as Christ did (see Romans 8:2). We can't afford to miss this distinction. Otherwise, we will either succumb to legalism—the burden of obedience without love, or to antinomianism—the delusion of freedom without obedience.

So, there *is* a law that we are under. But it is not the law of sin and death, and it is not the written code (regulations). Paul tells the Corinthians that he is "under the law of Christ" (1 Corinthians 9:21), and he commands the Ephesians to "obey the law of Christ" (Ephesians 6:2). James calls this the "perfect law that gives freedom" (James 1:25).

The fact that we are "not under the law" could not mean that we are now free to be "lawless." Nearly every contributor to the New Testament, including Jesus, condemned lawlessness as among the greatest of degradations to humanity. Therefore, we do have a rule of law in the Kingdom of God, and that rule is defined clearly by who the King *is* and what He is *like*.

But what is this law of Christ, this perfect law that gives freedom? The "law of the Spirit of Life" is that obligation which we are under to imitate the nature and character of Christ—love. The Holy Spirit teaches us to do this. Every verse of Scripture is intended to illuminate His character and is that to which we are obligated. Look at how the Apostle Paul puts it:

> So then, brethren, we are under obligation, not to the flesh, to live according to the flesh—for if you are living according to the flesh, you must die; but

> if by the Spirit you are putting to death the deeds of
> the body, you will live. (Romans 8:12)

So, our obligation is to live according to the Spirit, and the Spirit will teach us all things and remind us of everything that Jesus taught us (John 14:26).

To further bolster our understanding, let's take a few verses of Scripture into account. John's primary theme in his first two letters was to convey just what the love of God would look like in a believer. He says in 1 John 3:24, "The one who keeps His commandments abides in Him, and He in him." Also, in 2 John 1:6, "And this is love, that we walk in according to His commandments."

If we love God, we will want to be like God. God is faithful. Be faithful. God is merciful. Be merciful. God is honest. Be honest. God is generous. Be generous. The adventure of reading the Bible is discovering all the ways we can imitate our Father in heaven. If we fail to do so, we are not under condemnation but simply must come to Him in humility that He may help us better live as Jesus did. Learning this is the essence of the Christian life, that Christ may be formed in us (see Galatians 4:19).

Obedience is Love

The Apostle Paul describes his task in preaching the gospel in this way: "Through whom we have received grace and apostleship to bring about the obedience of faith among the Gentiles for His name's sake" (Romans 1:5). To what was he calling the gentiles? Obedience. Paul takes it a step further when he writes to the believers in Thessalonica: "If anyone does not obey our instruction in this letter, take special note of that person and do not associate with him, so that he will be put to shame" (2 Thessalonians 3:14). Here, there is a fine line between law-driven condemnation and Spirit-driven accountability to obedience. As the Church, we MUST grasp this vital difference.

The enormous importance of love-driven obedience is heralded by the apostles who heard it straight from the mouth of the Christ, who told them, "If anyone loves Me, he will *keep* My word" (John 14:23). This greek word, *tereo,* means to "watch over, to guard" and implies a prioritized vigilance. In other words, Jesus is saying something along these lines: "I'm giving you something extremely valuable in what I am teaching, be careful with it, pay close attention to it, and put it into practice."

In case it wasn't clear enough, however, He continued, "He who does not love Me, does not keep My words" (John 14:24). Pretty simple: obedience is love. Why? Because obedience to Christ is the most vivid and demonstrative expression of trust one can produce, and love cannot be mature without trust. We have been entrusted with an invaluable collection of truths, and we must watch over them carefully, guarding them and putting them into practice in our daily lives.

So, it's not only because we *have to*—because Christ is *dominant* (Lord), but because we *want to*—because Christ is *dear* (Friend), that we obey Him. Jesus summed up the law for the Pharisees by quoting this passage from Deuteronomy:

> "And He said to him, 'You shall love the Lord your God with all your heart and with all your soul, and with all your mind.' This is the great and foremost commandment." (Deuteronomy 6:4-7, Matthew 22:37)

Why must we obey Scripture? Because it describes what is most loving in how we relate to God and people. Love begins with choices and eventually produces trust. Choosing what is loving involves deference—choosing modesty or abstaining from the appearance of evil. Sometimes the best choice is sacrificial, involving patience or extreme generosity.

The Scriptures give us a clear picture of what is—or was, and what isn't—or wasn't, the most loving action in the circumstances of each Bible character. Paul's description of love in 1 Corinthians chapter 13 is a description of the nature and character of Jesus. Therefore, love will drive us; mad-love, in fact, will compel, control, and constrain us to imitate Jesus (see 2 Corinthians 5:14).

Some of what is in the Bible can be confusing, especially to new believers. But if you come at it from the two greatest commands, you will have fulfilled all the requirements of the law. Listen to what Paul says,

> "Owe nothing to anyone except to love one another; for he who loves his neighbor has fulfilled the law. For this, 'You shall not commit adultery, You shall not murder, You shall not steal, You shall not covet,' and if there is another commandment, it is summed up in this saying, 'You shall love your neighbor as yourself.' Love does no wrong to a neighbor; therefore love is the fulfillment of the law." (Romans 13:8-10)

Interpreting Scripture for Application

The accurate, faithful interpretation of Scripture is of paramount importance if we are to understand what God is like and what his expectations are for his people. Derek W. H. Thomas offers these guidelines as we approach Scripture for its meaning:

> To these various genres, distinctive rules of interpretation apply (history is to be read as history, parable as parable, apocalypse as apocalypse, and so on), ensuring that a "literal" interpretation is sensitive to the literary genre.

The interpretation of the law is a prime example. Moral laws are eternally fixed as primary obligations to anyone who would either know God or make Him known. These are the least difficult to understand, and of them, the Bible's intent for our responsibility is quite clear. However, there are some commands in the Bible that we are not under obligation to obey. Why is this? To better understand how to break down the Bible into what we are to do and what we are no longer required to do—out of love for God and others, it is vital to understand a couple of basics about the law.

First, the law was the means to righteousness, or right standing with God, for those under the Old Covenant. Under the New Covenant, Christ fulfilled the righteous requirements of the law for us (Romans 8:4), so the law can no longer provide us with a means to righteousness. Paul states it like this: "Not having a righteousness of my own derived from the law, but that which is through faith in Christ, the righteousness which comes from God on the basis of faith" (Philippians 3:9).

Secondly, the laws given in the books of Moses (the Torah, or the first five books of the Bible) had specific protective guidance for the Hebrew people. Many of these directives are bound by time, culture, or other circumstances. This may mean that they are not directly relevant to us but are still indirectly relevant. Some laws were written to direct the Hebrews in matters related to sanitation, social development, holidays and festivals, and foods. Sanitation is still pertinent but not handled exactly the same way commanded in Leviticus. Social life, food, feasts, and holidays are still relevant, but under the law of Christ, the law of love may have different applications to our culture and time. On the other hand, morality is always relevant because it is representative of God's nature; therefore, moral laws are to be adhered to entirely. Our duty is "accurately handling the word of truth" (2 Timothy 2:15).

To interpret Scripture through the eyes of love, one must be led by the Spirit. Genuine love is not of human origin. It is not rooted in your willpower to love. It *is* a choice, but it is one that is fueled by the Holy Spirit. In this manner of spirit, one reading the law may ask the Holy Spirit, **"What loving intention was at the root of this command?"** It will be easy to see as you read commands like "don't steal" or "don't murder," because these commands are rooted in core aspects of morality. You may have to do some digging and researching to understand why the Holy Spirit spoke what he did through Moses in some of the passages of Leviticus. But with hunger driving you and a desire to be conformed to Christ, you will light upon insights piled high, inspiring and directing your growth in the Lord.

This matter of love is evident in Paul's letter to the Romans, "the love of God has been poured out within our hearts through the Holy Spirit who was given to us" (Romans 5:5). What is loving cannot be determined by agents who are naturally selfish and unloving. We must be led by One whose nature is love. In doing so, the law is fulfilled, and we are not under its life-draining, human-powered obligations. For this reason, it is stated, "but if you are led by the Spirit, you are not under the law" (Galatians 5:18).

He states that Christ canceled the written code, nailing it to the cross and making a public spectacle of its having ended (see Colossians 2:14). He describes these directives as "things which are a mere shadow of what is to come; but the substance belongs to Christ" (Colossians 2:17). This is a clear indication that Christ would fulfill the law by always doing what is in the best interest of the Father and of the people. For this reason, Christ stated, "which is lawful on the Sabbath: to do good or to do evil?" Christ took their Sabbath regulations and redefined them in terms of what was most loving.

Paul describes legalistic regulations, void of the divine nature, thus:

> If you have died with Christ to the elementary principles of the world, why, as if you were living in the world, do you submit yourself to decrees, such as, "Do not handle, do not taste, do not touch!" (Which all refer to things destined to perish with use)—in accordance with the commandments and teachings of men? These are matters which have, to be sure, the appearance of wisdom in self-made religion and self-abasement and severe treatment of the body, but are of no value against fleshly indulgence. (Colossians 2:20-23)

The Holy Spirit knows what is loving—uniquely loving—for all people in all circumstances. For this reason, disciples must know and listen to the Holy Spirit. But one cannot simply claim to be "led by the Spirit" while living independently of biblical values. For this reason, it is furthermore essential to understand what is and isn't loving as we meditate on Scripture. To correctly ascertain a balanced interpretation of Scripture, entrust yourself to godly people who herald the inerrancy of Scripture, who have walked your path—loving the Lord with all their hearts, and who have good cause to be trusted in their walk with Christ (see Hebrews 13:7). Remember, Scripture is our measuring rod.

Learning to fly the AN-225 would take a lot of focus, concentration, and training. You would have to study a lot. You would have to practice alongside more experienced pilots—a lot. You would have to have critical attention to detail and disciplined respect for the laws of physics. You will need no less to follow Jesus, live by the Spirit, and grow in your private and public victory. Start with embracing by faith the great gift of the Word of God and commit yourself to interpret it correctly, do what it says, and so become like Christ.

Conclusion and Contemplation

Believe that obedience to Scripture is your love song to Christ. Will you believe that Christ's Word is His best for you? Will you imitate Christ out of a deep desire to be like Him?

Prayer of Commitment

Father in Heaven, Please help me see Your nature and character in Scripture. Help me rightly divide the word of truth and never subscribe to the idea that obedience to Jesus is the same as being under the law. Help me be under Christ as Lord, to be under the law of Christ, as the Apostle Paul was, and embrace this perfect law that brings freedom. I want to see You and Your nature when I read Your Word. Teach me by the Holy Spirit and remind me of everything Jesus has commanded me to do. Amen.

Discussion Questions

1. Explain how attitude affects success? What attitude did Christ have that we should also have?
2. Why does the Bible have lists of rules?
3. Should we expend our efforts to obey these lists of rules? How important is this? Why?
4. What is the relationship between obedience and repentance?
5. What does it mean to be "under the law?"
6. How is Spirit-empowered obedience different than legalistic obedience?
7. What is the role of love in obedience?
8. How can we interpret Scripture using the definition of love?
9. What is antinomianism, and what are its dangers?

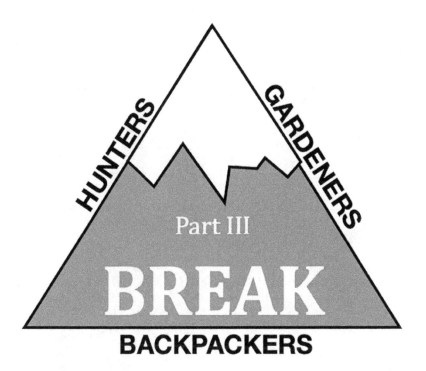

HUNTERS GARDENERS

Part III

BREAK

BACKPACKERS

INTRODUCTION

If you are ready to climb, take a knee! Desperation begins this journey, and brokenness continues it. In part three of *The Mountaineer*, we will move beyond the foothills and arrive at the Temple's Gate. Like courageous explorers, we will drag our pain and resistance with us until they vanish in awe of what we discover.

In this section, we will look at how hunters, backpackers, and gardeners all carry an expectation with them. They are looking, hoping, and searching for more, and they are willing to undergo spiritual "heart surgery" to find the Lord. These are the ones who discover the lovingkindness of God. The lovingkindness of God is what draws us to be reconciled with Him. Like a sprawling meadow of wildflowers in the foothills of the mountain of the Lord, His lovingkindness is our only hope that mercy will, in fact, triumph over judgment.

This alone is enough to bring us to our knees when we encounter Jesus, the Gate. Desperation for God and a broken, tender heart are those things that will invariably bring us into the courts of heaven, where we experience His presence.

Literary Support

When through the wood and forest glade I wander
And hear the birds sing sweetly in the trees

When I look down from lofty mountain grandeur
And see the brook and feel the gentle breeze
Then sings my soul, my Savior God to Thee
How great Thou art, how great Thou art
—Carl Boberg, *How Great Thou Art*

Valleys In the Shadows
Asiah Wedin

A picture of reversing hills
Are the valleys in the shadows
The morning air completely fills
The valleys in the shadows

Beneath the light and o'er the grass
Are the valleys in the shadows
All frights and fears will surely pass
In the valleys in the shadows

So if you find a place to lay
In the valleys in the shadows
Do watch the little fawns at play
In the valleys in the shadows

"The road took us to the most distant fountain of the waters of the mighty Missouri in search of which we have spent so many toilsome days and restless nights. Thus far I had accomplished one the those great objects on which my mind has been unalterably fixed for many years. Judge then of the pleasure I felt allaying my thirst with this pure and ice-cold water, which issues from the base of a low mountain or hill of a gentle ascent for half a mile. The

mountains are high on either end of this gap at the head of this rivulet through which the road passes. Here I halted a few minutes and rested myself." —Meriwether Lewis, on discovering the source of the Missouri.

God's-Acre
Henry Wadsworth Longfellow

Into its furrows shall we all be cast
In the sure faith that we shall rise again
At the great harvest, when the archangel's blast
Shall winnow, like a fan, the chaff and grain

Then shall the good stand in immortal bloom
In the fair gardens of that second birth
And each bright blossom mingle its perfume
With that of flowers, which never bloomed on Earth

Chapter VII

HUNTERS

In the Foothills of Lovingkindness

Imperative

*We must regularly encounter the environment
of God's lovingkindness.*

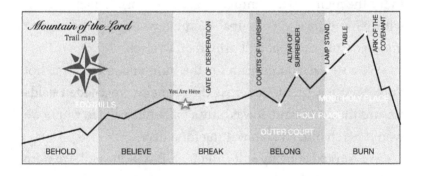

The Cackling Booth

November 2017

Gainesville, Missouri

Asher and I embarked upon his first deer hunt in the middle of November, 2017. We filled the car with our camping and hunting gear and set out for the Ozark Mountains. On the way, we ate a dozen peanut butter and jelly sandwiches and made a stop at Starbucks. After seven hours of twisting and turning roads, we pulled onto the gravel of "Wedin Way" and crossed the low-water bridge onto my dad's farm.

Deep in the Ozark mountains, autumn had settled on the woodsy acreage. Leaves in the auburn spectrum robed the birch, oaks, and elms in splendor, speaking in the visual poetry of the Creator. I mused at the seemingly impossible likelihood that such a Creator—who could speak into existence an enormity of delightful vistas and aromas such as are manifest in the profound pleasantness of fall—would let me have a relationship with Him. What kindness, what generosity, what tender mercy! I grew more and more satisfied in the goodness of God as I pitched our tent, inflated an air mattress, and tossed all our gear in for the night. That evening, we gathered together and visited with "Grandma and Grandpa" Wedin a while, and then Asher and I got into our tent and drifted off to sleep.

We rose early to gear up for the hunt and, after some hot Folgers coffee, set afoot across the crunchy, frost-laden fields toward the deer stand. It was only a half-mile or so to where we would perch ourselves in waiting for a deer.

We worked at being still and quiet. But in the end, we were far too interested in the euphoria of experiencing such an event. Three generations of Wedins sat atop inverted buckets in a pallet hut covered with camouflaged cloth, waiting with tear-filled eyes for something to shoot at. The pallet hut was indeed a brilliant innovation. Though it was much like a fort built by eight-year-olds, it was cozy, constructed of primarily free materials, and provided multiple places to rest one's rifle—supposing a deer would come into sight.

No deer ventured near the cackling booth, however, and our waiting proved to be unfruitful. Nevertheless, we returned to the house merry and forgetful of the underlying purpose of our adventure.

The daytime consisted of napping, eating, and shooting things. Later, in the afternoon, we were joined by a fourth Wedin, affectionately called "Uncle Andrew" by the youngest version of us all. Andrew aimed and missed with as many firearms as I did, and we laughed at the continual rendering of nonsense with which he addressed every motion and sound created by anyone or anything close enough to be incorporated into his non-stop improvisational comedy. Our bellies ached from laughing and overeating, but we continued to do both because the humor was so thick and the deer stew so irresistibly delicious.

Our second attempt at deer hunting was a warmer repeat of the first, except that, this time, it included Andrew, who sat sorely visible *outside* the pallet hut, where he added several decibels to what was already an overly noisy hunting party. Asher insisted that the deer were behind us and that he had seen them, but none of us could see anything because our aged eyes were clouded over with tears from laughing so hard.

When we finally gave up the hunt to the falling dusk, we walked over to where Asher had "seen the deer," and sure enough, there were three deer! A big buck and two does. They bounded away, glibly flashing their whitetails, as we gasped at the audacity and irony of our misdirected focus toward the empty field.

Guitars and cocoa were passed around the evening after the failed hunts. No one really minded that we didn't get a deer, as processing one is time-consuming, and we had only a short time to visit. Grandma Wedin brought forth more delicious food, pies, ice cream, and coffee, all with smiles and laughter— and the feasting continued.

As we were exchanging songs and stories, Grandpa Wedin unveiled his prized guitar. It had been his birthday gift from over twenty years before, and he said, "Asher, I want *you* to have this," handing him the beautiful instrument. Asher's eyes grew wide with unbelief. "Is he kidding?" he wondered. But he wasn't.

That generosity, benevolence, and environment of pure joy and peace found in a rural haven of quiet and rest called "Wedinville," is the essence of the lovingkindness of God. My dad's gift to Asher reminded me of God's generous gifts to us. In and through His lovingkindness, God gave His Son so that we could have everlasting life. In the same disposition toward all humanity, He continues to offer us both the environment of His goodness and the tools we need to work alongside Him, persevere in hardship, and to bring forth His purposes in the earth today.

Feel His Breath

Imagine sitting in a coffee shop with your favorite character from history, your favorite author, or an international figure from whom you had long desired to learn. Imagine a quiet corner with ambiance and focus where you can hang on this person's every word, close enough to feel their breath as they disclose secrets you'd long-held as mysteries. This is *"panim!"* This closeness, this proximity, this environment of apprenticeship learning is exactly what the Holy Spirit desires to create with you. He wants to get close to you, in your face, so to speak, so you will remember what you learned. Jesus made this closeness possible for all who believe.

This is the environment where the lovingkindness of God is transmitted to us. The truths you come to understand here will produce power in you, by which you will launch into victory. High voltage spiritual electricity will affect you in this environment, shredding cloaks of darkness that would otherwise obscure how deeply He loves those who fear Him.

To galvanize this point, look back to the first work of God on humanity. "Then the Lord God formed the man from the dust of the ground, and breathed into his nostrils the breath of life, and the man became a living being" (Genesis 2:7). In this creation event, God is looking at what He made. He could have settled for a sculpture, but He saw the potential for more. As He gazed upon the formation in His hand, He drew close to it, breathed into its nostrils, and it became a living being.

Intimate proximity to God has been fundamental to our relationship with Him and usefulness to Him from the very first interaction between the divine and the created. For the first time, Adam felt the breath of God upon his skin. Immediately, this work of creation was enlivened, enabled, and empowered toward action. It otherwise had zero potential.

Significance

Imagine for a moment that you have ascended beyond the small town below you into the foothills of the mountain. There you are entranced by the view ahead, the wildflowers at your side, and the way the trail bends and curves with the contours of the mountainside. You pause to let the sun warm your face, and you take a deep breath of the crisp air. Large birds wheel upwards above you, and small ones sing from their nests in the blossoming black cherry trees not far off the trail.

You are on your way to summit the hill of the Lord. You will meet with Him and gaze upon His beauty in His temple. He is drawing you there, and you are responding. These foothills are the place of His lovingkindness, where He reassures you and fills your heart with a vision for meeting with Him. The primary hope of this section is that you would seize upon greater tenderness in your heart, and you can get there by understanding how kind, gracious, and loving the Lord is toward you.

On such a journey upwards, some have stood in awe of the sheer mass of the mountains in their gaze. These mountains stand tall and imposing upon the earth, yet the earth hangs quietly in space, at quite a distance from even its Moon. From the Moon, the massive snow-capped ranges aren't even visible, let alone the person who beholds their wonder. And though the earth is a beautiful blue orb off the horizon of the Moon, it is a mere star from its nearest planet, a speck barely visible in our solar system. Beyond this, our world becomes an unnoticeable, indistinguishable molecule in the vastness of space.

No word of Earth need be spoken beyond our galaxy, for Earth is gone there, having vanished into depths irretrievable from such distances. Our galaxy is, according to NASA, over 100,000 light-years from side to side. But the Milky Way galaxy is only one of over 100 Billion galaxies in our Universe, which is around 93 billion light-years in its expanse. There are an estimated 200 billion trillion stars in the Universe, most of them much larger than Earth.

How could God love us? How could Elohim become a man on a planet barely visible outside its Solar System? Why would He love us, so small? Does our infinitesimally small home called Earth affect our value—our worth?

Could it be that we are beyond the reach of significance because we are so small in comparison to the Universe? Perhaps the One who created us *wanted* us to feel as if we were alone as we fly through empty space on this terrestrial ball. It seems He is underscoring our helplessness, our need—a precursor to the demonstration of his mercy and kindness.

In all reality, though, making us bigger would not make us more lovable. Did you know that? If Earth was a massive planet at the center of the Universe, we would not be more deserving of His love—we would not be more likely to "catch His attention." In fact, we could be even smaller and still be loved. We could all live on an atom, and in some respects—at least comparatively—we do!

Sand

It is estimated that there are more atoms in one grain of sand than stars in the Universe. Estimates range in the quintillions, some as many as one-hundred-quintillion, depending on the size and type of sand. Each atom has electrons buzzing around it at the speed of light. Tiny universes exist on every one of more than 7 quintillion grains of sand on the Earth. Right here on Earth, incomparably larger than the sand which warms our toes on the shores of a sunny beach, we disprove the "size equals significance" idea. Purported by atheists who blindly reach for meaning without hope of finding it, this idea is used to dismiss any notions of a personal God who loves His creation.

God is infinite. That doesn't mean God is enormous; it means God is measureless in any direction, on any scale. It doesn't matter how small we are! He can fill smaller hearts than ours. He can go to the nano-sphere and have a picnic or move galaxies with His breath. He is not material, nor is His love diminished by anything which carries in its very nature measurability. While we are made in God's image—indicating some likeness to Him—one of the most remarkable differences between God and us is that we are created and thus finite, while He is uncreated and infinite.

It is enough to state that God's infinite qualities exempt Him from the limitations imposed on the finite. However, it must be pointed out to assure our understanding of the subject that God is also Spirit in nature and is spiritually known. This is almost too logical to imply because it should be painfully obvious that anything material in nature is finite.

His love is conferred upon us from Spirit to spirit, and His means of communication is by His Spirit speaking to ours in spiritual words not easily understood in the carnal, physical world. Therefore, it is nonsense to conclude we are alone and unlovable simply by observation of the size of Earth in proportion to the Universe.

His love is immeasurable, and so is His kindness. His thoughts of us are more numerable than the sand (Psalm 139:17-18). He is bursting with love for us. We are the objects of His love because we are His own. He made us and is happy with what He created. He has made a way for us to know Him, hear Him, and interact with Him, and we can do that from anywhere in the Universe.

> Do you not know? Have you not heard? Has it not been declared to you from the beginning? Have you not understood from the foundations of the earth? It is He who sits above the circle of the earth, and its inhabitants are like grasshoppers. Who stretches out the heavens like a curtain, and spreads them out like a tent to dwell in. He it is who reduces the rulers to nothing, who makes the judges of the

earth meaningless. Scarcely have they been planted, scarcely have they been sown, scarcely has their stock taken root in the earth, but He merely blows on them, and they wither, and the storm carries them away like stubble. "To whom will you liken Me? That I would be his equal?" says the Holy One. Lift up your eyes on high and see who has created the stars, the One who leads forth their host by number and calls them all by name; Because of the greatness of His might and the strength of His power, not one of them is missing. (Isaiah 40:21-27)

Don't imagine for one moment that the one who can bring out 200 billion trillion stars and call each of them by name is beyond loving you. His love for you is incomparable—even to the vastness of the Universe—because it is infinite.

As such, "Your lovingkindness, O Lord, extends to the heavens" (see Psalm 36:5), and "as high as the heavens are above the earth, so great is his lovingkindness toward those who fear Him" (Psalm 103:11). Someday you will stand before this infinite Love and see clearly, "face to face" (1 Corinthians 13:12), and know just how much He does love you.

Therefore, let there be no doubt: we are loved. We are loved by the innumerable acts of kindness lifted into our reality by the Creator of reality. You once carried the weight of sin and the sentence of death in your soul, but His kindness came to you, forgiving and forgetting your sins (Hebrews 8:12). You were wounded by others and felt worthless, but He has come to you with healing in His wings (see Malachi 4:2). He did not treat you as your sins deserved (Psalm 103:10), but waited carefully, hopefully, for you to respond to the kindness of His conviction.

He is ready to share His balm with you, His salve upon your eyes, you will see Him with ever-increasing clarity, you will cry out to Him, "Son of David, have mercy on me!" He will call you to Himself, and you will come (Luke 18:38-40). There He will stoop to your lowered frame and bestow upon you His healing, mercy, and kindness (see also Mark 8:22-26, 10:47-52).

He is a Father to you who were fatherless, or whose fathers were absent; and He provides justice to the widow (see Psalm 68:5), He heals all your wounds and renews your youth like the eagle (see Psalm 103:3-5). He is the Father of mercies and the God of all comfort (see 2 Corinthians 1:3). He is the Father of the prodigal; waiting, searching, and yearning for you; He sees you, runs to you, embraces you, and kisses you (see Luke 15:11-32). He is standing on His porch, waiving as you arrive, eager to share His kindness, deer stew, and guitars with you.

Kindness Leads to Brokenness

When I consider His love for me, I am stalled with gratefulness. I am undone and wrecked by His everlasting mercy, His enduring compassion, and His mighty kindness. This is the place where we begin to break and really break. Sorrow over sin can break a man down, but not to the degree of gratefulness for mercy. When we understand the mercy of God toward us, His ever kind disposition, and baffling patience, we will break down. And this breaking down is instrumental in His building us back up as we need to be.

God's lovingkindness is at the root of His patience with our tendency toward sin, foolishness, and rebellion. He created us fearfully and wonderfully; He is endeared toward us because He formed us (see Psalm 139:13), and this will never change. In fact, lovingkindness is so central to His nature, it is included in the most heralded description of God in the Bible:

> Then the Lord passed by in front of him and pro-claimed, "the Lord, the Lord God, compassionate and gracious, slow to anger and abounding in lov-ingkindness and truth." (Exodus 34:6)

> "The Lord is compassionate and gracious, slow to anger and abounding in lovingkindness" (Psalm 103:8).

> "Now return to the Lord your God for He is gracious and compassionate, slow to anger, abounding in lov-ingkindness and relenting of evil." (Joel 2:13)

It is written that "the kindness of God leads you to repen-tance" (Romans 2:4). Almost nothing is more practically expe-riential in the Christian life than this! There is absolutely no way we could ever come to understand the extent of our sinful hearts and behaviors without the kindness of God expressed through His Holy Spirit. Why would an infinite God, who cre-ated the entire Universe, even care if I have a sinful thought? That seems absurd. And yet He does. And this truth implies just how significant we are—that He would warn us about our mis-deeds and guide us into truth. What kindness that He speaks through His written word and into our conscience to show us our errors!

Knowing the wrong we've done, He then enables us by the Holy Spirit to believe that He is good and willing to forgive. And we make our confessions and find in Him the forgiveness of sin that restores our hearts and consciences before Him. Consider the words of the Psalmist:

> He will not always strive with us, nor will He keep His anger forever. He has not dealt with us according to our sins nor rewarded us according to our iniquities. For as high as the heavens are above the earth, so great is his lovingkindness toward those who fear Him. As far as the east is from the west, so far has He removed our transgressions from us. Just as a father has compassion on his children, so the Lord has compassion on those who fear Him. (Psalm 103:9-13)

What kindness and generosity that we do not have to carry the guilt of our sins any further than to His generous forgiveness! He removes them from us!

It is hard to be motivated to go up to meet with the Lord when you are cowering in shame over your choices. Preferably, you would pay attention and obey the Lord in all things, keeping a clear conscience before the Lord. But if you do sin, Christ stands before the Father in our defense, contending for the dispensation of His lovingkindness toward us, over and above His wrath. (See 1 John 2:1)

Don't let guilt keep you from Him! He wants you to come up the mountain and meet with Him. Along the way, He will help you deal with your heart, and you will come down from that time in the hills with His righteousness, peace, and joy in the Holy Ghost.

Conclusion and Contemplation

Fall upon the kindness of Jesus Christ and be broken to pieces. Will you break down before Him and trust Him with all your heart?

Prayer of Commitment

Father, thank you for loving me, healing me, strengthening me, and being my help in every way and every need. I am grateful that You think of me so often and for always being near to me. Help me to grow in my understanding of Your vast love and incalculable kindness toward all of humanity. Amen.

Discussion Questions

1. What does intimacy with God look like to you? Do you believe God wants to spend time with you?
2. How is understanding God's kindness a key to a deeper relationship with Him?
3. Why is significance unrelated to our physical size in proportion to the Universe?
4. Why does the kindness of God lead to repentance?
5. How has God shown kindness to you? How did you feel when you first realized the ways in which He had shown you His lovingkindness?
6. Do you believe God's kindness will run out? If you continue to fail in your personal growth, will He always tolerate you? Why?
7. How is gratefulness related to an understanding of God's lovingkindness?

Chapter VIII

BACKPACKERS
The Gate of Desperation

Imperative
We must be desperate in order to have broken, tender hearts.

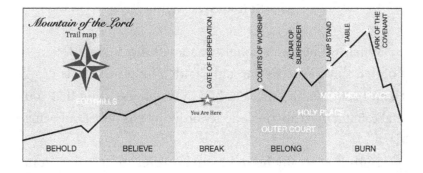

Expectations of Grandeur
May 2019

Two cousins created comedy in the backseat of the rusted Subaru Outback. Behind them, a stack of backpacks reached the ceiling, obscuring the rearview. As we pulled away from the girls, my heart ached for the 6 days we would be away from them, but Asher and I were en route to his first experience of hiking the Appalachian Trail.

135

The following day, with bellies and backpacks filled, we pulled into the A.T. access parking lot and spilled out of the car like a kicked anthill. It was the final opportunity to ditch or hitch anything in question. Gear was strewn across the gravel as eyes darted from one necessity to the next, contemplating weight and value to see which would win.

Thoughts raced through my head as I tried to imagine what I was about to experience. What would I see? I knew resolutely that it would amaze me, and the anticipation alone was satisfying, but curiosity and adventure would not be satisfied until my feet were on the trail.

Faith Requires Action

When we believe strongly in something, it shows. James pointed this out when he said, "faith without works is dead" (James 2:26). Faith cannot only be a simple assertion that you make, but it must also include action, or it runs the risk of being "dead."

Faith is eternally bound to and forever inseparable from the pursuit of God. "And without faith it is impossible to please Him, for he who comes to God must believe that He is and that He is a rewarder of those who seek him" (Hebrews 11:6). If you have faith that God exists, you will want to seek Him because you genuinely believe that indescribable beauty lies ahead. If you seek Him with all your heart, He will reward you. Listen to Jeremiah:

> Then you will call upon me and come and pray to me,
> and I will listen to you. You will seek me and find me

when you search for me with all your heart. I will be
found by you declares the Lord. (Jeremiah 29:12-14)

What a promise! It was faith that led Moses up the hill to
seek the Lord. It was faith that led King David up the hill to
the temple where he would gaze upon the beauty of the Lord.
It is faith that will lead you up the mountain. Faith makes
mountaineers.

William Penn

The sun bounced off bright green leaves and illuminated
parts of the forest floor. We took our first steps into the woods,
then crossed an old railway bridge that spanned a small river.
Where rain was expected, heat persisted as we climbed 1600
feet to the ridge. The temperature finally dropped as the clouds
darkened and the wind picked up.

Poison ivy reached toward Asher and me with 3-pronged
claws, hoping to settle into our sensitive skin. Some hikers
trudged fearlessly through it, claiming immunity, but I cau-
tioned the brazen behavior.

The trail rolled down into shaded forests and elbowed at
entrancing precipices, which slowed our pace. On some of these
bluff-side views, the hike was stalled so we could capture each
vista with a photo. Our bodies often stood in front of the beauty,
downgrading the awe, but a few good shots kept our photo-
graphic ambitions at the top of our priorities.

The stony pathway soothed and smoothed into soft forest
topsoil, from which hundreds of ferns reached toward the raindrops. Now only eighteen inches wide, the trail maintained a
downward grade—almost unnoticeable—as it snaked through

the deciduous cover toward our destination for the day, the William Penn Shelter.

The Gate of Desperation

If you are going up the mountain to seek the Lord, you will eventually arrive at the place of His throne or His temple (Ezekiel 43:7). The first thing you will discover here is the gate facing east, or The Gate of Desperation. It is referred to as The Gate of Desperation because if a person wants to break through and find God, they must seek him in the spirit of humility and desperation. A humility that leads to desperation is one of God's terms on the mountain, one of His conditions for discovery, a requirement not a single human may dodge or shortcut. For this reason, in this chapter, we will place a lot of emphasis on understanding humility and desperation.

Jesus said, "Strive to enter through the narrow gate" (Luke 13:24, NKJV). The word "strive" used in this verse is translated from the Greek word "agonizomai," which means to "struggle" or "contend with." It is here at the gate that your faith requires action. Your first deed of faith is to "humble yourself under God's mighty hand, that he may lift you up in due time" (1 Peter 5:6). This humility is a sign of true faith. This was the response of Ezekiel when he, in his vision of the temple, came to this place:

> "Then he led me to the gate, the gate facing toward
> the east; and behold, the glory of the God of Israel
> was coming from the way of the east. And His voice
> was like the sound of many waters; and the earth
> shone with His glory. And it was like the appearance

of the vision which I saw, like the vision which I saw when He came to destroy the city. And the visions were like the vision which I saw by the river Chebar; and I fell on my face. And the glory of the Lord came into the house by the way of the gate facing toward the east and the Spirit lifted me up and brought me into the inner court; and behold the glory of the Lord filled the house." (Ezekiel 43:1-5)

Humility is the first fruit of genuine faith. Ezekiel saw the glory of the Lord, and his first response was to humble himself. Then the Spirit lifted him up and took him into the inner court, where God was enthroned. When we humble ourselves before the mighty hand of God, the Spirit will lift us up and bring us before the Throne of Heaven (See 1 Peter 5:6).

Without a biblically-based anticipation of the Glory of the Lord being revealed, however, we may not possess the awe and reverence that leads to an actual act of humility before Him. Let me reiterate that genuine faith will always lead to an act of humility.

Humility is pretty simple: get low and mean it. If you *believe* that there is an infinite Creator seated on an indescribable throne in heaven—and that this Being is infinitely powerful, wise, knowledgeable, loving, and kind—you *will* bow down in reverent humility. If you don't, there are only two possibilities for why: Either you don't really believe this God exists, or you don't know how desperately in need of Him you really are.

This entire lesson of entering through the gate is summarized by Jesus in his declaration: "I am the gate" (John 10:9, NIV). At the gate, we must ask the Holy Spirit to reveal the glory of Jesus to us. Ask yourself right now, are you beholding the glory of Jesus? Are you gazing upon the beauty of the Lord in His temple? If not, you need your eyes opened because you are blind. Like Bartimaeus, your opportunity to see Jesus is passing. Will you cry out as he did?

> And *later*, as He was leaving Jericho with His disciples and a large crowd, a beggar who was blind *named* Bartimaeus, the son of Timaeus, was sitting by the road. And when he heard that it was Jesus the Nazarene, he began to cry out and say, "Jesus, Son of David, have mercy on me!" Many were sternly telling him to be quiet, but he kept crying out all the more, "Son of David, have mercy on me!" And Jesus stopped and said, "Call him *here*." So they called the man who was blind, saying to him, "Take courage, stand up! He is calling for you." And throwing off his cloak, he jumped up and came to Jesus. And replying to him, Jesus said, "What do you want Me to do for you?" And the man who was blind said to Him, "Rabboni, *I want* to regain my sight!" And Jesus said to him, "Go; your faith has made you well." And immediately he regained his sight and *began* following Him on the road. (Mark 10:46-52)

When you cry out to Jesus from your bedroom floor, desperate to see Him, your flesh will scorn you and tell you that you are acting foolishly. Like Bartimaeus, you will hear many voices telling you to be quiet. But if you persist in desperation, Jesus will give your heart eyes with which to behold His beauty. The apostle Paul wanted the Ephesians to see with their hearts:

I pray that the eyes of your heart may be enlightened, so that you will know what is the hope of His calling, what are the riches of the glory of His inheritance in the saints, and what is the boundless greatness of His power toward us who believe. (Ephesians 1:18-19)

It's interesting to note that the first thing Bartimaeus saw when his eyes were opened was Jesus. Then he saw others around Jesus. Later, he likely saw himself. Do you have the faith to believe that Jesus can make you see Him? Will you cry out to Him to open your eyes? If you do, Jesus will help you see, and you will want nothing else than to follow Him along the road.

With the glory and wonder of our Savior alive in our hearts, here at the gate, we must make several acknowledgments. You might speak these acknowledgments like this:

- *Father, You are The Lord God Almighty, You exist, and You are present with me here, now. I believe that I will find you when I seek you with all my heart.*
- *I humble myself before You. You are highly exalted, seated on the throne above all else. I do not deserve Your goodness or mercy.*
- *Jesus, You are the gate. I cannot draw near to God except through the gate, which is You. I cannot enter the temple on my own merit.*
- *I am drawing near to You, oh God, and I know that You will draw near to me because You are faithful to Your promises.*
- *Holy Spirit, You dwell in me. You are my Guide. I have come to meet with You so that I may know You more*

deeply and go out and help others to know You as well. Lead me now, fill me now.

Faux Hawk

The shelter peered out into the lofty atmosphere through the trunks of oaks and elms from its mountainside perch. Also perched on the mountainside was "The Leech," whose faux-hawk and $300 hiking sneakers spelled "poser" to Tom. Nevertheless, his pervasive body odor convinced us that he really had been on the trail for two months and was indeed headed to Georgia.

Soon the shelter floor was carpeted with sleeping gear, and meals-ready-to-eat were rehydrated around a campfire. Wet kindling had given way to Tom's expertise, and everyone came around to enjoy the flickering campfire entrancement.

"The Leech" was already snoring when we all piled into the shelter and sank into our bags. Several comical descriptions were assigned by the cousins to "The Leech's" obnoxiously loud breathing, such as "chainsaw," "weed-eater," "lawnmower," and certain levity lending bodily functions. With the discussion came teary laughter from the boys and the decision that he should change his trail name to one of these.

The jokesters eventually concluded that it sounded most like flatulence and, between each rattling snort, voiced a relieved "excuse me" and then burst into bellowing laughter again only to repeat the charade. Grandpa, intent on his rest, scolded the comedians to sleep, and "The Leech's" buzzing fell down the Appalachians into the otherwise quiet mountain valley.

Who was "The Leech"? What was his name? Who was the real person behind that high-tech gear and under that faux-hawk? We couldn't tell, but God could.

Humility Leads to Discovery

One of the best examples of humility is given in the parable Jesus told about the Pharisee and the tax collector. See if you can identify the "poser" in *this* story:

> And He also told this parable to some people who trusted in themselves that they were righteous, and viewed others with contempt: "Two men went up into the temple to pray, one a Pharisee and the other a tax collector. The Pharisee stood and was praying this to himself: 'God I thank you that I am not like other people: swindlers, unjust, adulterers, or even like this tax collector. I fast twice a week; I pay tithes of all that I get.' But the tax collector standing some distance away, was even unwilling to lift up his eyes to heaven, but was beating his breast, saying, 'God, be merciful to me, the sinner!' I tell you, this man went to his house justified rather than the other; for everyone who exalts himself will be humbled, but he who humbles himself will be exalted." (Luke 18:9-14, ESV)

Humility means coming to grips with the truth. It means acknowledging that which is *accurate* about ourselves, our needs, our faults, failures, shortcomings, and our sin. It is to disown inaccuracies in our self-evaluations. It is arriving at an agreement about what is true of God, His limitless mercy, immeasurable wisdom, and infinite love. To some motivating degree, it is realizing His exaltedness and His vast difference from us, then responding to that with words of heartfelt desperation. Humility's task is to separate the wheat from the chaff, truth from falsehood, reality from fantasy, and then display the results before God.

To humble one's self before God is to move into discovery mode. We first discover the truth about ourselves, then we discover God! The God described in the Bible exists; make no mistake, and He is discoverable! His first term of discovery is humility. Though often demonstrated in physical expressions like kneeling, humility is much more than getting our bodies closer to the ground. Humility puts us in the right mindset to be desperate before God—we *realize* our need. Desperate is what really hungry people are, and God always feeds the hungry (See Matthew 5:6).

At The Gate of Desperation, you acknowledge that there are no "qualifiers" and no "dis-qualifiers" for seeking God. You can't be good enough—like the Pharisee—to "deserve" to seek God, and you can't be bad enough—like the tax collector—to *not* "deserve" to seek Him. You simply come to Jesus with your life and lay it at His feet in humility. He *won't* receive anyone *without* humility, and He *will* receive anyone *with* humility. Whether or not you feel worthy is irrelevant. Whether or not you've done well or poorly is irrelevant. Whether or not you come in the joy of victory or the pain of defeat is irrelevant. Discovery mode *always* starts with humility. Bring Him nothing except your life and humble yourself, placing your confidence in the righteousness of Christ as your merit—your singular qualification.

In *The Life of God in the Soul of Man*, Henry Scougal states:

> Humility imports a deep sense of our own weakness,
> with a hearty and affectionate acknowledgment of
> our owing all that we are to the divine bounty, which

is always accompanied with a profound sense of submission to the will of God.

Desperation is the indicator that we know our need for God's mercy. Such realization brought George Whitfield to lay face down all day in the open fields of England before the Lord in prayer. With such a grasp of our needful disposition before the Almighty, Moses lay face down before Him for 40 days and 40 nights, desperately pleading for the lives of the Israelites.

Poncho Strategy

The trees creaked and swayed high above me as I sipped my richly anticipated coffee from a camping mug. Nothing could be heard but the menagerie of mountain birds and a periodic breeze that whooshed through the treetops. I was alone while others rested, and I began to speak to the Father, thanking him for his majesty expressed in the forested beauty. I again gazed deep into the terrain ahead of me and wondered what I would see. I had little imagination of what was coming, yet I couldn't wait.

Not much later, we were on the trail again. Dewdrops caught on long, slender blades of grass caused the morning sun to bounce as we descended into the deciduous sparkle. The trail morphed from stony to gravelly to muddy and back to stony. Euphoric gazes persisted on our faces as we marched along to the sound of our footsteps and trekking poles.

Ascending into an evergreen forest, pine needles and boulders became the trail. Another scenic overlook was within steps of the trail, so we stopped to take some photos and feed some chipmunks, who were surprisingly friendly.

Below us, far away in the distance, lay sleepy towns with idling people, unaware that, along such a mountain ridge, we were in discovery mode. We thrust our packs back onto our backs and resumed our exploring. Hiking changed to bouldering, and the trail seemed invisible atop the granite landscape.

The wind was blowing with subtly increasing force, and the sunshine was less prominent as darker clouds moved in. Rain fell all at once, heavily. Asher frowned as his poncho failed to keep him dry. His frustration rose to anger when his poncho pointed sideways in the watery wind.

This is where Asher broke on the Appalachian Trail. He changed here for good and grew into a new dimension of strength and determination. But it came through the challenges he faced and as he embraced them in all their dismal effects, with a heart willing to do anything it took to reach a better place.

Drenched, he tore the poncho off and slammed it to the ground, putting on his rain jacket and flipping up its hood. We encouraged him, though he seemed as if he would give up the quest. He eventually discovered how much more effective his jacket was. A smile returned to his face, and he sped vigorously to the front of the group. Later that day, he dissected the advice of his Grandpa, who stood firm under the poncho strategy—dry, and smirking behind his square glasses and long, grey beard.

A very rocky and very rainy trail eventually led us to a waterfall paradise, where the speedier Tom had already set up camp. After a failed attempt at acquiring functional real estate, we found a dry place to pitch our tent. We then cooked up some dinner and fell finally, happily, asleep.

Humility Brews Desperation

Desperation drives a man to his knees before God; it's what causes him to cry out for sight like Bartimaeus, it's what compels him to pound his chest with his fist—like the tax collector. Desperation is another stepping stone on the path to true brokenness. It causes a man to stop, look at his circumstances and do what is necessary to create change. God often uses circumstances to show us our need for change. Like the poncho, which failed in the wind and rain, circumstances may indicate a need for heart change. But you must embrace its reality, or you will not experience change.

Now we are getting down to business! Humility like this, which flourishes within a genuine acknowledgment of need, will always produce desperation. Desperation is often called "hunger" or "thirst" in the spiritual language of the Bible.

Jesus said, "blessed are those who hunger and thirst for righteousness, for they shall be satisfied" (Matthew 5:6). Look at how deeply King David desired the Lord:

> As the deer pants for the water brooks, so my soul pants for you, O God. My soul thirsts for God, for the living God; when shall I come and appear before God?" (Psalm 42:1-2)

> O God, You are my God; I shall seek you earnestly; My soul thirsts for You, my flesh yearns for You, in a dry and weary land where there is no water." (Psalm 63:1)

Realizing the truth about yourself and your situation can lead to a desperation that causes you to "cry out" to God. This is common throughout scripture and is a condition upon which God is pleased to respond. Look at the urgency with which Jeremiah writes to the Israelites:

> Their heart cried out to the Lord, "O wall of the daughter of Zion, let your tears run down like a river day and night; give yourself no relief, let your eyes have no rest. Arise, cry aloud in the night at the beginning of the night watches; pour out your heart like water before the presence of the Lord, lift up your hands to Him for the life of your little ones who are faint because of hunger at the head of every street." (Lamentations 2:18-19)

Again the Psalmist shows us the route up the hill of the Lord:

> Then they cried to the Lord in their trouble, and He brought them out of their distresses. He caused the storm to be still, so that the waves of the sea were hushed. (Psalm 107:28-29)

And Jonah found himself in desperate circumstances, but not too far for the hand of the Lord to save—after he humbled himself:

> I called out of my distress to the Lord, and He answered me. I cried for help from the depth of Sheol; You heard my voice. For you had cast me into the deep, into the heart of the seas, and the current engulfed me. All your breakers and billows passed over me. I descended into the roots of the mountains.

The earth with its bars was around me forever, but
you have brought up my life from the pit, O Lord my
God." (Jonah 2:2-3,6)

At The Gate of Desperation, we bow low, acknowledge Him,
and wait for His Spirit to show us the truth of our hearts—reality,
as it were. Then will we cry out to Him with all our hearts, and
then will He lift us up, in His time, and take us into His courts.
Quite often, there is work to be done while we wait. Work to be
done from an attitude of faith, humility, and desperation. Before
we pass through the gate, we must walk through the garden.

Waterfall

The second morning of the trek was even better than the
first, owing primarily to the gentle and steady percussion of
the waterfall against the stony creekbed. I thought about the
goodness of God. It poured into my heart like a waterfall from
heaven with abundant and consoling mercies.

The valley in which we camped opened up to a blue morning
sky, and the first bursts of sunshine crept down the opposing
mountainside toward our camp. Again, I enjoyed a hot coffee,
black in my blue cup. In the invigorating bliss, I spoke to the
one who created all of that which I delightfully observed and
kindly situated me to enjoy it. I felt honored—and humbled—to
be in the presence of such exquisiteness.

Familiar anticipation filled my soul as I considered what else
I might encounter in the exploration ahead of us. I wanted to
know what was down that trail. I had been on the path ascending
"the hill of the Lord." I was seeking, searching, and believing that
I was moving into His glorious goodness. I wanted to summit

the mountain again to experience the colors, smells, sounds, and scenery. I believed beauty lay ahead, and I was willing to take up my pack, deny myself ease and comfort, and follow the path.

Conclusion and Contemplation

To break, we must be desperate; to be desperate, we must be humble. Come to grips with the truth about yourself and your need for God. Are you desperate for Him?

Prayer of Commitment

Father, I bow down now and begin my prayer with a demonstration of humility in my bodily demeanor. I acknowledge that I cannot do anything eternal for myself; I must reach toward You to find help beyond this life. I need You to forgive me, I need You to assist me, I need You to restore and renew me today. I am glad that You have helped me see how deeply I need You and ask You to show me more. Help me never rely on my own strength, skills, gifts, or talents. But help me to always rely on Your Holy Spirit. I love You, O, Lord, and I bow low before You. Amen.

Discussion Questions

1. What is humility?
2. How are faith and humility linked?
3. How is desperation linked to brokenness?
4. What does it mean to see with your heart? How can we come to do this?

5. Describe why the tax collector in Jesus' parable went home justified before God.
6. Do you ever feel like you've done so well that you deserve to seek God? Have you ever felt so ashamed that you thought you didn't deserve to seek God? Explain.
7. What is the one source of merit for coming into God's presence?
8. How are humility and desperation linked?
9. Why should we be desperate? What happens when we are?
10. Why aren't we more desperate for God?

Chapter IX

GARDENERS
Divine Transformation of the Heart

Imperative

We must embrace the divine responsibility to guard our hearts.

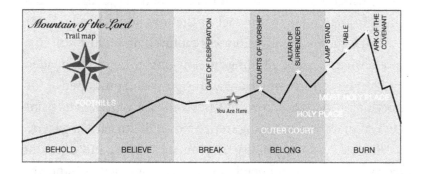

Patio Paradise

April 2018

Louisville, Kentucky

Lime green and violet-colored aliens invaded an insipid, grey planet. With a full spectrum of hues as their weaponry, their colors and scents were foreign to land. They had visited there before, but their effect had died away and was all but forgotten. These were the pleasant sort of aliens, though, both in sight and aroma, and the transformation they delivered was as immersive as the variety and detail with which they produced it.

The soggy, winter-deadened landscape became host to the vivid changes of spring, when up from the ground and out upon limbs returned certain strangers with broadening blades, burgeoning blossoms, and billions of banners, green and gregarious. Embarrassingly naked branches, unsightly and drab, were clothed in thick foliage and stood proudly in majestic splendor. Flowers of red, yellow, white, orange, and blue came to adorn nearly every stationary life form, evangelizing the world with the message of renewal from the pulpits of their gardens.

Owners and renters of just about any sized plot of earth upon which these effects could occur manicured and molded them to maximize the impact of the invasion. They had realized that unless the invasion was cultured, it could result in a totalitarian reign of all things green—including such dreaded and foreign species which are as unsightly and unwanted as the horrific thistle. Thus, rows of roses and isles of irises were situated so that the flourishing frenzy fed its life to garden gazers.

Lawns resumed vitality over once browned and dormant terrestrial carpets and neighbors walk across them, to-and-fro, like barbers of acreage, sculpting them into perfect conformity. Vineyards were pruned and tuned with hopes that the fruit of the vine would soon glisten burgundy in crystal glasses on a white-cloth table.

Just between crisp and comfortable, exhilarating warmth emanated from a less-far-away sun, whose proximity was restored and whose touch was once again felt. Spring: when the soul of man is catapulted into a season of sunny ecstasy, nearly forgotten in the dungeon of deadness from which the world was resurrected.

One morning, during such a transformational coup, wherein the greeneries of spring had overthrown the dead and frozen government of winter, I sat in my patio chair, reading near the daffodils. The aroma of Goodfolks Coffee Roasters billowed up and out from their chimney and over the neighbors' roofs, spilling into my backyard sanctuary, adding a scent of caramelized toast to the floral mixture. Monarchs flapped their wings as they lit upon the hyacinths and begonias, and cardinals sat in trees across from blue jays and exchanged songs like the bands of local football teams.

I spent many evenings and Saturday afternoons creating and perfecting this refuge of brick, stone, and plants. I was no stranger to the totalitarian tendency of this invasion and was strictly opposed to many undesirable visitors. So I stood up and examined the hostas, plucking a weed from their raised bed. I checked the azaleas, almost ready to bloom, and adjusted the mulch around their bases, keeping the ground moist and tender. I pulled up a tuft of grass between the bricks and then analyzed the rose blossoms. I had pruned those rose bushes quite a bit, "would they flourish now?" I wondered.

The Heart is a Garden

In the life of man, the heart is such a world, such a garden. The heart regularly gravitates toward seasonal deadness, and it must be revitalized. It awaits invasion. Springtime is to the year, as morning to the day when His lovingkindness and compassion are renewed (see Lamentations 3:22-23). For some, spring seems to never come, and His mercy is never known. For others, who have come nearer to the Son, the warmth of His proximity brings forth a flourishing faith and a manifold fruitfulness.

The heart, like a plot of earth, is entrusted to the person in whom it is situated—and they must tend to it. This is a divine responsibility because it has been given to us by the Divine One, Jesus. If you have given your heart to Jesus, you have done well, and He is delighted to *own* it. But like the owner of the vineyard, He has *entrusted* it to your care and is expecting your faithfulness (see Matthew 21:33). Of paramount importance is this divine responsibility, given to man, to tend to the garden of the heart. "Watch over your heart with all diligence, for from it flow the springs of life." (Proverbs 4:23).

As you war against those tendencies of the heart to stray, entertain temptation, and forget about Jesus, He sees your genuine love for Him. Love always fights for what is loved. The wildflowers of sacrificial love bloom on the battlefield. As you keep your heart pure for love, He will be honored—and He deserves all the honor we can give!

Jesus describes the kind of soil best suited for the invasion. He wants His seeds to flourish when planted. But sometimes they don't:

> "When anyone hears the word of the kingdom and does not understand it, the evil one comes and snatches away what has been sown in his heart. This is the one on whom seed was sown beside the road. The one on whom seed was sown on the rocky places, this is the man who hears the word and immediately receives it with joy; yet he has no firm root in himself, but is only temporary, and when affliction or persecution arises because of the word, immediately he falls away. And the one on whom seed was sown among the thorns, this is the man who hears

the word, and the worry of the world and the deceit-
fulness of wealth choke the word, and it becomes
unfruitful. And the one on whom seed was sown on
the good soil, this is the man who hears the word and
understands it; who indeed bears fruit and brings
forth, some a hundredfold, some sixty, and some
thirty." (Matthew 13:19-23)

Disciples are gardeners of the heart. But spiritual sluggards, in a lapse of sound judgment, have left their hearts in ruins, overcome by thorns, weeds, and hardened ground. Solomon observed:

I passed by the field of the sluggard and by the vineyard of the man lacking sense, and behold, it was
completely overgrown with thistles; its surface was
covered with nettles, and its stone wall was broken
down. (Proverbs 24:30-31).

The Nature of the Heart and of Hardness

To develop spiritual green thumbs, we must understand the human heart. It is naturally hard. The heart is innately inclined toward fruitlessness and solidity. As a garden unattended produces less fruit and more weeds, the heart unattended is host to less fruit of the Spirit and more sin. As soil grows harder over time, the heart returns to its hardness when unattended. The heart of man defaults to distance, death, and hardness. There is no autopilot mode for following Christ; you will return to your old ways unless you carry a cross, crucify the flesh, and break up the hardened ground.

No human being can avoid a barren hardness of heart without directly addressing it in humility and desperation before the Lord. This must be done regularly, as a gardener tends the soil and the plants. Hardness of the heart is a condition in which the word of God has no lasting effect on the person (see Matthew 13:20-21). Hardness of the heart is the necessary condition for weeds to grow. This naturally fatal condition is exacerbated by unholy influences or a disobedient lifestyle. It is a condition in which any spiritual growth is halted and impossible.

Hardness of heart is a condition in which all spiritual activity—if there is any—is fruitless and driven by duty rather than a love for the Lord. It is the condition in which the old man returns to the converted soul to reinstate those behaviors and tendencies which were once put off in repentance and faith (see Ephesians 4:20-24). Like a creeping vine, this old nature grows back upon the garden from which it was once removed, and any remaining outward demonstration of faith is a mere show. Hardness of heart is the necessary condition for legalism to thrive, and its fruit is condemnation.

The following are some indicators that your heart is growing hard. You will tend to live independently of God, growing more confident in your own abilities. You will grow angry and resentful, believing others owe you much more than they do. You will find much difficulty in praying beyond a mealtime prayer, worshipping passionately, or entering into any level of intimacy with God. You will harbor secret sin and have a hidden life, increasing duplicity in your social and spiritual spheres. You find reading the Bible unprofitable, dull, or a waste of your time. You will wonder who is at fault for your fallen state and seek a bullseye for your fiery darts of blame.

You will become as Israel had become, entranced by the "world" around them, running after worthless idols, having abandoned the Lord. And He will find you as He did them:

> O Lord, do not your eyes look for truth? You have smitten them, but they did not weaken; you have consumed them, but they refused to take correction. They made their faces harder than rock; they have refused to repent. (Jeremiah 5:3)

These words came after Josiah began to purge Judah and Jerusalem of their high places, altars, and evil priests. Jeremiah wrote these words not to a people who never knew the Lord but to a people who had turned away. He said, "For their rebellion is great, and their backsliding many" (Jeremiah 5:6, NIV).

Jeremiah loved Josiah and lamented his death (see 2 Chronicles 35:25). Josiah demolished the high places and restored the functionality of the temple, and the Lord said,

> Before him there was no king like him who turned to the Lord with all his heart and with all his soul and with all his might, according to all the law of Moses; nor did any like him arise after him. (2 Kings 23:25)

The hearts of the people were nevertheless calloused, hard, and unwilling to be broken. Thus, while the people pondered why God could possibly be angry with them, Jeremiah prophesied their enslavement to Babylon:

> It shall come about when they say, 'why has the Lord our God done all these things to us?' Then you shall

> say to them, 'as you have forsaken Me and served
> foreign gods in your land, so you will serve strangers
> in a land that is not yours.' (Jeremiah 5:19)

And so it is for those who do not tend to their hearts: they grow hard, unrepentant, and end up in slavery. Sin is destructive, but hardness of heart is the *reason* we sin. Thus, it is *hardness* that should alarm us more than anything. A man may very efficiently hide this condition from the public eye and therefore seem like an upstanding citizen—all the while a hard and defiant heart hangs in his chest. Make no mistake, behavior must be managed. Chiefly, however, it is heart change that God is after. This is because the heart is the wellspring of life, from which our words and actions spring, whether in the public eye or not (see Matthew 15:18-20).

The opposite is true of the person who maintains a tender heart like soil turned over and readied for the seed. This person depends entirely on the Lord and knows the foolishness of relying on their strengths, no matter how refined their gifts may be. This person serves others and doesn't believe they are owed anything. They can easily slip away into rich times of prayer and worship and are strong to lead out in public settings. Their behavior concerns them but holds no contest to their concern for a tender heart. They harbor no secrets but are open, honest, and forward-moving in their growth and maturity. They love the Word of God and regularly search it to know the Lord more deeply and follow him more faithfully.

Gardeners are Humble

Recognizing the tendency for the heart to grow toward hardness, the earnest disciple will take action. The first means by which one may tend the garden is through humility.

Humility is synonymous with submission as it relates to God. You cannot at the same time be humble and rebellious. Humility, to be exact, requires submission of your nature to His nature. In humility, you resign as the chief architect of your life and render your soul obligated to His directives. In the truest sense, it is a total act of trust and surrender, releasing the right of control to Him to whom it rightly belongs.

Francis Frangipane, in *Holiness, Truth, and the Presence of God*, wrote:

> In our desire to know God, we must discern this about the Almighty: He resists the proud, but his grace is drawn to the humble. Humility brings grace to our need and grace alone can change our hearts. Humility therefore, is the substructure of transformation. It is the essence of all virtues.

When a person expresses faith in Christ for the first time, they must humble themselves, or they will not be saved. Submission and surrender to the Holy Spirit allow Him to bring forth His fruit in us. While this is often painful, it is indeed the birth pangs of the new birth. In this "new creation" of the "new man" event, faith, humility, and grace are the mid-wives. These virtues also have in their progeny the immersion of one's soul into the presence, power, and purpose of the Holy Spirit.

If a man is humble, he is given grace and faith. If he has faith, he will humble himself and receive grace. If he has grace, he will believe. If a man believes and seeks, he will find. The interconnectedness of these workings of the Holy Spirit in the surrendered heart is the breaking up and preparing of the soil. They are the readying of the heart for the divine transformational coup of man's entire spirit, soul, and body.

This transformational coup is the establishment of the government of Jesus and the disestablishment of the will of man. Your will must die for you to be under the Lordship of Jesus, for you to be filled with the Spirit, and for you to be born again. A dying will's *last* breath is humility, and a living faith's *first* breath is humility. Dead faith cannot save, only living faith; Dead faith cannot be filled with the Holy Spirit, only living faith. Saving grace is not given to the proud, only to the humble.

Some people think they must only be saved from the fire of Hell, and perhaps this is all they will ever experience. And these will enter Heaven as those "escaping through the flames" (1 Corinthians 3:15, NIV). But our hope is to be saved not just from fire in Hell but from ice on earth. We want to be saved from a cold, hard heart. We are desperate to be saved from the status quo, saved from the ordinary, saved from the dull, drab, and dismal existence, which is absent of summits and narrowly knows there is even a mountain to be climbed. But only faith, driven by genuine humility, can save us from this.

Dead "faith" will not be accompanied by a hearty acknowledgment of need, resulting in desperation before Almighty God. But with such an acknowledgment of our need, in a spirit of desperation, all heavenly saving faith is released. This is faith that will, through repentance, save a man and transform him from death unto life, yielding the new birth. This faith will transform a person from a world of ice to one of fire, a world of flatlands to one of mountains, and from wastelands to wonders.

If we go up to the temple to pray arrogantly, relying on our own achievements and merit, we are no different than the Pharisee of Jesus' parable in Luke 18. Neither can we, as believers, seek God without faith-inspired humility before His mighty hand. Ezekiel certainly wasn't lost, but it wasn't until he humbled himself under the mighty hand of God that the Spirit lifted him up and ushered him into the inner court of the temple, where the Glory of the Lord was revealed in full measure.

We must not go too quickly, though. We must go as the Publican of the same parable in Luke 18, standing at a distance and humbling ourselves before God. The wisdom of the tax collector was to realize his shortcomings and display them in his demeanor. Pride, however, produces overconfidence and nonsensical rambling.

Pick up the gardener's tool called *humility* and put it to work before the Lord. You will soon see how he is "near to the broken hearted" (Psalm 34:18) and a friend of the meek.

Gardeners are Desperate

Gardeners are desperate. They know that their hard hearts must be broken to pieces, so they cast themselves upon the Son of God. They know that "he who falls on this stone will be broken to pieces, but on whomever it falls, it will scatter him like dust." (Matthew 21:45). And in a moment of realization about the genuine reality of their hearts, they employ the tools of gardeners to get the heart tender, rich, and ready for the seed of the sower.

They will heed the direction of Jeremiah:

> For thus says the Lord to the men of Judah and to Jerusalem, "Break up your fallow ground and do not sow among thorns. Circumcise yourselves to the Lord and remove the foreskins of your heart, men of Judah and inhabitants of Jerusalem, or else My wrath will go forth like fire and burn with none to quench it, because of the evil of your deeds." (Jeremiah 4:3)

They will also follow the guidance of Hosea:

> Plant the good seeds of righteousness, and you will harvest a crop of love. Plow up the hard ground of your hearts, for now is the time to seek the LORD, that he may come and shower righteousness upon you (Hosea 10:12, NLT).

It will not be enough to casually acknowledge you have been distant, independent, and on your own. It will not be enough to walk past your garden and think, "Wow, *that* needs work." You must grip reality. This hardened ground requires immediate attention by a person humble enough to recognize that the Owner of the garden deserves far more than this.

Horrified

It is nowhere implied in Scripture that a wildly neglected, dry, and hardened ruin, overgrown with thorns and weeds, is acceptable in the sight of the Lord. Listen to Joel address Israel when they had yet again allowed their hearts to grow hard, distant, and full of the weeds of foolishness:

> "Yet even now," declares the Lord, "Return to Me
> with all your heart, and with fasting, and weeping
> and mourning; and rend your heart and not your
> garments." Now return to the Lord your God, for
> He is gracious and compassionate, slow to anger
> abounding in lovingkindness and relenting of evil.
> (Joel 2:12-13).

Garments were torn in Hebrew culture in moments of unspeakable grief and horror; and as a gesture of absolute loss, particularly the death of a loved one. We find Jacob tearing his robe when he believes that Joseph is dead (Genesis 37:34). Also, David and his men rent their garments upon hearing of King Saul's death (2 Samuel 1:11). There are many other examples of similar expressions of abhorrence.

The high priest tore his robe when he heard Jesus confess to being the Christ. He considered this blasphemy and was appalled by it, thus rending his garment (Matthew 26:65). Paul and Barnabas tore their clothes in horror when they learned that the people thought they were gods and wanted to sacrifice to them (Acts 14:14).

Joel directs the Israelites to take this attitude to their destitute hearts, placing themselves in total agreement with the perspective of the Lord toward their rebellion: that it is an unbearable atrocity that demands instant, urgent action.

You will not be able to rend your heart if you are not horrified. You must understand that there is no situation where the Holy Spirit will bless half-hearted, casual repentance. Part of you has died; rend *your heart*! You have lied to the Holy Spirit; rend *your heart*! You have taken control of your life, seated yourself on the throne of your own heart, and become an idol, *rend your heart*! Get down on your knees and beat on the floor with your fist as you cry out to God for mercy. Raise your voice as you call on Him to help you break up the hardness in your own heart.

Hidden Error

It is pretty simple to be *forgiven*—come honestly into agreement with God and His word. In other words, acknowledge that you were in the wrong and ask for the forgiveness provided for you by the death and resurrection of Jesus. Forgiveness is not appropriated to man's heart until sin is confessed and renounced, and forgiveness is requested (see 1 John 1:9).

However, identifying your error is not always straightforward and will be even more difficult if your heart is hard. Breaking up hardness of heart requires time and attention to expose its often-inconspicuous tendencies. God wants you to see if you are sincere. Sincerity is a petal on the wildflower of sacrificial love. If you give up too soon, your sincerity can be weighed by the lack of persistence. But if you endure—waiting and persisting—until you break through, seeking until you find, you will discover rare and beautiful jewels which can only be discovered by the diligent explorer.

The Psalmist faced this dilemma and said, "Who can discern his errors? Acquit me of hidden faults" (Psalm 19:12). Not knowing the Word of God also can make it challenging to understand your errors, so soak your heart and mind in the Word. Ask the Holy Spirit to reveal any offense in your heart, and in His timing, He will. "Search me, Oh God, and know my heart; Try me and know my anxious thoughts, and see if there be any hurtful way in me, and lead me in an everlasting way (Psalm 139:23-24).

If you have never done this, you will likely feel foolish and criticize yourself. This would be the flesh scorning you for attempting to take it to the cross. But you must persist, determined to have a broken heart before God. As long as it takes, take the time to know that you have truly humbled yourself before the Lord and found the brokenness of heart He desires. To assist with this, the following guidance may help you to identify how your heart has grown hard in the first place.

The Quadruplex of the Heart

The heart houses four fundamental characteristics from which all sin evolves. It is a quadruplex in which are deep pools of rebellion, arrogance, fear, and greed. Giving attention to these one at a time provides the opportunity for a thorough heart examination.

It is essential to point out that while introspection—looking deeply into one's own heart—is an important facet of approaching God, it is also a path we must not permanently tread. There is a danger in looking only into one's heart, and that is that we may begin to feel that we must deal with *every* aspect of immaturity in our hearts. We may try to eliminate every inclination toward sin, all in one time of prayer and repentance, but this is not the way of the Lord.

Instead, we must simply pray that God brings us forward in humility. We must declare to Him that nothing is hidden, and we are ready to deal with anything He reveals. After we have given sufficient time, His peace will rest on us, and we can then return to worship, thanksgiving, and praise. In this way, we will again focus on Him and His character, trusting that He has dealt with us in the way He wants to for this time.

With this in mind, walk through your garden, looking for the following weeds, thorns, and stones.

Rebellion

Rebellion can be understood as rejecting or *neglecting* the Word of the Lord. Neglecting to do what God has commanded results from having His word as less than your highest priority. Thus, because something else has risen above the value of God's word in a person's life, they have rebelled. Neglect may not always be a conscious choice, but rejection of the Word of the Lord is a conscious decision to do otherwise than He has directed. This is most certainly rebellion. The case study for this state of heart is King Saul, who was rebuked by the prophet for his choices.

"For rebellion is as the sin of divination…because you have rejected the Word of the Lord" (1 Samuel 15:23a). Why is rebellion as unto the sin of divination? It is like witchcraft because, in rebellion, one rejects the power of God and embraces a power foreign to the throne of Heaven. Rebellion is instant hardness, like Quickcrete of the spirit. The writer of Hebrews says, "Today when you hear his voice, do not harden your hearts as Israel did when they rebelled" (Hebrews 3:15, NIV). Furthermore, rebellion places a person on the wrong side of the battle, and they will eventually have Almighty God as their enemy who fights against them. "But they rebelled and grieved His Holy Spirit; therefore He turned Himself to become their enemy, He fought against them" (Isaiah 63:10).

Rebellion claims ownership of the garden yet hates the ways of gardening. It knows nothing of stewardship and boldly states, "This is my life and I can do what I want!" It boasts that all berries can be consumed, and all fruits are "good for food" and "a delight to the eyes" (Genesis 3:6). Rebellion renders disaster where order was decreed and disowns any responsibility for it. It welcomes the sowing of "tares among the wheat" (See Matthew 13:25). This wild and unbridled soul knows nothing of the adventure of following the Lord, and in its blind ignorance, it imagines that it can create for itself a more beautiful life than can the Creator.

Such a state of heart must be dealt with by asking these specific questions and by taking time to consider carefully each one:

- Am I *eager* to obey the Lord?
- Am I *reluctant* and *resistant* to obey the Lord?
- Have I *rejected* the word of the Lord?
- Have I *neglected* the Word of the Lord?
- Am I *ignoring* God's Word?
- Have I *disobeyed* the Word of the Lord?
- Do I see obedience as *optional*?
- Do I value my *opinion* above Scripture?
- Am I pursuing my *own* interests first?
- Am I *lazy*?
- Am I *undisciplined*?
- Is Christ *Lord* over me?

In the humility of heart discussed in the previous chapter, the discoverer of God will bow low to the ground and cry out for mercy.

Father, forgive my rebellion! Forgive me for considering my own opinion above Your word. Forgive me for rejecting the truth and embracing the ideas of the world. Deliver me from this rebellious heart, have mercy on me and cleanse me by the blood of Jesus Christ. I submit totally to You, acknowledging You again today as Lord of my life and Lord of all.

Arrogance

The second half of Samuel's rebuke of Saul was about arrogance. He said, "And arrogance is like the evil of idolatry. Because you have rejected the word of the Lord, he has rejected you as King" (1 Samuel 15:23b, NIV). Arrogance is like idolatry because you decide that you don't need God and can rely entirely on your own efforts. In your imagination, *you* are the king. You have replaced God with yourself and have enthroned yourself as the ultimate authority, giving approval to your choices even when they are contrary to His word.

God eventually rejects these kings and dethrones them. "But I thought God was for us!" You might say. No, He is for the humble. "God is opposed to the proud but gives grace to the humble" (James 4:6). If you are such a king in your fantasy world, you must embrace reality and step down, get low, and get humble before the real King.

This independence is not one of the fruits of the Spirit. It is one of the forbidden fruits. If it grows in your garden, you need to uproot and destroy it. John warns that this thinking has its origin in the *world*, another word for the kingdom of Satan. "For all that is in the world, the lust of the flesh and the lust of the eyes and the boastful pride of life, is not from the Father, but is from the world." (1 John 2:16).

To deal with arrogance in the heart, you need to dig deep into the soil of your heart and examine yourself by asking these questions:

- Have I considered myself above others?
- Have I sought to exalt myself?
- Is there anyone I need to forgive?
- Am I waiting for someone to apologize?
- Have I dreamt about the praise of man?
- Have I longed for the approval of others?
- Have I worked for my glory rather than for the glory of God?
- Have I strutted about, feeling confident in myself?
- Have I grieved the Holy Spirit, acting like nothing happened?
- Have I sought power or position?
- Am I holding on to my rights?
- Am I often losing my patience?
- Am I demanding of others?
- Am I criticizing, gossiping, or acting divisively?
- Am I speaking of myself with many words?
- Am I consumed with my outward appearance?
- Am I lying or fabricating stories to elevate myself.
- Am I operating in secrecy or deception?

Move slowly through these questions, and ask the Holy Spirit to reveal any other pits of arrogance or pride in your heart. Repent and commit your way to the way of humility. Pray this prayer:

Father, I humble myself before Your mighty hand. You are enthroned both in Heaven and in my heart. I am not first; you are, and then others. Let me consider the needs of others above my own. Help me find ways to serve others and move away from the praise of man. Help me to seek Your glory and Your honor above all else. Help me to always choose humility and reject arrogance. I depend on You for all my strength, all that I need, and life itself. Help me not to believe the lie that I can go on without You.

Fear

In the third room of the Quadruplex is fear. Fear is faith aimed in the wrong direction. It is faith that God won't act. Fear rises as rationale replaces reality. Reality is found in Scripture, and fear is found in conjecture. Fear puts a blindfold on us and tells us to run, but faith opens our eyes and tells us to rest. Ignorance of God's nature and character breeds fear and dissolves communion with the Holy Spirit.

Fear will allow upon the stage of the mind those things which bring destruction, deprivation, and delusion. And these vain imaginations will provide convincing performances on this stage, which can lure our allegiance. Short of breath by the demoralization and doom depicted, we succumb to fear.

Faith awaits placement on the same stage. Faith will depict the promises of God for those that fear only Him. Faith would underscore the character of God and illuminate His nature as a Father, Protector, Provider, and Guide. Scripture is the script of this mind-staged, reality-production of the truth of God's word. Faith allows only that which aligns with the Word of God to be depicted on the stage of the mind.

Thus, the one who would seek the Lord can say He "delivered me from all my fears" (Psalm 34:4). The person who trusts His word knows, "He will not fail you or forsake you, do not fear or be dismayed" (Deuteronomy 31:8). And, "Do not fear, for I have redeemed you; I have called you by name; you are Mine!" (Isaiah 43:1).

How can I get free of fear? 1 John 4:18 states that "perfect love casts out fear." You must encounter the perfect Love of God toward you. You must encounter the Father's love. This love is felt—you will feel, too—although love is not a feeling. This love is much *more* than feelings, but it is not absent from feeling. Genuine love causes people to feel genuinely loved. How would you like it if you *didn't* feel love? Or worse, felt unloved. It is not enough to know the *fact* that God loves us; we must *experience* His love by interacting with Him in the place of His presence.

You must know that you have been loved by the Father; otherwise, the fruit of His love could miss your basket and land elsewhere. For this reason, the Apostle prayed for the Ephesians that they would "know the love of Christ which surpasses knowledge, that you may be filled up to all the fullness of God" (Ephesians 3:19). Being filled to all the fullness of God will provoke feeling!

Our mortal bodies should *experience* an influx of divine life from Divine Love. Perfect love goes beyond only ever having read about your Father in a publication—having never met Him—to fishing with Him, speaking to Him, and feeling the warmth in His embrace. *This* love delivers from fear.

Of such love, John H. Jowett, in *The Best of John H. Jowett*, stated,

> Love is a tremendous reality of which the reason
> itself can offer no explanation. And when reason
> makes a venturesome attempt to explain it, the result

is always grotesque. Have you ever read what professes to be an intellectual explanation of love? Take any book of moral philosophy, and wander down its highroads of detailed analysis of human affection, and then return to your own love of your fiancee, or of your wife, or of your child. And it is like returning from some dull herbarium, where everything is dry and withered to the wild flowers of nature and to the wandering perfumes of the honeyed woods. Love itself is a glorious reality. But intellect has no lamp to disengage its secrets. We can be perfectly sure when we are in love even if the philosopher is dumb.

You are experiencing fear because you are not experiencing the love of the Father. You are not experiencing His love because your heart has grown hard, you have abandoned the truth of His word for your own reasoning, and you are giving way to the lust of your flesh to believe more in the strength of the enemy than in the Sovereign power of Almighty God.

"God has not given us a spirit of timidity, but of power and love and discipline" (2 Timothy 1:7). Ask the Holy Spirit to visit you and reveal your mistake in trusting the message of fear rather than the message of the Gospel. It is time to visit the third quadrant of the heart, in which is housed all the reasons you have abandoned the protective promises of God for the pulsating power of fear.

Ask yourself these questions and acknowledge your wrongdoing, seeking the mercy and forgiveness only available through Jesus.

- Have I worried that God would not do as He has promised? (Fear of abandonment)
- Have I worried what others would think? (Fear of man)
- Have I been afraid of persecution? (Fear of suffering)
- Have I had fear that I would not have my needs met? (Fear of deprivation)
- Have I been afraid that harm would overcome me? (Fear of harm)
- Have I been afraid of those who can harm the body rather than of Him who can throw the whole body into Hell? (Fear of death)
- Am I afraid of how I look or sound or of my personality? (Fear of rejection)
- Have I been afraid of being alone? (Fear of isolation)
- Have I lied or deceived to avoid shame? (Fear of embarrassment)

Sometimes it's important to cut off influences that stimulate fear in your life. This might be certain types of movies, books, music—or other media sources. It might mean stopping or walking away from specific conversations that are centered around fear. These things can cause thorns to grow up in you and choke you out. Don't let them. Pray this prayer:

Father, I am guilty of believing the voice of fear more than Your voice. I repent! Please forgive me for listening to fear. Forgive me for filling my life with influences that produce fear. I repent and turn from these things. I choose to trust You and what You have spoken through Your Word. You have promised to deliver me from all my fears, and I need You to do that now. I no longer fear what others think about me, I no longer fear loss, I no longer fear death,

I no longer fear injury, sickness, discomfort, or lack. I trust that You will protect me, that though a thousand fall at my side, and ten thousand at my right hand, it will not come near me. Amen.

Greed

Finally, in the fourth room of the Quadruplex is greed. Greed pops up in many ways but can be defined as *having excessive want for something beyond need and right.* Greed can be expressed in conjunction with any need a person has, whether for food, money, relationships, power, respect, or other material things.

Jesus said, "Beware, and be on your guard against every form of greed; for not even when one has abundance does his life consist of his possessions." (Luke 12:15). Lust, covetousness, jealousy, and envy are all forms of greed. In greed, you want what another person has to satisfy your own desires. Greed is the foundation of covetousness, and the words are often used interchangeably in the Bible. Greed is the root of envy and jealousy. The problem is that greed is insatiable. The only answer to greed is to repent, cutting off its nasty head with the double-edged sword of contentment and generosity.

Paul wrote in Colossians 3:5-6, "Therefore consider the members of your earthy body as dead to immorality, impurity, passion, evil desire, and greed, which amounts to idolatry." Greed is idolatry because it moves the heart's affection from God to temporal things. The mind is buzzing like a hornet's nest with thoughts of want and urgent desire, no peace to be found except in the moments of reception and consumption. Then back to anxious wanting. Greed is a mighty stronghold used by Satan to ensnare the heart and mind of a person who spreads their idolatrous adulations across as many objects as it can imagine having. And it wants them with ravenous fury. The greedy heart has abandoned Christ and His call for those things which tantalize its fleshly cravings.

Paul offers a solution to the person who finally comes to their spiritual senses and repents of greed. In 1 Timothy 6:6-10, he writes:

> But godliness actually is a means of great gain when accompanied by contentment. For we have brought nothing into the world, so we cannot take anything out of it either. If we have food and covering, with these we shall be content. But those who want to get rich fall into temptation and a snare and many foolish and harmful desires which plunge men into ruin and destruction.

James offers a rebuke to those whose voracious greed has earned them a mountain of wealth with which they continually soothe their own lusts, forgetting that there are many around them in deep need. In James 5:1-5, He writes:

> Come now, you rich, weep and howl for your miseries which are coming upon you. Your riches have rotted and your garments have become moth-eaten. Your gold and your silver have rusted; and their rust will be a witness against you and will consume your flesh like fire. It is in the last days that you have stored up your treasure! Behold, the pay of the laborers who mowed your fields, and which has been withheld by you, cries out against you; and the outcry of

the those who did the harvesting has reached the
ears of the Lord of Sabaoth.

One must be careful in examining the heart for indications
of greed. It hides behind pride and deception and can be challenging to identify. Here are a few questions to ask to get you
started, but take the time you need to wait on the Holy Spirit
and truly turn over the soil of your heart.

- Have I been content?
- Am I generous?
- Am I conscious of the poor and those who have little?
- Is there anything for which I have excessive thirst or
  lust?
- Do I want or try to have more than I need? (General
  Greed)
- Do I envy those with wealth? (Money Greed)
- Am I striving to accumulate nicer things? (Material
  Greed)
- Am I hanging on tightly to things I don't need?
  (Hoarding Greed)
- Can I fast and pray, or must I always eat? (Food Greed)
- Am I able to make time for prayer, or must I sleep on
  and on? (Sleep Greed)
- Do I strive to protect my reputation? (Respect Greed)
- Am I thirsty for authority over others? (Power Greed)
- Does position at work or type of work reflects my value?
  (Status Greed)
- Am I lustful? (Body Greed)
- Am I manipulative in my relationships? (Emotional
  Greed)

- Am I addicted to alcohol or other substances? (Substance Greed)
- Have I placed my own gratification as a priority? (Pleasure Greed)

Having asked these questions and examined your heart, take time to pray like this:

Father, please deliver me from the deception that I have been under. I have believed I needed things that I didn't. I have accepted that my wants were my needs. I have felt that having more things would satisfy me, and it hasn't. I have been selfish, wanting what would make me more comfortable and happy, and I have not considered the needs of others. I repent of greed! Help me give up everything for my relationship with You and for the purposes You have for me in this life. Help me love Jesus and the Gospel more than the things in this world. Please cleanse my heart with the blood of Jesus Christ and make me whole again. Amen.

When you have taken the time to walk through your garden, identifying any weeds, thorns, thistles, or stones that don't belong, you will sense the blessing of the Holy Spirit upon you. You will sense His working in your heart, and you will feel as if He loves you deeply. This is the beginning of discovering His beauty and glory in the temple. Take a while after this just to worship, offer your life in surrender, and enjoy communion with the Holy Spirit.

Conclusion and Contemplation

Break up the hardness of your heart and prepare to receive the seed of His word. Is your heart hard right now?

Discussion Questions

1. What is the default state of the human heart?
2. Who has been given responsibility for your heart? Why?
3. What does it mean to rend your heart, not your garment? What was the significance of rending garments in Hebrew culture?
4. Which should alarm us more: the behaviors of sin or hardness of heart? Why?
5. Will God honor a casual pursuit of Him? Why or why not? What scriptures support this?
6. Is it sometimes challenging to identify sin in your heart? Is it difficult to be forgiven? Why does God require us to wait on Him—quietly and carefully?
7. Why is rebellion like sorcery? Why is arrogance like idolatry?
8. How are fear and faith similar? Why do we choose to fear?
9. What is greed? Is greed always for material things?

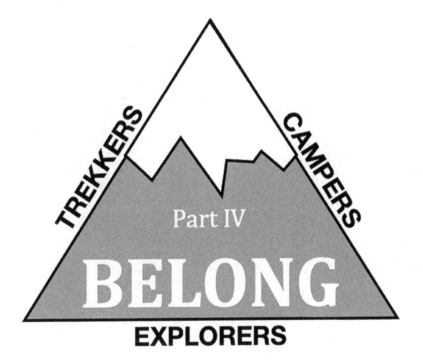

TREKKERS

CAMPERS

Part IV

BELONG

EXPLORERS

INTRODUCTION

Summiting the Mountain of God can go no further without our Guide, given to the explorer bent on the most profound discoveries. In part four of The Mountaineer, prepare to be infiltrated by the wondrous beauty and delight of the Holy Spirit. Here you will learn to whom it is that you belong. You and all you possess—both material and otherwise—belong to Him under an eternal covenant of love. By constantly renewing this covenant in an attitude of surrender, His flame will consume you.

During this section, you will see how important it is to cultivate and maintain the dispositions of surrender, brokenness, and total consecration to God. Anything less than this constitutes idolatry, and the Holy Spirit will wait for you to recognize that and repent of it before revealing more of His Glory to you.

You are close to the summit now, on the verge of a significant breakthrough. Press into Him, search hard for Him—with all your heart, climb, reach, stretch…and find Him.

Literary Support

"Follow the light into the sun, leading me back where I belong
I was a fool, fading away when autumn was brown, winter
was grey."
— *Home*, by Gabriel Martinez

Joy floods my soul, for Jesus has saved me,
Freed me from sin that long had enslaved me,
His precious blood He gave to redeem,
Now I belong to Him.
—*Now I Belong to Jesus* by Norman J. Clayton

There's a sound of awakening, and it's shut up in my bones,
There's a rumbling and a rattling, the wind is starting to blow
We are people of the mountain, and we embrace the climb
Our DNA is the wilderness, we were born for this time
—*Anthem of Awakening,* by Ryan Bain

The Hills
Madison Cawein

There is no joy of earth that thrills,
My bosom like the far-off hills!
Th' unchanging hills, that, shadowy,
Beckon our mutability
To follow and to gaze upon,
Foundations of the dusk and dawn.
Meseems the very heavens are massed,
Upon their shoulders, vague and vast
With all the skyey burden of,
The winds and clouds and stars above.
Lo, how they sit before us, seeing,
The laws that give all beauty being!
Behold! to them, when dawn is near,
The nomads of the air appear,
Unfolding crimson camps of day,
In brilliant bands; then march away;

184

And under burning battlements,
Of twilight plant their tinted tents.
The truth of olden myths, that brood,
By haunted stream and haunted wood,
They see; and feel the happiness,
Of old at which we only guess:
The dreams, the ancients loved and knew,
Still as their rocks and trees are true:
Not otherwise than presences,
The tempest and the calm to these:
One, shouting on them all the night;
Black-limbed and veined with lambent light;
The other with the ministry,
Of all soft things that company
With music—an embodied form,
Giving to solitude the charm
Of leaves and waters and the peace,
Of bird-begotten melodies—
And who at night cloth still confer,
With the mild moon, that telleth her
Pale tale of lonely love, until,
Wan images of passion fill
The heights with shapes that glimmer by,
Clad on with sleep and memory.

Chapter X

TREKKERS

Adoration in the Courts of Worship

Imperative

*We must be fascinated with the beauty
of the Lord in His Temple.*

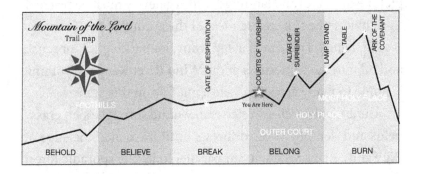

Cirque of the Towers
September 2021
Lander, Wyoming

We turned right off the highway onto a gravel road that seemed to have no end. It rolled over the hills into the distance until it narrowed into nothing on the horizon. The sky was broad, blue, and bright, with enormous clouds suspended unevenly. Pronghorns darted away in the distance in groups of

20 or 30, and cattle roamed without fences in the open territory. Southern Wyoming's wilderness welcome kept us pointing, smiling, and full of anticipation.

After an hour and a half of gravel, Travis Grimes and I arrived at the Big Sandy Campground and parking area. It began to rain as we made final adjustments to our packs. It was 4:30 PM, and we had three hours till sunset. That was just enough time to cover the 6.5 miles to Dad's Lake.

Here would a pair of legs and lungs cry out for quitting. This journey up and over streams and stones was at a grade dismal to comfort. Reaching nearly 12,000 feet, the entrancing trail draws hundreds through the deluge of difficulty with hors d'oeuvres of picturesque lakes and landings. Still, a gateway must be reached to sit before the full course meal of the Cirque of the Towers.

Big Sandy Trail leads away from the parking lot, obscure, and off into the wilderness of the Wind River Range. Wyoming is home to many arresting vistas, but few on this scale.

The amiable, well-traveled trail wound through open grassy fields and densely wooded forests until it reached the edge of Big Sandy River, where it ran parallel to it. The sporadic forest patches were scattered between meadows of knee-high grasses, browned under the late summer sun. The trail narrowed and cut deep into the soil, dividing the meadows unequally.

If rain and storms were there to deter us, they didn't. To climb a mountain is a noble feat, and we would always prefer favorable conditions. But, since they were not, we pushed through. We were fortunate to do so since the rain clouds eventually broke up. It was just as we came out of the forest again and into another meadow. Grey and blue and purple were the thunder clouds, now with patches of blue sky between them, and these clouds were moving more quickly. Some hung seemingly still in the distance, behind the lofty mountains, and looked climbable.

We followed the trail trustingly, and it brought us to a brook that cut through the meadow. In the brook were trout, and I wanted to catch them, but we didn't have much time before it would be dark, so we pressed on. Beside Mirror Lake, I saw more trout and lamented to leave the scene without casting my line.

The trail ascended steeply from there, up past a waterfall that ripped over the crags of a steep gorge. The tumultuous trail took sharp turns as it switched back and forth up the hillside, between the inferno of Aspen leaves, blazing golden orange against their white bark.

The descent onto Dad's Lake came with a family of black-tailed deer crossing the trail and curiously casting glances at us. As we closed the distance between them and us, they bounded into the forest and disappeared. Dad's Lake sat in the perfect position to catch the sunset. The various densities, colors, and shades of the evening clouds hung on the horizon and were reflected by the still waters of the lake.

We found a campsite on the lake's edge, elevated by the granite bluffs that lined its southern shore, and fell into it abruptly. Patches of grass grew amid the stone platforms, and one was level and large enough for the tent.

In the morning, I had time for a trout conquest. Sadly, they eluded me and ignored my very real-looking trout fly. I cast it from behind some tall grass in an attempt to not scare them away, still no bites.

Morning coffee was abnormally delicious and perked up my wearied body. The first day's hike would be the easiest, but

I wasn't acclimated to the elevation nearing 10,000 feet at Dad's Lake. It rained again while we were packing up camp, which meant I was carrying a wet tent.

The sunshine was back midday and gave color back to the scenery. Marm's Lake was a spectacle that earned a thirty-minute gawking and photo session. The land, which slipped easily down into the lake, was speckled with trees—mostly evergreens, and boulders—mostly buried. A marmot watched us from a safe distance with an expression of disdain. Small beaches rounded the corners of the lake, and when the sun hit the water, it either reflected the sky or illuminated the sand beneath it. The water of Marm's Lake was quite clear and created the imagery of a Caribbean beach with hues of light green and blue. It was so captivating that we wanted to jump in and swim around, but we knew this water would mean hypothermia.

The gully that led out of Marm's lake was not too challenging and landed us in a broad valley at the intersection of the Shadow Lake Trail and the Continental Divide Trail. We turned right toward Shadow Lake, and more accommodating clouds allowed the sunshine to warm our skin as we trekked through the valley toward Texas Pass.

Burgundy and golden ground cover sprawled across the browned grasses and under hunter-green boughs of pine needles. Up from the edges of the picturesque valley, granite spires shot heavenward and towered over us like a wilderness skyline. Washakie Creek is twenty-five feet wide in some places and looks waist-deep. I could see no fish there, but wanted to. We had to cross the waterway several times and were fortunate to find our way atop protruding stones. Rippling down from above at Texas Lake, through Billy's Lake and Shadow Lake, the creek bolstered every photo and magnetic moment of breathtaking site-seeing.

We meandered through shoulder-height boulders at Shadow Lake and pushed aside the branches of fiery yellow Ligustrum shrubs. It was evident by its dark blue-green tone that Shadow Lake was deeper than the other lakes. Colder, too, I suspected. We filtered and drank its water, and it cooled our insides and refreshed our weariness. After a lunch break, we continued up to Texas Pass. Boulders grew larger as we approached the last lake before the ascent. Some were twenty feet tall and tempted a micro-summit. A pleasant, increasingly prominent sunshine greeted us as we fell into the grass and rested on the wind-busied shore of Texas Lake.

Not long after sprawling flat on my back under the golden rays of the sun, I began to collect frigid water from the lapping shore of the lake. We devoured our afternoon snacks and repositioned our gear before attempting the climb.

Texas Pass requires an elevation gain of approximately 1,000 feet over a span of about one-third of a mile. With our packs on, we surveyed the most strategic route, which would be the least annihilating to our energy and strength. We made the distance a bit longer by zig-zagging across the mountainside but still could only take a dozen or so steps at a time before having to stop and catch our breath.

The view from behind us also stole our breath. Texas Lake seemed smaller and took its place below the colossal walls of the mountainsides between which we had ascended. The beige basin was carpeted in late summer grasses, which stretched down the long passage and took most of the space between the elevated pinnacles above them. The creek, a barely visible line through the valley, connected the lakes, which looked like puddles, and pines blurred together like dark blemishes on a toasted valley rug.

Finally, the summit was in view, and we knew we had it in our back pocket. Our ambition grew with each exhausting step until we forgot our weariness for the joy of the summit.

We had arrived at 11,800 feet of elevation and could see for miles beyond our position. A sign that once said "Texas Pass" had fallen apart. We nevertheless stood by it and took pictures of the valley behind us.

Turning toward the enormous basin, fittingly called Cirque of the Towers, we stood quietly, taking in what was before us. The wonder of God's creation and the certainty of His help in getting us there was overwhelming and more penetrating than the frigid gusts of wind. His marvelous presence and thoughts of His goodness tore through our souls with fury and innovation, lighting fires long extinguished. It was terrible and wonderful to have come to such a place, where the body was virtually incapacitated, but the spirit was so richly invigorated.

Down below us, waterfalls and brooks flowed toward Lonesome Lake, and the sun lit up the backs of War Bonnet and Pingora peaks. We knew we had to make our way down to a suitable campsite before sunset, but we didn't want to leave this place, this moment.

I slept better that night than the first. I was more exhausted, but also there was no altitude sickness or headache to interrupt my sleep, only wind. Howling wind—in fact, growling wind, whipped angrily against our tent. It sounded like grizzly bears at one point, and I was awakened. For a moment, eyes rounded and staring upward at the roof of my fabric shelter, I felt like a meal—packaged and laying on the lawn of a bear's habitat. I dismissed my fears, however, and went back to sleep under the stars and spires of Lonesome Lake.

It was still dark when I decided to get moving. I saw some headlamps traversing the upper-base of Pingora. Climbers, I suspected. Slipping quietly out of the tent, I gathered my coat and boots and prepared to watch the sunrise.

Lonesome Lake is situated so that the longer banks are on its north and south sides, and a river flows out of its narrowed East end. There, the water converges with the V-shaped horizon trickling away between the monstrous Mitchell and Lizard Head peaks.

There had been a massive fir growing near the lake's shore, and it had long ago fallen away from the lake's edge toward the shore. The lake had risen, but just enough to turn the massive trunk into a pier, connecting the shore to a position over the water. I stepped up onto the broad, old tree and shuffled out over the water, where I took a seat, legs dangling.

Behind the dark silhouettes of the mountains, the sky began to brighten, and clouds came into view with ominous orange bellies. Firs along the bases of the mountains remained almost black as the mountains grew grayer and more visible. Patches of rose and red appeared along their highest points where the first rays of morning descended into the Cirque.

The sky, now golden above the exiting waters of the lake, faded back to dark blue above my head, where stars could still be seen. Morning broke into the Cirque of the Towers with a delightful array of colors and beauty, reminiscent of heaven's grace invading the dark word of humanity. The Lake, now a mirror of what was beyond it on the horizon, looked painted with pinks, oranges, and light blues swirling across its surface.

The trees became green again, and beyond their pointed tops, pointed mountain tops glowed red hot from the light of the sun still tucked below the horizon.

Trout flinched below me in the water, and cold air cracked my lips. I mused at the grace which had such form and presence scarce beheld by the eyes of men. Prayers and songs lifted easily from my chest, up through my voice, and into eternity. I longed for God with aching in my soul and joy that just barely surpassed it.

Never in my life had I sat in such a place, but always had I wanted to. I knew I was right where I belonged. I also knew that what I saw was not a discovery but a revealing. I heard no voice calling me but felt as if the Holy Spirit was responsible for getting me up, out, and upon that log with an invitation that echoed in my soul, "Come to Me and I will answer you, and I will tell you great and mighty things which you do no know" (Jeremiah 33:3).

The Court of the Temple

When you have taken time to honor the Lord in His majesty at the Gate, not rushing in and trampling upon his courts (see Isaiah 1:12), but going carefully before Him, falling down in humility before Him, His Spirit will lift you up and take you into the courts as He did with Ezekiel (see Ezekiel 43:5). I certainly felt lifted by the Spirit as I climbed up Texas Pass, and then descended into what seemed like the courts of heaven— the Cirque of the Towers. After humbling myself before the Lord, I have also felt the Spirit lift me up and bring me into His presence.

The courtyard of the temple was where the people of God gathered to celebrate the atonement of their sins and offer God various sacrifices like thank offerings and free-will offerings. This is a place of celebration, thanksgiving, and praise. Consider this scene during the reign of Hezekiah:

> He then stationed the Levites in the house of the Lord with cymbals, with harps and with lyres, according to the command of David and of Gad the King's seer, and of Nathan the prophet; for the command was from the Lord through His prophets. The Levites stood with the musical instruments of David and the priests with the trumpets. Then Hezekiah gave the order to offer the burnt offering on the altar. When the burn offering began, the song to the Lord also began with the trumpets, accompanied by the instruments of David, king of Israel. While the whole assembly worshiped, the singers also sang and the trumpets sounded; all this continued until the burnt offering was finished. Now at the completion of the burnt offerings, the king and all who were present with him bowed down and worshiped. Moreover, King Hezekiah and the officials ordered the Levites to sing praises to the Lord with the words of David and Asaph the seer. So they sang praises with joy, and bowed down and worshiped. (2 Chronicles 29:25-30)

What a wonderful picture of how we must conduct ourselves as we enter into the courts of our Lord. Such an expression of reverence, humility, gladness, and thanksgiving was this time of worship for the people of Israel—kneeling down together with their king to worship the Lord God and dedicate themselves to Him!

Total consecration to the Lord is a precondition to worshipping in Spirit and in truth. As mentioned before, devotion, or consecration, is the entire surrender of everything in a person's heart and hands to the Lord. All dreams, possessions, and energies belong to Him by means of trust-driven surrender. Consecration stems from a covenant that we enter into through repentance, faith, and baptism. We are His as a husband and wife who belong to one another. This is why the Lord is jealous for us and grieved by an adulterous people.

If needed, renew your covenant with the Lord, and return to your first love. These gestures of trust, commitment, and belonging are worth more than all the songs you could ever sing. This is what the word of God teaches about surrender: "Present your bodies a living and holy sacrifice acceptable to God, which is your spiritual service of worship" (Romans 12:2).

One of the true signs of humility is gratefulness. This is the time to begin to thank Christ for His atoning work on the cross. To declare that you could never come into this place of His glory on your own merit. King David wrote:

> "Enter his gates with thanksgiving and his courts
> with praise; give thanks to him and bless his name.
> For the Lord is good and his lovingkindness is
> everlasting and His faithfulness to all generations."
> (Psalm 100:4-5)

In the courts of heaven, John saw, among many things, the following:

Then I looked, and I heard the voice of many angels around the throne and the living creatures and the elders; and the number of them was myriads of myriads, and thousands of thousands, saying with a loud voice, "Worthy is the Lamb that was slain to receive power and riches and wisdom and might and honor and glory and blessing." And every created thing which is in heaven and on the earth and under the earth and on the sea, and all things in them, I heard saying, "To Him who sits on the throne, and to the Lamb, be blessing and honor and glory and dominion forever and ever." (Revelation 5:11-13)

If this scene is going to occur in heaven, where God Almighty is enthroned, and we are commanded in Scripture to approach this throne (Hebrews 4:16), then we would be wise to do what every living creature in the universe will be doing: Praise him! Use this passage as a source for your wording as you lift up praise to God. Take a cue from Hezekiah and praise the Lord with the words of David and Asaph. Go to the Psalms or other passages where various Bible characters lifted up praise to God and learn how they did it.

Clasp His Feet

"Come, let us worship and bow down; Let us kneel before the Lord our Maker. For He is our God, and we are the people of His pasture and the sheep of His hand" (Psalm 95:6-7). Getting down to the feet of Jesus is essential to worship. Notice that King Hezekiah and the entire assembly knelt before the Lord and worshipped him in the Court of the temple. Imagine what

Hezekiah could have been saying to the Lord while his forehead was touching the ground. Perhaps he said:

> It is good to give thanks to the Lord and to sing praises to Your name, O Most High; To declare Your lovingkindness in the morning and Your faithfulness by night, with the ten-stringed lute and with the harp, with resounding music upon the lyre. For You, O Lord, have made me glad by what You have done, I will sing for joy at the works of Your hands. How great are Your works, O Lord! Your thoughts are very deep. (Psalm 92:1-5)

Women, who were looking at the tomb of Jesus after his death and burial, encountered him on the road as they ran to tell the others what an angel had said to them. "Suddenly, Jesus met them, 'greetings,' he said. They came to him, clasped his feet and worshipped him" (Matthew 28:9-10, NIV). With their faces so close to his scars, did they open their eyes to see them? What thoughts filled their minds as they possessed in their hands the feet of their Maker who became their Messiah? What must they have thought or said while in such a posture of adoration and worship before Him who conquered death and walked out of the tomb on wounded feet? Perhaps this,

> Surely you took up our infirmities, Jesus, and carried our sorrows, yet we considered you stricken by God, smitten by him, and afflicted. But you were pierced for our transgressions, you were crushed for our iniquities; the punishment that brought us peace was upon *you*, and by *your* wounds we are healed. We,

> like sheep, have all gone astray, each one has turned
> to his own way, and yet Yahweh has laid on you the
> iniquity of us all. (Isaiah 53:4-6, adapted paraphrase,
> italics mine)

When you come to the Gate, you have come to Jesus (see John 10:7). And when you come to Jesus, you find your need for His forgiveness, healing, and mercy. One such person came to Jesus at a dinner held by a Pharisee named Simon. She brought the most valuable possession she had, an alabaster jar of pure nard—and expensive perfume—worth a year's wages. She, too, went to His feet.

> And standing behind Him at His feet, weeping, she
> began to wet His feet with her tears, and kept wiping
> them with the hair of her head, and kissing His feet
> and anointing them with the perfume. (Luke 7:38)

Jesus told the Pharisees that anyone who had been forgiven much would love much, but he who had been forgiven little would love little (see Luke 7:47). This kind of love is driven by understanding our *need* for forgiveness. Those focused on quantifying the *number* of their sins will love little and seldom seek mercy or forgiveness. Yet "If anyone is guilty of breaking the law at just one point, he is guilty of breaking all of it." The chasm created by sin between people and God is not quantifiable. If you think your sins "aren't that bad," you're thinking like a Pharisee.

Your holiness is not better than this woman's, it's not better than the tax collector's, it's not better than the homeless addict you drive past on the way to work. You need Christ's redemption just as much as any person on Earth. Approach Him with that mindset and you will find yourself pouring out love and affection upon His feet in gratitude for His mercy and forgiveness.

The Pharisees had a desperate need for forgiveness, but many didn't realize it. Thus they received no forgiveness. The woman, recognizing her deep need for the Redeemer, came in brokenness, pouring out all that she owned upon Him, bowing down and with all of her heart offering her love, adoration, and worship.

If you have broken up the hardness of your heart, you will want to do little else than to lay hold of the feet of Jesus, your healer, and worship. We must come through the gate and then into the Court of Worship. Go to your knees at the Gate and understand that "Out of the heart come evil thoughts, murders, adulteries, fornications, thefts, false witness, slanders." (Matthew 15:19).

Every heart has some element of rebellion, arrogance, fear, and greed in it. David understood this and thus prayed, "Who can discern his errors? Acquit me of hidden faults" (Psalm 19:12). After letting the Lord deal with you "ever so severely," your humility before the "mighty hand of God" will be rewarded; and the Spirit of the Lord will "lift you up and take you into the courts." Then you will be able to worship like Hezekiah, the Marys, the woman with the alabaster jar, and myriads upon myriads of angels around the mighty throne of the risen Lamb of God.

Agreement And Confession

Agreement is one of the fundamental components in both confession of sin and confession of praise. You agree that you were wrong and ask forgiveness. Coming into agreement with God, even in the place of having sinned, honors Him and expresses His place as Redeemer and our place as those who need to be redeemed. Subsequent to confessing the truth of our nature and deeds to God is confessing the truth of His nature and deeds. This is fundamental to all worship, adoration, praise, and exaltation in the presence of the Lord.

When you come into the courts of the Lord, you may feel that you have little to say. This is ok for a while, but at some point, you need to activate your speech with words of praise. Not only does this produce focus for a mind that may otherwise wander, but it is also another function of devotion that is attractive to the Lord. He hears your praise and allows you to discover more of who He is, and you will begin to feel in your Spirit something similar to what you might feel when looking out from such a vista as we did from above the Cirque of the Towers.

God always looks for active faith in His people. When He knows that you can't see the beauty, but you are already declaring it, He will open the eyes of your heart and spirit, and you will behold the beauty of the Lord in His temple (see Psalm 27:4).

Songs and Shouts of Praise

Not a singer? No prob. Just shout. When you get up on your feet after pouring your perfume on the feet of Jesus, enter the enormous and incomprehensibly loud rock concert that is booming in the courts of heaven right now. If you're going to heaven, you *must* believe what the Scriptures describe is happening there and has been for a very, very long time. At loud concerts, one can sing, shout, dance, jump, and just be rowdy.

Find all these behaviors in Scripture. My motto for worship and praise has long been "all things biblical." Do anything in the Bible, and you can be sure you're in good order. But beware, the Bible's prescriptions for praise are rowdy!

"Saying with a loud voice..." (Revelation 5:12). Loud shouting and singing of praise to God is a big part of the culture of the Kingdom of heaven, which includes the temporal world of Earth. People who see the King can't keep silent. If they do, even the stones will cry out.

> As soon as He was approaching, near the descent of the Mount of Olives, the whole crowd of the disciples began to praise God joyfully with a loud voice for all the miracles which they had seen, shouting: "Blessed is the King who comes in the name of the Lord; Peace in heaven and glory in the highest!" (Luke 19:37-38)

King David understood the culture of praise in the Kingdom of God. He danced before the Lord so wildly that his wife scorned him. (See 2 Samuel 6:22). He wrote these words:

> Praise the Lord! Sing to the Lord a new song, and His praise in the congregation of the godly ones. Let Israel be glad in his Maker; Let the sons of Zion rejoice in their King. Let them praise His name with dancing; let them sing praises to Him with the timbrel and lyre. For the Lord takes pleasure in His people; He will beautify the afflicted ones with salvation. Let the godly ones exult in glory; let them sing for joy on their beds. (Psalm 149:1-5)

If you are hitting a wall in your worship and praise before the Lord. Take a cue from Joshua and the Israelites, "So the people shouted, and priests blew the trumpets; and when the people heard the sound of the trumpet, the people shouted with a great shout and the wall fell down flat" (Joshua 6:20). You may have to march around that wall seven times, but if you believe and shout, you will have victory.

Mirth in Heaven

The culture of heaven is celebration. It is us celebrating the might and power of our God and King, but it is also Him celebrating the uniqueness and wonder of each of us, whom He knit together in our mother's wombs. We are fearfully and wonderfully made (see Psalm 139:14)! The fact is that God is so excited for what you are that HE IS SINGING AND DANCING in heaven:

> Sing aloud, O daughter of Zion; shout, O Israel! Rejoice and exult with all your heart, O Daughter of Jerusalem! The Lord has taken away the judgments against you, He has cleared away your enemies. The King of Israel, The Lord, is in your midst; you shall never again fear evil. On that day, it shall be said to Jerusalem, "Fear not, O Zion, Let not your hands grow weak. The Lord, your God, is in your midst, a mighty one who will save; He will rejoice over you with gladness, He will quiet you by His love, He will exult over you with loud singing." (Zephaniah 3:14-17, ESV)

This passage indicates an atmosphere of mirth in heaven. The word "rejoice" is translated from the Hebrew "sun" or "sis" which can be translated to "make mirth." Mirth is a party atmosphere, a "we just won the championship" kind of mindset; it's the attitude of the fans flooding onto the football field when the championship game is won. It is the team dumping Gatorade on the coach and shouting for victory. It is Travis Pastrana after doing a double backflip on a motorcycle at the X-games. It is Nacho Libre after defeating Rameses. Mirth is celebration, and this celebration goes on and on and on into eternity and we can join in it now. Elohim is a dancer and a singer and His songs are about you! Let's make noise about Him and see if we make a connection to Him we didn't know could be made.

Take your time as you worship the Lord in praise and thanksgiving; in this way, you will stoke the flames on the altar— flames you will need soon. Know that He has qualified you by the righteousness of Jesus to come before His throne, and give thanks for that. Know also that by venturing in this direction, something in you is dying, and it will cry out to prevent your advancement. That something is the you that must be crucified with Christ. Like climbing up through the boulders and stones along the path up through Texas Pass, you must endure until you break into the atmosphere of His beauty and the unequaled place of His glorious presence.

Conclusion and Contemplation

You belong in the courts of the Lord, where His people join with heaven in worship and adoration. Will you bow down and clasp His feet?

Prayer of Commitment

Thank You, Jesus, for making way for me to enter the courtyard of heaven. You are the only way to the Father, and I trust that You will bring me into fellowship with Your Holy Spirit. I bring You nothing today that is good in me to prove my worth, and I lay down my guilt over my shortcomings and failures. You make me worthy by clothing me in Your righteousness, which I receive by faith. I celebrate having a clear conscience before You, and I am ready at any moment for Your Holy Spirit to show me if there is any offensive way in me. I love You, I trust You, and I worship You in the splendor of Your holiness.

Discussion Questions

1. Why is a sense of belonging important?
2. Do you believe that you belong in the courts of heaven? Why or why not?
3. What were some of the things that the Israelites did while in the temple courts with King Hezekiah?
4. What is happening in the courts of heaven around the throne right now?
5. What should we do when we come into the courts of heaven?
6. What does it mean to come into agreement with God through confession?
7. Should we praise God when we don't see or feel anything? Why?
8. Describe celebrating God? Are you comfortable with that? Why or Why not?

Chapter XI

CAMPERS

Belong in the Presence of the Lord

Imperative
We must be wholly consecrated to
God, belonging entirely to Him.

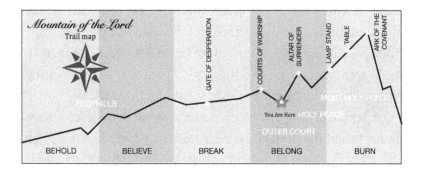

Christmas Campout
December 2016
Bardstown, Kentucky

F all closed up shop and handed a deadened world to winter. Not, however, before the first-ever primitive "Wedin Campout!" We stuffed our packs with primarily clothes and sleeping gear and piled it all on top of the car. It was a colorful afternoon. The weather was in the mid-'60s, and sunshine beamed through the golden-auburn ocean of leaves, still dancing in the treetops.

With a giant dog and a family of four packed into the microbe-sized Saturn, we launched toward our destination—a Kentucky State Park in Bardstown. A perforated muffler muffled next to nothing during the hour-long commute, and the bleating motor flat-lined our minds. We stared into the last visages of autumn, eager to get un-cramped and out of the car and into the aroma and ambiance of our one-night home in the wooded wonder.

With our backpacks on and legs stretched, we set afoot down the drive that led us deep into the forest. Asher carried his first-ever pack and performed well with it. The winding pavement concluded at the trailhead, where we stepped into nature's euphoric buffet for the senses and descended into the valley. Buddy—our massive, furry, white Great Pyrenees—sniffed to his heart's content and told the world of animals he was visiting with each sprinkling of trailside shrubs and tree trunks.

After crunching our way across the forest floor of leaves, we finally found the perfect site near a creek. We pitched our tents and built our fire, and soon the dark night fell on our rustic scene. All that could be heard over the crackling fire were the groans of distant cattle. Carving sausage roasters out of saplings was Asher's camp job, and he worked at it diligently with his pocket knife.

Meanwhile, Buddy, tethered to a tree with a twenty-foot leash, meandered through his plot of forest, tying himself into a knot of total immobility amidst the thicket of a dozen small trees.

A super moon crept up over the silhouetted horizon, and the woods were eventually illuminated by the blue-grey beams of the lesser light. After a meal of brats, Asher and Asiah followed me along a hiking trail for an expedition of exploration through the shadows of a moonlit night.

The hike was buddy's first adventure without a leash. Faithfully, he stayed right at my side. Eventually winding back through the valley haven of oaks, birch, and walnut giants, we arrived at our creekside tent home and parked our chilled noses and fingers in front of the blaze.

Anne Marie passed out granola bars and gleaming smiles while we laughed and shared memories of past family experiences. Some memories were, perhaps, on par with the indescribable felicity bubbling up in each of us during *these* moments of fireside delight. The Moon seemed to have halted directly above us like a parking lot light. When the stories ran thin, and the fire ran thinner, we began our migration into our tents. Our goal of warmth was initially achieved in our bags, but as the night stretched on, we cooled, and cooled, and writhed in the cold.

A single thread of smoke rose from a ring of stones at daybreak, up through the forest canopy, where it dissipated into the sunless, blue sky. I stirred the coals and added sticks, and the crackling flames that followed drew slumbering little Wedins from their one-night hibernations.

First, faces peered out from partially unzipped tent doors. The campsite looked different in the daytime than it had at night. Buddy had not figured out how to untangle himself, so he slept in his fixed location. When he looked up at the awakened children, it gave the cue for daylight forest fun, but not until after breakfast over the coals.

The day's hikes produced better photos. From the crevasses of mossy monoliths, Anne Marie, Asher, and Asiah smiled for the camera with wintery puffs proceeding from chilled lips.

Creekside, we found rocks to skip, fossils to keep, and more picturesque moments. Buddy's nose found no rest among the nearly infinite range of aromas only he could detect. We found an overhang two hundred feet long and more than thirty feet high. Asher and Asiah followed groundhog tracks while Buddy played in the water.

After packing up gear and climbing back out of the valley, we piled into the car again and drove home. Everyone, dog included, crashed into a sound sleep until only the constant hum of my old car could be heard.

I thought about the bittersweet stage in life that I was in. Nearly so perfect, there's a tinge of sadness in knowing it would one day pass. My children will grow into adults, and new phases will begin. But I loved *this* phase.

I thought about how it would be Christmas in a few days. But this was the only gift I wanted. The gift was having the opportunity to make depth, create real wealth, and do it out of such an exploit as a camping adventure. My family is my wealth; I could be no wealthier.

As emotionally rich as a family memory can be, and as profound as is the trust that grows from it, it's important to know that this, too, is but a shadow. This is a temporary family, but we also have an eternal family to which we forever belong. And the Eternal Father is even more interested than any earthly father in building a wealth of depth and meaning into our relationship. He is building a family. He does this by sharing with us the invigorating and revitalizing Person of His Holy Spirit.

On our journey up the mountain of the Lord, we must camp here. We must take a while and consider the scenery on this vital part of our journey. We must explore the pathways of this often obscured truth: that we cannot belong to the Father *and* to the world. Here again, there is no neutral stance. Either you belong to one or the other—*not* both, *not* neither.

Let us look deeply and understand clearly that belonging is at the root of love-driven obedience and sacrificial surrender—no matter to whom one belongs. If you love the world, you will obey its demands and sacrifice much to affirm that belonging. The fact is, you were *created* to obey and sacrifice as demonstrations of love and belonging. This campsite is where we *make sure we know* to whom it is that we belong.

We Belong Here

In the last chapter, we saw how the Court of the Lord is a place of worship. In this chapter, we will continue our exploration of this glorious place and find that it is the place where we discover, develop and deepen a sense of belonging.

As you've seen in the climb up Texas Pass, we can't expect to get to such a place easily. We must know that God's terms of discovery are that you seek Him with all your heart. Like any climb up a mountain, you may find yourself weary at times, out of energy, or even out of breath. You may wonder why you are doing this, what you are looking for, and whether you should give up. But if you persist, pressing on toward the goal of the upward call of God in Christ, you will find unspeakable beauty. You will be shown things tremendous and unsearchable.

You climbed up and came through the gate in humility, desperation, repentance, and brokenness of heart. Now you are in the Courts of Worship, and this part of your journey is a time to reinforce belonging. It is a hike with your spouse, kids, and the family dog down into a creekside campsite where belonging solidifies like mortar between souls.

Did you know that we belong to the Lord? We are His property, and He is an infinitely good steward. We were purchased from our enslavement to sin at the price of the broken body and shed blood of the Son of God. As ones who belong to Him, we belong in His presence, and His presence is given to us through His Holy Spirit.

One of the first fruits of the Holy Spirit in our lives is that of solidifying our identity in Christ as children of God. He does this in two ways, when a person is born of the Spirit and when they are led by the Spirit. It is not that complicated to understand that if we are "born of the Spirit," we are his children, spiritually speaking. Perhaps simpler still is the idea that if we are children and He is our Father, we will follow Him around doing what He does.

That is why it is so important that we not just follow a Christian code of ethics and hope that our attempt at "being good" will get us to Heaven. No, actually, "if anyone does not have the Spirit of Christ, he does not belong to Christ." No matter how tingly a worship song feels at church or how much time you spend eating donuts and drinking coffee in the church lobby, you don't belong to Christ if you don't have the Spirit.

Belonging to God means NOT belonging to the world—neither to the Prince of the world, nor to the pattern of the world, nor to the people of the world. In John 8:44, Jesus said to the Pharisees, "You belong to your father, the Devil." How could Jesus tell that they didn't belong to Him? They didn't listen to Him and couldn't hear Him. He said, "He who belongs to God hears what God says, the reason that you do not hear is that you do not belong to God."

Do you belong to Jesus? You can only belong to Jesus or to the world. When you belong to Jesus, it is similar to being in a marriage. You forsake all others. This is another picture of consecration and covenant. Don't cheat on Jesus!

Some Christians think that imitating the world will help them get people saved. Actually, acting like the world does not produce fruit for the Kingdom. It might produce friends who don't belong to Jesus, but in the end, they will still land in Hell. Only the abandonment of the world and its ways establishes the kind of soil in which the Word of God can grow and produce fruit.

In the following several paragraphs, we will examine the *Prince* of the world, the *pattern* of the world, and the *people* of the world. Look to see if you have aligned yourself with the values and culture of the world. Take time to repent, read Scripture, and renew your covenant of belonging to Christ.

The Prince of the World

What does the Bible mean with the phrase, "the world?" Well, first of all, it refers to him who is the ruler of "the world" and of the kingdom from which we, who are believers, were delivered:

> And you were dead in your trespasses and sins, in which you formerly walked according to the course of this world, according to the Prince of the power of the air, of the spirit the is now working in the sons of disobedience. (Ephesians 2:1-2)

The god of this world is Satan (see 2 Corinthians 4:4). Satan has a literal kingdom according to Jesus, who said, "If Satan casts out Satan, he is divided against himself; how then will his kingdom stand?" (Matthew 12:26). And thus, we understand that to refer to worldliness is to refer to the culture of the kingdom over which Satan is Lord, and to belong to the world is to belong to its ruler.

There are only two kingdoms in the spiritual realm to which a person can belong. One is ruled by Jesus (the eternal kingdom), and the other is ruled by Satan (a temporal kingdom). There is no neutral place; you belong to one or the other. If you belong to any other kingdom than the Kingdom of God, over which Jesus is Lord, you belong to Satan. If you abandon the Lordship of Jesus Christ, make no mistake, you embrace the vilest and most destructive creature in all the universe as your master, and you will share his eternity. The following are ways to identify if you have deceived yourself into believing in dual citizenship.

The Pattern of the World

First, take a hearty evaluation of the patterns in your life. The Bible teaches us, "do not be conformed to the pattern of this world, but be transformed by the renewing of your mind" (Romans 12:2, NIV). The pattern of the world is a sinful, "futile way of life inherited from your forefathers" (1 Peter 1:18). The pattern of this world is the culture of this world, and culture is quite resistant to change.

A godless world in rebellion to Christ is driven by the impulses of the carnal nature rather than the divine nature. Paul gives it this description, "for you are still fleshly. For since there is jealousy and strife among you, are you not fleshly?" (1 Corinthians 3:3). It can be deduced that Paul's expectation was that the Corinthian church would "come out and be separate," to be consecrated unto the Lord by the mortification of the flesh and the subjection of their will to the will of the Lord Jesus. They, however, had not done so and remained in the flesh. Therefore, it is apparent that the mindset we are to have is this: that to be in the "flesh" is synonymous with being in the "world." This *modus operandi* is the root of what the Apostles were pointing at in their writing on worldliness, the carnal nature, and a general tolerance of sin in the believer's heart.

The following is a general description of those things that would indicate the pattern of the world. It is taken primarily from the outline given in 1 John 2:15-17 and from the list of qualifications for worldliness Paul offers in Galatians 5:16-21.

Lust of the Flesh: Debauchery
The Philosophy of Hedonism

It is difficult to understand a form of Christianity in which the mortification of the flesh is a foreign concept. Yet this is perhaps the most pervasive perversion of what it means to be a Christian in all of Christian history. Men believe they can go on living a carnal life and avert the destruction it produces, and thus they are deceived. Hedonism suggests that pleasure (the satisfaction of desires) is the highest good and proper aim of human life. Under the guise of "freedom from the law," hedonists posing as disciples of Christ are clothed in lust and pursue all their heart desires with no restraint.

But the flesh of men expands to license every inclination of the heart to be expressed in limitless thoughts, words, and actions with no thought of their imminent destruction. "The mind set on the flesh is death," says the Apostle Paul (Romans 8:6). The hedonist acts on the philosophy that "my pleasure is the highest good" regardless of the destruction it brings anyone else.

That pleasure, which the hedonist seeks, might very well be of many distinctions, but all are rooted in self-interest and self-love. The mind of sinful man is superior in its adaptation to self-interest. It is angered by all who stand in its self-interested way and is easily offended by anyone who might be inclined to teach it to be thoughtful. Arguments and divisions are the standard modes of the flesh, for pride rules this heart, and everyone else is wrong and ill-informed.

The mind of the flesh is dead to others, and in the instance where it appears generous, it does so to show its superiority in giving, relieving some pressures of guilt. A hedonist will run like a mouse through a maze to get the fleshly fulfillment it smells. No cost is too high. Neither sleepless nights nor 80-hour workweeks will stay the hand of him who labors to love his flesh.

Hedonists have no hunger to learn but only to feel. Because of this, whatever feels right is justified, regardless of which moral boundaries are crossed. As the soul of such a person darkens, the horizon of evil behaviors broadens with new possibilities, all of which feed the hungry monster of their flesh. Debauchery will fill this cup to overflowing until this man's mind is only evil all the time.

Lust of the Eyes: Idolatry
The Philosophy of Materialism

In the last 250 years, since the onset and maturing of the industrial age, the potential for materialism has blasted beyond anything previously imaginable. Circled by idols, like buzzards over a malodorous carcass, today's materialist is as dead in spirit as a man has ever been.

Materialism can be looked at from two perspectives. First as a tendency to consider material possessions and physical comfort as more important than spiritual values. This is the fruit of a materialistic philosophy: the doctrine that nothing exists except matter and its movements and modifications. This idea includes the declaration that consciousness and will are wholly due to material agency.

Interestingly, in 1859 a strict materialist who thought of himself as a Christian cooked up a philosophy that rendered existence nothing more than the succession of random chemical changes in life forms. With *The Origin of Species*, Charles Darwin summarized in pseudo-scientific terms the philosophy needed to move the material age into the most powerful religion of idolatry ever to exist. "You Are a Bag of Chemicals" has become the fireside song led by ukulele strumming evolutionists who sing former creationists to sleep. With every stroke and strum, more inspiration is given to backsliding believers to pursue worldly wealth and ignore the dying of their spirit.

Marx rejoiced at Darwin's innovative work and stated in his letter to Ferdinand Lassalle, "Darwin's book is very important and serves me as a basis in natural science for the class struggle in history." Marxism purported that wealth and power were intrinsically united, and thus materially minded people struggled to advance themselves into greater stratospheres of control over others. Many Americans denounce Marxism while unwittingly playing his game.

"Will others admire my possessions?" asks the idolatrous heart, and it extends itself toward acquisition at all costs. With hopes that a flashy new possession will fill the soul with permanent bliss and elevate stature to that of gods, men bow lower and lower to all of the demands which will secure this end. Cars, homes, clothing, and jewelry are all carefully evaluated in the light of this worship. Marriages are lost tugging at idols, and children move through adolescence angry unless they have the latest fix of material security.

Honestly, the worldly man has nothing else for which to live. Whoever once said, "he who dies with the most toys wins," left off one word at the end… "nothing." This poet of materialism did not realize that he who lives with the most toys has no real security either. Having gained the whole world, he often loses everything in this life and his soul in eternity.

But the spiritually-minded person combats the idolatry of materialism by hating the idea of supplanting the Lordship of Christ with something material and rejects idolatry with a holy hatred. This person also carries a double-edged sword, with generosity on one side and contentment on the other. With this sword, the chords of deceit are slashed and destroyed, and the words of truth from the Lord ring into eternity: "For one's life does not consist in the abundance of his possessions" (Luke 12:15, ESV).

Pride of Life: Self-sufficiency
The Philosophy of Humanism

The pride of life is the sensation a person feels when they believe they have fulfilled the lust of the eyes and or the lusts of the flesh. Now in full boasting mode, the mind of a carnal man is proud of his conquests.

Humanism puts man in the center of the universe with his value as supreme and his glory as of the fundamental goal of all his activity in life. Contrary to this is the idea that God is the creator of the universe, is thus most valuable, and is to be glorified above all else and to all ends. Thus, humanism is quite the opposite of the Gospel of Jesus Christ and the reality that "all have sinned and fallen short of the Glory of God." But many "Christians" are self-enthroned humanists.

In the words of Mad TV's Stuart, the worship song in the temple of self is "Look what I can do!" Idolaters scream from the rooftops the gospel of self-worship, citing their achievements and acquisitions in an ongoing dialogue of self-adulation. Whether preachers, politicians, or plumbers, a man's reputation is as important to him as the air, he breathes. Furthermore, winners at "king of the mountain" look disdainfully down at others; and men of "no reputation" (see Philippians 2:7, KJV) are "despised and abandoned" (Isaiah 53:3).

Everyman, either patting his own back or thirsting for the right to do so, lies low in the temple so as to create as much distance from the floor where they grovel to the idol of self they have erected. Disguised as disciples, these delusional idolaters arrive at church ready to face their fellow men and see if they have risen above them.

If they are outdoing the crowd in their blind estimation, they float hot-headed like hot-air balloons up into the atmosphere of their idolatrous world to look down on their subjects, who stand amazed at their height. These subjects engage in envious and delirious imaginations as they dream with their mentor, Maslow, of achieving the pinnacle of "self-actualization," and all the while, the call of Christ to "self-denial" falls short of their hearing.

The measurements for god-status in this temple are how you look, where you were educated, your IQ, and how many short years you have produced a compelling story of success. Success is defined in this culture as no more than to what degree you have fulfilled the lust of your eyes or the lust of your flesh. "If I wanted it, I went and got it," they say to a group of self-condemning nodders who respond with, "What you want is what you need!"

Worshippers in this temple will not mind or mention any more than you do your failure at family, your fractured friendships, or your avaricious addictions. They will not berate you for your lack of integrity or your foul mouth, for you have risen above your peers on the only landscape of life that has any meaning: that of the "success" story.

Success here can be defined first by wealth, then power, and physical appearance. With pretentious smiles, worshippers of themselves do all in their ability to convince everyone of their beauty. Spending thousands of dollars for clothing and style, they wink at themselves in the mirror with a gesture of adoration.

In the ministry, men who pose as men of God are really men of self and menaces to society. They broaden stages and fill them with outwardly beautiful people whose occupancy of loveliness on the outside distracts from the vacancy of holiness on the inside. In a final blow of death to the spirit, the man who feeds the pride of life sings along with Frank Sinatra: "I did it MYYYYYYY way."

The Six Patterns

There are six important areas of influence in which the pattern of the world can readily be seen and has cornered the market in destructive force. These six are relationships, finances, business, parenting, entertainment, and fashion. Deeply evaluate your life in light of the questions offered with each of these six.

What is the pattern of the world in relationships? Are you self-serving and needs-focused? Are you easily offended and slow to forgive? Do you resist anyone who brings your wrongdoing to light? Are there two versions of "you"—one known by others and one by you and God? If you answered yes to any of this, you are following the pattern of the world in relationships.

What is the pattern of the world in finances? Are you self-serving your self-interests? Are you more interested in gaining than in giving? Do you pursue your own comfort and pleasure before a thought arises of those in need around you? If you answered yes to any of these, you are following the pattern of the world in its handling of wealth. "Therefore, if you have not been faithful in the use of unrighteous wealth, who will entrust the true riches to you?" (Luke 16:11). "In this case, moreover, it is required of stewards that one be found trustworthy" (1 Corinthians 4:2)

What is the pattern of the world in business? Do you engage in manipulative and deceptive practices? Are you working on getting sales at all costs, even the cost of authentic business relationships? Is the immediate more important to you than the long-term benefit? Do people mean nothing compared to profit? If this is your mindset, you are following the pattern of the world in business. "But we have renounced disgraceful, underhanded ways. We refuse to practice cunning or to tamper with God's word" (2 Corinthians 4:2).

What is the pattern of the world in parenting? Are your children an inconvenience to you? Do you send them away because they are in the way? Are you emotionally charged and driven by irritation? Have your transferred your responsibility to teachers, coaches, and pastors? Who is teaching your children, engaging them in discussions about character and wisdom? If it is not you, you are following the pattern of the world in parenting. "Fathers, do not exasperate your children, so that they will not lose heart" (Colossians 3:21).

What is the pattern of the world in entertainment? Is entertainment constant in your life and time-consuming? Do you relish corrupt humor and violence? Are you amused with adultery and immorality? If you can answer yes to any of these, the culture of the world is ruling your heart; you are its disciple.

> But among you, there must not be even a hint of sexual immorality, or of any kind of impurity, or of greed, because these are improper for God's holy people. Nor should there be obscenity, foolish talk, or course joking, which are out of place, but rather thanksgiving. (Ephesians 5:3-4)

What is the pattern of the world in fashion? Is your fashion immodest and sensual? Is fashion so important to you that you would waste Christ's money on excessive, expensive, and flashy style? God is not opposed to fashion; He is opposed to idolatry. The pattern of the world is to dress to become an idol for others to look on in admiration. If this is your pattern, it is because you have conformed to the pattern of the world. Do you belong to the world? To the fashion consumed ladies of Pontus, Galatia, Cappadocia, Asia, and Bithynia, Peter wrote these guidelines:

> Your adornment must not be merely external—braiding the hair, and wearing gold jewelry, or

putting on dresses; But let it be the hidden person
of the heart with the imperishable quality of a gentle
and quiet spirit, which is precious in the sight of God.
(1 Peter 3:3-4)

The People of the World

The people of the world are the original haters, according
to James, Paul, and John. They are the haters of God (James 4:4,
Romans 8:7, John 15:18-19). In the business world, we sometimes say, "change your people, or change your people." If your
people don't align with your standards, get new people.

In the kingdom, you must make your stand; whoever follows
you as you follow Christ continues to be your friend. Everyone
else: goodbye. Solomon wrote, "The righteous should choose
his friends carefully, for the way of the wicked leads them astray"
(Proverbs 12:26, NKJV). James rebuked the church with these
words: "You adulteresses, do you not know that friendship with
the world is hostility toward God? Therefore, whoever wishes
to be a friend of the world makes himself an enemy of God"
(James 4:4).

This is important, especially for new believers, because your
friends can draw you back into your old identity as a worldly,
sinful person. When I was 13, I started skateboarding. After
that, I skateboarded nearly every day of my teenage life, and I
got pretty good at it.

I had become a Christian and left behind much of the mis-
chief and foolery that characterized my friends and me. But few
of my friends were also living for Christ, and it began to draw
me away. By the time I was 18, I had learned to share my faith
and had become an evangelist.

One day all my skater friends jumped into my car, and we made the rounds to some pretty great skate spots. But these jokers were using loads of profanity, playing terrible music on my car stereo, and shoplifting everywhere we went. At the end of the day, I sat down with these kids and had a talk.

"I can't skate with you guys," I said. I'm trying to live for Christ, and you are not, and it's not good for me to be around you.

They didn't like this very much because I was the only one who had a car and could get them to the best places to skate.

"We'll stop cussing," they pleaded.

"Yeah, we'll stop stealing stuff, too!" They continued.

So I made a deal with them. I said, "if you come to my Bible study every Thursday, I will take you skateboarding after that."

Three of them came! After several weeks, these three guys gave their hearts to Christ, and then I baptized them in the apartment complex swimming pool!

Change your people or change your people.

To really encounter the Lord deeply, we must know with certainty that we belong to God and not to this world. We must know that we DO NOT belong to the devil!

Do you belong to the *Prince* of this world, the *pattern* of this world, or the *people* of this world? Ephesians 2:19 says, "So then you are no longer strangers and aliens, but you are fellow citizens with the saints, and are of God's household."

Belonging is Initiated When We Are Born of the Spirit

It is the Holy Spirit who does these critical works in the believer to confirm our identity as his children. As mentioned above the first work of the Spirit in us is to be born of the Holy Spirit (John 3:5-6). It is very likely that if you have humbled yourself before God, cried out to Him to break up hardness in your heart, and repented of all known sins you are either born again, or are about to be.

But don't think that some acknowledgements made with the mind and mouth are enough to bring forth a new birth. As is evident by millions of people who go forth during altar calls to ramble and repeat things they don't understand, only to be deemed a "Christian" and leave entirely unchanged, it is possible to fake a conversion. Unfortunately, it happens all the time because many preach forgiveness without repentance.

You might as well say "Jesus is Lord" in a language you don't understand. It is no different to say it in English, not knowing what it means. You *must* understand what it means to take up a cross, deny yourself and follow Him if you are to understand what it means to have Him as Lord over your life. True repentance and a truly broken heart before Jesus are the first fruits of genuinely coming under His Lordship.

After this occurs, you will most certainly and without exception, in His timing, experience an undeniable physical change in your mortal body. This change will be characterized by a powerful inward surge of "life and peace." It is for this reason that the Apostle writes,

> "And if the Spirit of him who raised Jesus from the
> dead is living in you, he who raised Jesus from the
> dead will also give life to your mortal bodies through
> his Spirit who lives in you." (Romans 8:6)

Life to your mortal bodies! Your body will be electrified with the heavenly life force of the Holy Spirit. For some people, the work of the Spirit in the new birth is almost immediate upon them, humbling themselves, and this is for reasons only the Spirit knows. But for others, like 19th-century revivalist Charles Finney, it took hours of prayer and repentance in the woods, followed by more hours of prayer indoors, before he was born a new man. Coming in from hours on his knees in the forest, he recalled:

> As I closed the door and turned around, my heart seemed to be liquid within me. All my feelings seemed to rise and flow out and the thought of my heart was, 'I want to pour my whole soul out to God.' The rising of my soul was so great that I rushed into the room back of the front office to pray.

> As I went in and shut the door after me, it seemed as if I met the Lord Jesus Christ face to face. It seemed to me that I saw him as I would see any other man. He said nothing, but looked at me in such a manner as to break me right down at his feet. It seemed to me a reality that He stood before me, and I fell down at his feet and poured out my soul to him. I wept aloud like a child and made such confessions as I could with my choked words. It seemed to me that I bathed his feet with my tears, and yet I had no distinct impression that I touched him.

> As I turned and was about to take a seat by the fire, I received a mighty baptism of the Holy Spirit. Without any memory of ever hearing the thing mentioned by any person in the world, the Holy Spirit descended upon me in a manner that seemed to go

through me, body and soul. I could feel the impression, like a wave of electricity, going through and through me. Indeed it seemed to come in waves of liquid love, for I could not express it in any other way. It seemed like the very breath of God. I can remember distinctly that it seemed to fan me like immense wings.

No words can express the wonderful love that was spread abroad in my heart. I wept aloud with joy and love. I literally bellowed out the unspeakable overflow of my heart: These waves came over me and over me and over me one after the other until I remember crying out, 'I shall die if these waves continue to pass over me!' Yet I had no fear of death."

Even for others, like world-changing preacher George Whitefield, it took months of pursuit and constant humility with fasting. But in the timing of the Holy Spirit, this man emerged as one of the most powerful witnesses the world has ever had the privilege of seeing. Take Whitefield's account, which occurred while he was in seminary, into consideration:

"God showed me that I must be born again, or be damned. I learned that a man may go to church, say prayers, receive the sacraments, and yet not be a Christian...."

Whitefield began a series of increasingly ascetic disciplines in order to get himself born again. None of these things seemed to work, though he lay prostrate on the ground for days at a time, wore uncomfortable clothing, took a vow of silence, fasted for weeks on end; and by it all brought his physical well being to such a concern to his doctor that he was confined to his bed. He truly made "every effort to enter through the narrow gate!" Yet it seemed he was "not able to." This went on from fall to spring. Desperate for change and with no more branches of self-denial upon which to ascend, he relinquished himself into the merciful hands of God:

> "God was pleased to remove the heavy load, to enable me to lay hold of his dear Son by a living faith, and by giving me the Spirit of Adoption to seal me, even to the day of everlasting redemption.
>
> O! with what joy—joy unspeakable—even joy that was full of and big with glory, was my soul filled within, the weight of sin went off, and an abiding sense of the love of God broke in upon my disconsolate soul! Surely it was a day to be had in everlasting remembrance. My joys were like a springtide and overflowed the banks."

When you have repented of sin, placing your faith in Jesus to forgive you and justify you before God, and you believe you have given it your whole heart, rise from that place and begin to worship. When you sense the Holy Spirit filling you, you will want Him more and more. You will also begin to hate your old way of living as His presence produces in you the fear of the Lord. The more you bless and acknowledge His glory and goodness, the stronger His presence will be. God has given you or *is* giving you, if it is the first time, the Spirit of sonship. As

His presence continues to grow and be made experiential to you, you will cry out, "Abba, Father" (Romans 8:15).

This is the purpose of the courts of the Lord, that is, to provide a place for those who belong to the Lord to proclaim the worth of the Lord. In this place, the Holy Spirit will testify that you are a child of God (see Romans 8:16). If you have this testimony in the Presence of the Lord, you can be assured that you are born again. If you haven't, continue in this way until that moment comes, and don't give up. This is the way of faith in practical expression.

Belonging Is Affirmed As We Are Led By the Spirit

The second thing the Holy Spirit does to declare that we belong to Him is to lead us. "Those who are led by the Spirit of God are Sons of God" (Romans 8:14). When we know that the Holy Spirit is leading us, we know that we belong to Him.

If you are walking in the sinful nature, stop! You are denying your identity as a child of God. It is possible for Christians to become confused about their identity and begin to act like the old man they once were. If you are not certain at any moment in the day that the Spirit of God is leading you, take a pit stop, spiritually speaking. As you quiet yourself, purpose to listen to and follow the Holy Spirit, and this will provide you with a profound sense and affirmation of who you are in Christ.

Isaiah said this to Israel: "Your ears will hear a word behind you, saying, 'this is the way, walk in it'" (Isaiah 30:21). If you are unsure how to be led by the Holy Spirit, you need to do little more than acknowledge who you are as His child and ask Him to lead you. You are about to go very deep with God, to meet with Him in a most profoundly impactful way. But you cannot proceed in this manner of devotion without the Holy Spirit leading you. Wait, listen, then follow.

"Hey kids, follow me; I want to show you something." And I took them deep into the forest, where many wonders were discovered.

Conclusion and Contemplation

You belong to the Lord by means of a holy covenant. He has called you to come out of the world and be separated unto His purposes. To whom do you belong?

Prayer of Commitment

Father in Heaven, thank You for making me Your child. Thank You for loving me so deeply and with such action, providing a way for me to be forgiven and have a relationship with You. I know that I belong to You and right now, I renew my love and commitment to You. I do not belong to myself, I do not belong to this world, I do not belong to the ruler of this world, and I do not belong to the people of this world. I belong to You, and I am committed to living according to the principles of Your Word. I abandon the principles of this world and the ways of evil, and I embrace You and the truths of Your Kingdom. Amen.

Discussion Questions

1. What are two ways the Holy Spirit confirms that we are children of God?
2. Can we be citizens of Heaven and belong to the world? Why or why not?

3. Who is the Prince of the World? What is he like?
4. Describe the people of the World.
5. What is the pattern of the world? In what areas does the pattern of the world show up?
6. Is it possible for Christians to become confused about their identity? What usually follows this confusion? How can it be corrected?

Chapter XII

EXPLORERS
Offerings at the Altar of Surrender

Imperative
We must be fully surrendered to God in absolute trust.

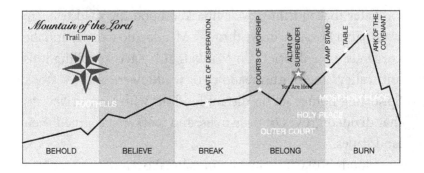

Redwoods and Rivers
January 2015
Crescent City, California

E arly in the morning, I slipped out of bed and knelt in the dark hotel room. Raindrops pattered on the windowsill in a soothing rhythm. I love waking up to the sound of rain, but not when I'm on vacation. We had landed at the San Francisco airport, picked up a rental car, and drove to Santa Rosa, where we spent our first night as a family in Northern California.

I meticulously planned each day's events and did my best to be prepared for everything. But I hadn't any control whatsoever of the weather or of what could be the outcome of this road trip up the 101. Would it rain the whole time? Would giant trees be exciting? I didn't know. But I genuinely *wanted* to see the goodness of the Father.

So, I asked Him for that. I reiterated to Him that I understood I had no control over what was about to happen and whether it would deepen the bond in our family. I surrendered the trip to the Father and got up to start the day. I entrusted all to Him in an attitude of faith, believing He would make more of it than I could.

Later that morning, we embarked upon the road trip. Up from Santa Rosa, we drove through Mendocino County and the gorgeous wine district. Vineyards that lay across rolling hills and valleys met with meadows of wildflowers and livestock. Sprawling homes sat on distant foothills with long driveways that divided groves of pear trees, and workers groomed their landscapes.

Clouds broke into massive marshmallow puffs that took on the shapes of things we'd seen. They morphed, then dissipated— and were gone. The sun showered a full spectrum of light down upon the scenery, bringing a myriad of colors and tones into view, mostly in greens and blues. Above the wondrous vista, not a single cloud remained; pure azure filled the expansive atmosphere. Surprisingly, because experts on weather channels predicted storms for the whole week.

The Russian River ran beside us and sliced through the lush landscape with a sparkle on top, but cold weight and momentum below its dark-blue ripples. We came to a quaint village outside Ukiah where farmers' markets spilled into parking lots from antique-looking buildings. As we wound along through rustic towns, opportunities for wine samples seemed as frequent as the stripes on the narrowed roadway. An arched sign reached overhead and declared that we had come to the beginning of giant territory. Asher and Asiah wondered what kind of giants could be living in the mountains just ahead of us, and with widened eyes, their faces scrunched with concern.

Rivers and creeks of various sizes took turns running alongside us and a railroad, too, for a time. The rolling hills grew sharper and rose higher into peaked mountains, and the trees seemed to grow taller with every passing mile. It was the land of the redwoods, whose trunks were sometimes broader than our house and reached hundreds of feet above the ground.

The 101 seemed to wind randomly through the forests while the mysteriously large trees beckoned us to stop and place our amazement at their feet. We gave way to the urge for exploration and pulled down a drive into a roadside park. The Eel River curbed the enchanted grove of Redwoods. We strolled along the flowing and falling trail with heads thrown back until we reached the water's edge. There we stopped to skip rocks across the emerald eddies of the Eel.

Our drive took us past Arcata to a small coastal town called Trinidad. A guess landed us on a mystical beach, fit for stories of pirates and kings. Asher and Asiah hopped from rock to rock above the receded tide and scoured the dampened terrain for starfish and crabs. Asher announced with a trumpet voice that he had discovered "a whole city of starfish," so we all made the slippery journey across barnacles and seaweed to deliver an observation.

Just then, a family of white-spotted seals caught our attention. They basked atop distant rocks catching the last few minutes of daylight as the sun set over the picturesque Pacific cove. Eventually, the seals noticed our intrigue and wiggled nervously away from us.

We left the brownish-grey sand and the protruding black rock formations below as we ascended back up precisely 224 steps to the lighthouse and parking lot. We discovered that gas-station-Mexican-food was better than we expected, and we even made some friends with the people who ran the place.

Darkness shrouded the remaining hours' drive into Crescent City. We eventually arrived at the Curly Redwood Lodge, a very spacious, clean, and 60's style motel with the singular amenity—sleep.

I woke early to take a walk and pray. Asher heard my stirring and whisper-shouted, "Dad, can I come with you?" And I gladly accepted his company.

We walked along the marina with a flock of seagulls above us and some at our feet. Out on the waterfront, sea lions were spread across the enormous stones. They were fascinating for Asher to see, but they projected a foul smell, so we turned and walked along in a different direction discussing Sponge Bob Square Pants, and the sound of sea lions faded behind us.

When we had eaten and prepared for the day, we began our drive along Howland Hill Road, deep into the forest of giants. As we crept along, the one-lane dirt road wound through the woods and across creeks for about 8 miles until it reached Smith Grove, a place for hikes and millions of photo ops.

Bursting out of the car, Asher and Asiah ran to greet the beauty and climbed everything conquerable by their proportionately tiny frames. We gawked at the majesty in these trees, some of which had been standing there through the life of Christ, the Dark Ages, the Reformation, and the American

Revolution. Needless to say, we spent the day admiring trees. A hike and a sky-ride gondola lift at Trees of Mystery brought us even more fascination as we absorbed the incredible variety rendered ours by the infinitely innovative King of us all.

We ended the day with a return to the sea and another hike, this time out to an island lighthouse. The honey-colored sky merged into a golden ocean as the sun, once again, set across the waters of the Pacific. Anne Marie and I relished the moment in the salty sea air as our children bounced from stone to stone above the sloshing waves.

On day three, we were back in the car and saying goodbye to Crescent City. We set out for the passage through the Klamath Mountains and eventually came to partner our passageway with the Trinity River. I admired the beautiful river gorge from high above as the road slowly bent around the mountain peaks. I hoped for a moment to stop, but the route remained elevated above the river.

A descent began, and I smiled. I kept looking at that river, which looked bigger as we approached it around each bend. I could see something like sandy shores on the other side but saw no way to get over there.

Anne Marie noticed a bridge ahead and recommended we cross it and go exploring. So we found a parking place along the road and hiked down toward the river. Our discovery was breathtaking.

From hundreds of feet above, an igneous quartzite batholith cascaded sharply into the sparkling river, which roamed around its heavy base. Jeweled and jagged, the faces of the mountainside were bearded with evergreens and had aged well through millennia of erosion and wear.

A small beach was formed at the bend of the waters, so we settled there and soaked in the beauty. A backdrop of sunlight beamed through the tree limbs, and an infinitely deep blue sky hung behind Asher, Asiah, and Anne Marie as they dug their toes into the warm sand on the river shore. Wading in the water got Asiah closer to some fish but made frozen skin, and she dashed back to the incubating sand.

The sun warmed us too, and the moment was so treasured that we knew this perfect gift had come down from the Father of heavenly lights. My prayer was for experiences that Asher and Asiah would never forget, and He was answering! One after the next, memorable moments burst forth from Heaven until our hearts were full of love for Him and His great name.

Christ on the Altar of Atonement

In the temple court was a great altar where sacrifices were burned for various purposes. Before the coming of Jesus Christ, many of these offerings were made to atone for the sin of the people. A spotless, unblemished creature was slaughtered and burnt up in the flames, symbolizing that death is the price of sin. Since the time when Adam and Eve first sinned and an animal was slaughtered to provide a covering for them, this was a pattern in Scripture and eventually became a requirement of God. In fact, "Without the shedding of blood, there is no forgiveness" (Hebrews 9:22). The death of an innocent creature would provide a covering for the corrupt heart of man. It would be offered to remove guilt and restore a clear conscience before God's perfect majesty.

But the coming of the Messiah replaced this need for a sin offering, and His offering was final, complete, and all-sufficient.

In this conclusive moment in the story of the atonement for sin, it was Christ upon the altar, the unblemished Lamb of God, who died, shedding His own blood for your sins. You need not pay the price for your sins; simply come in the humility required to repent of them and seek His forgiveness by faith in the beautiful work of Christ.

And He does forgive; the Scriptures state: "As far as the east is from the west, so far has he removed our transgressions from us" (Psalm 103:12), and "if we confess our sins, he is faithful and righteous to forgive us our sins, and cleanse us from all unrighteousness" (1 John 1:9).

The permanence of His work can be no more clearly seen than in the following passage:

> For Christ did not enter a holy place made with hands, a mere copy of the true one, but into Heaven itself, now to appear in the presence of God for us; nor was it that He would offer Himself often, as the high priest enters the holy place year by year with blood that is not his own. Otherwise, He would have needed to suffer often since the foundation of the world; but now once at the consummation of the ages He has been manifested to put away sin by the sacrifice of Himself. (Hebrews 9:24-26)

With our faith in Christ's sacrifice on the altar, the cross, we can have our sins forgiven. But we also have *access* to the throne room of Heaven: "For through Him, we both have our access in one Spirit to the Father" (Ephesians 2:18). This is where our relationship with God takes on a sacrificial characteristic, just as Christ's did. We don't enter the Most Holy Place, drawing near to God, only for ourselves. This is a place we go on behalf of others, just like the high priest went year after year on behalf of Israel. Understanding this is critical to moving beyond the foothills to the summit, from the outer courts into the Most Holy Place.

Look at how the message to the Hebrews conveys the reality of our passage by prayer into the Most Holy Place:

> Therefore, brethren, since we have confidence to enter the holy place by the blood of Jesus, by a new and living way which He inaugurated for us through the veil, that is, His flesh, and since we have a great priest over the house of God, let us draw near with a sincere heart in full assurance of faith, having our hearts sprinkled clean from an evil conscience, and our bodies washed with pure water. (Hebrews 10:19-22)

The only question that remains at this point is, "Why don't we enter? Tozer, in *The Pursuit of God*, answers this perplexing question like this:

> With the veil removed by the rending of Jesus' flesh, with nothing on God's side to prevent us from entering, why do we tarry without? Why do we consent to abide all our days just outside the Holy of Holies and never enter at all to look upon God? We hear the Bridegroom say, "let me see thy countenance, let me hear thy voice: for sweet is thy voice and thy countenance is comely." We sense that the call is for us, but still we fail to draw near, and the

years pass and we grow old and tired in the outer
courts of the tabernacle. What doth hinder us? What
is it? What but the presence of a veil in our hearts?
A veil not taken away as the first veil was, but which
remains there, still shutting out the light and hiding
the face of God from us. It is the veil of our fleshly
fallen nature living on, un-judged within us, un-cru-
cified and un-repudiated.

Christians on the Alar of Surrender

The point is that we will never pass beyond the veil if we
bypass the altar. In actuality, we can't bypass the altar, which is
the cross we are called to carry. We will never enjoy what Jesus
made possible for us by rending the veil of His body if we don't
follow Him first to the cross. Let's carefully examine the simple
truth that to summit, we must surrender.

The promise of atonement has been provided and was com-
pleted at the cross of Christ; there is now no longer a need for a
physical altar of sacrifice. But let's not forget that the temple was
a replica of what is in Heaven. If we can approach the Throne of
Grace, we can enter into the very courts of Heaven as we draw
near to God. When we approach God, we will find an altar (see
Isaiah 6:6, Hebrews 13:10, Revelation 6:9, 8:3-5).

Romans 12:1 says, "therefore, I urge you, brethren, by the
mercies of God, to present your bodies a living and holy sacrifice, acceptable to God, which is your spiritual service of worship." The apostle was not directing the Romans to lay down on
the altar of sacrifice, which was standing in the Court of Priests
during his writing. On the contrary, he was speaking of this

heavenly altar, this place where an eternal fire never goes out and can be seen in the eyes of Heaven's King.

To this altar, every Christian must go, continually, year after year, day after day, moment after moment, second after second. There is no other way to abide in Christ and maintain unbroken fellowship with the Holy Spirit than to be wholly yielded to him as one whose life is stretched across the grid above the flames. To this altar you must go while in the Courts, if you wish to progress into the Holy Place and then into the Most Holy Place.

Intimacy with God and usefulness to God come at the cost of surrender, total surrender, into the flames of His Spirit. Don't imagine that you can become useful to God without any intention of yielding all you are. Consecration is the setting aside of something for use in holy purposes. When we are at first consecrated unto the Lord in baptism, it is our confession to the world that we are set apart unto the Lord to be used as He sees fit. We belong to Him, a bride, entirely in covenant with the Bridegroom. But like Israel, we are, at heart, an adulterous people. This consecration must be affirmed and renewed at least daily, if not more often than that, lest our hearts drift, our commitments wane, and our usefulness to the Master evaporate. Through Him, then, let us continually offer up a sacrifice of praise to God, that is the fruit of lips that give thanks to His name" (Hebrews 13:15).

An Offering of Trust

At the Throne of the Almighty Creator, you would lay down an offering of trust. This is a thank offering, a goodwill offering, a fellowship offering; it is that offering of your very life. It is you who goes above the flames on the altar here; you who is consumed in the fire of the Holy Spirit; you who becomes a fragrant offering unto the Lord.

It could make one wonder why we don't trust Him more than we do. What can we make of our moments that He can't make better? What can we produce for ourselves that He can't provide better and more fulfilling? Why do we try to hang on to control?

Trusting God can be a challenge, especially if you are just beginning to know Him. But if you believe that He is infinite in goodness and kindness, what could you possibly lose? Tread upon your fears and make an offering of trust to the One who is worthy of everything you have to offer.

Fear is powerful. You may meet more deeply rooted fears when you decide to surrender all you are, own, control, and all you aspire to do or be into His hands. But there is a place where you can release everything in His control, and it is a place you must go if you are to progress in your relationship with Him.

It is interesting to note that on all wilderness expeditions, you are, to a certain unavoidable extent, subject to the volatility of the forces of nature. You must be willing to operate under the conditions that nature produces, whether favorable or otherwise. Some of my best camping experiences have been snowed on, some of my favorite hikes rained on, and some of my most cherished moments chapped my lips. Surrendering to these uncontrollable factors is part of getting up the hill. Get up the mountain with whatever comes, but get up the mountain! Embrace the challenge as it morphs, and the reward will only be better.

True Surrender is Consecration

There can be no other way to summarize the blessing of God in the lives of men than to note that they are both intimate with Him in deep communion of spirit and partnered with Him to see His purposes prevail on the earth. But these attributes of the Christian life are wholly dependent on a rendering of complete trust to God in all aspects of life. In the words of Andrew Murray, "The condition for obtaining God's full blessing is absolute surrender to Him."

Furthermore, in the words of Charles Finney:

> Entire consecration to God is indispensable to the prayer of faith. You must live a holy life and consecrate all to God—your time, talents, influence—all you have and all you are to be his entirely. Read the lives of pious men, and you will be struck with this fact: that they used to set apart times to renew their covenant and dedicate themselves anew to God; and whenever they have done so, a blessing has always followed immediately.

Consecration is, therefore, at the heart of surrender. True surrender is to be set apart for the Lord, His work, and His love. When you surrender to the Lord, you will climb the stairs of this heavenly altar, lie down on it, and die to everything you own and control, everything you want and aspire to be, everything that represents you.

> Therefore, if you have been raised up with Christ, keep seeking the things above, where Christ is seated

at the right hand of God. Set your mind on the things above, not on the things that are on earth. For you have died and your life is hidden with Christ in God. (Colossians 3:1-3)

This is the fabric of consecration—to be hidden with Christ in God. One will never arrive at this state of consecration while remaining willful, self-interested, and in control. It is the picture of a spiritual reality that you must face if you are to know God. To truly be Christ's disciple, spiritually speaking, you must carry a cross as He did, die as He did, and you will be resurrected as He was. Christ called us to take up our cross and follow Him because He knew that we could not be genuinely His unless we were dead first.

The cross you must carry is *symbolic,* just like the altar it represents. The "letting go" and surrender, however, is *real.* It is as real as Jesus, to whom you must surrender everything. This reality can no more powerfully be known than in the trust that surrender requires and the connectedness that consecration to Him facilitates.

Faith Drives Surrender

Many have failed to see that, though faith in Christ's work on the cross can be expressed in a single saving moment, resulting in the new birth, faith must not halt there. Faith must continually be expressed in Christ for the entirety of the life of this new creature in Christ, not only for the purposes of atonement but for the purposes of advancement.

Surrendering to God is essential to discipleship, essential to fellowship, and essential to completely becoming God's workmanship. Living faith springs from a dead will. Vibrant communion with God is born as we share in the fellowship of His suffering (see Philippians 3:10), carrying our cross to our own Golgotha, becoming like Him and dying there; that we may know Him in the power of His resurrection.

Paul, the Apostle of Surrender, states:

> But whatever things were gain to me, those things I have counted as loss for the sake of Christ. More than that, I count all things to be loss in view of the surpassing value of knowing Christ Jesus my Lord, for whom I have suffered the loss of all things, and count them but rubbish, so that I may gain Christ. (Philippians 3:7-8)

Certainly the Apostle was not trying to obtain atonement for his sin, certainly he was not trying to earn his way to Heaven. Not after such assertions against the works of the law as were written to the Galatians, just pages before in your Bible! No, Paul understood that if he was going to know Christ deeply he would have to lose something. Yet he considered that even those things of greatest value to him were already equal to loss compared to the invaluable intimacy available to him with Christ. Such a fellowship, camaraderie, and depth could not otherwise be attained, than in the intentional devaluation of his own endearments.

Paul understood that this included even such necessities as food, comfort, shelter, and basic human dignity. He wasn't proposing that he would give up something; he was considering all things as loss. He was implying that there was absolutely nothing more valuable to him than knowing Christ deeply. He believed unswervingly that he would gain Christ, and no cost was too high. It was faith working in him that enabled him to do this.

Furthermore, the Apostle wasn't writing this to the Philippians to demonstrate to them his own piety and devotion or in any kind of effort to outdo everyone. He was writing this to them in hopes that they would follow his example as he followed Christ's basic instructions for discipleship:

> Then Jesus said to His disciples, "If anyone wishes to come after me, he must deny himself, take up his cross and follow me. For whoever wishes to save his life will lose it, but whoever loses his life for my sake will find it. (Matthew 16:24-25)

Worthy of It All

Many have been willing to lay down everything for a sport, a career, or a bit of success in some way. Many have been happy to lose all, even their marriages and relationships with their children, for fame or fortune. Others surrendered to the status quo at the cost of the excellent. In doing so, these idolaters purchased an unauthorized version of themselves at the cost of their devotion; they took a path they were never intended to walk. That path was wide, and its course led to destruction. When God was looking for Daniels, they bowed down like the people of Babylon to an enormous fake, and they went to the altar of their god and surrendered everything. They didn't do anything differently than Jesus asked His followers to do; they surrendered everything, they lost their lives. The problem is that they went to an idol that was not worthy, could not save them, and would leave them with nothing in the end. To these, Jesus said the following:

> For what will it profit a man if he gains the whole world and forfeits his soul? Or what will a man give in exchange for his soul? For the Son of Man is going to come in the glory of His Father with His angels, and will then repay every man according to his deeds. (Matthew 16:26-27)

The heartbeat of surrender is worth. To you, is Jesus worthy? People surrender their lives, love, and material possessions for such temporal achievements as respect and recognition because they value these things above all else. Ask yourself if you genuinely value your relationship with Christ. Yes? Does the ambition with which you pursue Him tell the same story?

Total Surrender Required

Imagine if only *some* of the Nazis surrendered to the Allies at Reims, France. Would the rest of Europe and the United States have been satisfied with that? Of course not! They were not satisfied until the entire regime was unconditionally surrendered and ultimately destroyed. On May 7, 1945, the High General Alfred Jodl signed the document which enforced the absolute relinquishment of power to the collective nations and thus ended the reign of terror led by Adolph Hitler.

> At first, General Jodl hoped to limit the terms of the German surrender to only those forces still fighting the Western Allies. But General Dwight Eisenhower

demanded the complete surrender of all German forces, those fighting in the East as well as in the west. If this demand was not met, Eisenhower was prepared to seal off the western front, preventing Germans from fleeing to the west in order to surrender, thereby leaving them in the hands of the enveloping Soviet forces[3].

If Christ means nothing to you, it doesn't land you on neutral ground. It lands you in enemy territory. You *should* surrender to Christ because of His surpassing worth. But you *must* surrender everything to Jesus because if you don't, you have an enemy waiting for you. This enemy hates us and gladly takes whatever is not consecrated to the Lord. There is no partial commitment to Jesus; it's all or nothing.

So, this is the attitude of Christ toward the militant rule of selfish ambition in your heart. He doesn't want a tiny gesture of surrender while your flesh remains predominantly in power. He wants to help you end the reign of terror led by your carnal man. He wants to destroy your old nature by burning it up in the fire of the Holy Spirit. The difference in this war, however, is that Christ will not plow over you with militaristic force. He could, but He won't—until you face him on Judgement day. Now, here, during your life, He wants trust, He wants relationship, He wants depth; for that, your participation is required—and the first step is surrender.

---

[3] www.history.com "Germany Surrenders Unconditionally to the Allies At Reims." History. A&E Television Networks. November 5, 2009.

Betray the Flesh

The concept of surrender is touched on by the Apostle Paul in chapter 13 of his letter to the Corinthians. He makes it clear that surrender must be driven by love. To surrender to Christ, your work here must exceed the yielding of control over aspects of your life and possessions. It must go beyond there and include your life itself. But if it is not motivated by love for Christ, it will be for nothing. You cannot do this as a means to an end, thinking, "If I surrender to Christ, I'll have a thriving business, ministry, career, etc." You must surrender to him as one who goes off to prison.

In 1 Corinthians 13:3, he writes, "If I surrender my body to be burned, but have not love, it profits me nothing." According to Strong's Concordance, the word "surrender" or *paradidomi* in Greek means to "hand over, entrust, pledge, deliver, betray, or abandon."

Interestingly, the word *paradidomi*, or its variants, is used by Jesus when He told His disciples he would be "**handed over** *to be persecuted*" (Matthew 24:9, NIV). It is also the word that is translated as "entrusted" when Jesus tells the parable of the talents and says, "For it is just like a man about to go on a journey, who called his own slaves and entrusted his possessions to them (Matthew 25:14). He surrendered his property to them. Furthermore, it is used by Jesus to reveal the coming treachery of one of His disciples when He said, "*Truly I say to you that one of you will **betray** me*" (Matthew 26:21). In other words, "one of you will hand me over, deliver me up, and abandon me to those who will put me to death."

Application of the meaning of surrender in this context would sound something like this:

- *I deliver up my life into Your hands and abandon my instinct to do as I wish.*
- *I pledge myself to You and entrust myself in a complete surrender of my own power of faculties to You.*
- *I betray my flesh to You, Holy Spirit, and hand myself over to become a slave of Christ.*

That has a nice ring to it, doesn't it! *I betray my flesh!* How many times has your flesh betrayed the intentions of your spirit? Now it is time to proactively go before the Altar of God and betray your sinful nature to His divine nature.

Hand it over to be crucified in the same way Christ was handed over: "No one has taken it away from Me, but I lay it down on My own initiative." (John 10:18). The word "initiative" is *exousia* in the original language and means power or authority. Christ used His authority to surrender Himself to men so that men could use their authority and surrender themselves to Him.

If you are to know Christ spiritually, then your natural, carnal, sinful nature must be crucified with Christ. This is not done for you; you must lay your life down of your own accord.

Here are some beginning prayers to pray as you lay your life down on the altar of Heaven:

Lord, I surrender every aspect of my life to you. I am committed to you in complete and faithful obedience. You may have me, to use me in any way you desire.

- *Take my job; I surrender it to you*
- *Take my home; I surrender it to you*
- *Take my car; I surrender it to you*

- *Take my friends; I surrender them to you*
- *Take all my money; I surrender it to you*
- *Take my dignity; I surrender it to you*
- *Take my family; I surrender them to you*
- *Take my dreams; I surrender them to you*
- *Take my plans; I surrender them to you*
- *Take my time; I surrender it to you*

You can plan your life down to the minute. But you will never be able to create a better path than He has for you. He won't show you all He's going to do with you in advance; you'll have to trust Him. And to trust Him, you'll have to surrender. But know this, His promises are reliable, and as you surrender to Him, you will see His goodness. Who knows, you might even find yourself digging your toes into the warm sand of a riverside beach, sharing an exhilarating moment with the Creator.

Conclusion and Contemplation

Belonging to God is synonymous with betraying the world, the flesh, and the devil. You must hand over your life, dreams, talents, and possessions to the Lord if you are to surrender to Him. Will you trust Him on the Altar of Surrender?

Prayer of Commitment

Show me, Lord, if there is any other thing in my life that I hold more dearly than my relationship with You. I am ready to surrender it to You now. I am ready to lay down on Your altar with these things and be consumed in Your fire. Holy Spirit, I ask You to come and consume my offering in Your fire. Burn me up and leave only what is pleasing to You, useful to You. Let fire fall from Heaven on this altar. Come Holy Spirit, I surrender to You now. Amen.

Discussion Questions

1. Explain Romans 12:1. What is a living sacrifice?
2. What is the purpose of surrender?
3. How is faith related to surrender?
4. Why is there a cost to know Christ and make Him known? What is this cost?
5. What does *paradidomi* mean? How does this change your perspective on what it means to surrender?
6. Describe what it means to betray your flesh.
7. Who is in charge of whether or not you surrender?
8. Was Jesus' life taken from Him, or did He lay it down with His own authority? Describe how we should respond to that.

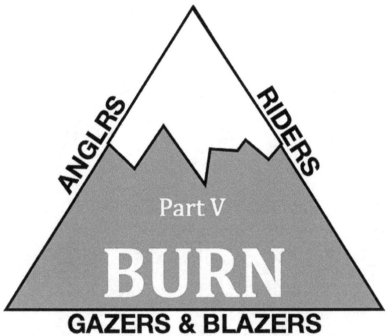

ANGLRS RIDERS

Part V

BURN

GAZERS & BLAZERS

Introduction

In part five of *The Mountaineer*, we enter into the peaks of the summit—the Holy Place and the Holy of Holies. You will meet with the work of the Holy Spirit both in and through you as you move beyond His Altar and into His Throne Room. Learning more specifically about His nature, character, and purposes, you will ascend to the summit where His blaze will set you aflame. Don't turn back, though your flesh cries out in disagreement, persist in His way until a fire burns within you as you are face to face with Elohim, the maker of Mountains.

Literary Support

Thou sacred mount, on whose pale forehead now
A desert quiet reigneth, ere the soul
Goes up to sit in meditation there,
She shall put off this world, with all its cares
And fading glory, to commune alone
With God, and with herself, on themes divine!
Thought, on swift wing, darts o'er the dubious waves
Where things promiscuous, by three thousand years,
Are swept together in one shadowy deep,
And rests on Olivet!

She here beholds,
Fleeing for refuge from a wicked son,
And with a wounded spirit bowed to earth,
The minstrel king, in bitter anguish come,
Showering the mountain with a father's tears
For his rebellious child!
But richer drops,
From purer eyes, and by a mightier One,
For thousands sunk in sin, have since been shed,
Where David mourned the guilt of Absalom!

The King of kings stood here; and looking down,
Wept o'er Jerusalem! Here, too, he led,
From the last supper, when the hymn was sung,
His few grieved followers out, in that drear night,
When, in the garden, on the mountain's slope,
His agony wrung forth the crimson drops!
While these sad pictures, hung upon thy sides,
Thou consecrated height, dissolve the heart
In pious sorrow; yet thy brow is crowned
With a bright, glorious scene!
Now, O my soul,
On the blest summit light a holy flame!

From the last foot-print of the Prince of peace,
The Conqueror of death, let incense rise,
And enter heaven with thine ascending Lord!
Shake off the chains and all the dust of earth!
Go up and breathe in the sweet atmosphere
His presence purified, as he arose!
Come! from the Mount of Olives pluck thy branch,

And bear it, like a dove, to yon bright ark
Of rest and safety!
—Hannah Flagg Gould, *Mount Olivet*

"I press toward the goal for the prize of the upward call of God
in Christ Jesus" (Philippians 3:14, NKJV).

"Prayer must be a flame, its ardor must consume. Prayer
without fervor is as a sun without heat." E.M. Bounds

"I feel my heart beating out of my chest, I wanna stay forever
like this. Let the flame of my heart always be lit, I wanna burn
forever like this." —*First Love*, by Kari Jobe.

The world is perishing for lack of the knowledge of God
and the Church is famishing for want of His Presence. The
instant cure of most of our religious ills would be to enter the
Presence in spiritual experience, to become suddenly aware
that we are in God and that God is in us. This would lift us
out of our pitiful narrowness and cause our hearts to become
enlarged. This would burn away the impurities from our lives
as the bugs and fungi were burned away by the fire that dwelt
in the bush. —*The Pursuit of God,* by A. W. Tozer

Fire of God, Thou sacred flames, Spirit who in splendor came,
Let Thy heat my soul refine, Till it glows with love divine.
—*Fire of God Thou Sacred Flame* by Albert F. Boyle

Chapter XIII

ANGLERS
The Sevenfold Spirit

Imperative
We must always be thirsty for the Holy Spirit.

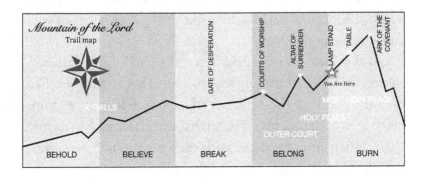

Zoeller's Pond
June 2014
New Haven, Kentucky

G olden dusky sunbeams dropped a sepia-tone sensation on the virgin landscape of Mike Zoller's enchanting property. I knew something rich, meaningful, and memorable was about to happen again. We crept slowly down his twisting driveway until we reached the house, barns, and pottery workshop that made up his homestead. Like a country doorbell, our crackling across the gravel brought Mike out of his house to greet us. Grandpa (Tom) began to talk to him immediately, smiling and shaking hands.

Mike showed the kids where and how he makes pottery. Their hunger for the art grew with his every word and with the display of his finished products. With clay on our minds, we stepped out the back door of the workshop and onto a wide forest trail.

The woodsy hike down to the pond was delightful, crossing meadows and dried creek beds. Mike and Tom discussed different trees and how well they did in a wood stove. Anne Marie and Grandma (Jan) chuckled and commented as they watched Asher and Asiah darting like young deer from one wild entrancement to the next.

At the dock, Grandpa mustered the children and demon-strated the skill of threading a worm with a hook. They watched intently, checking their mother's face to see if this was inhu-mane or not. Her smile told them that worms were ok to torture. Their anticipation escalated with each mention of how much fish like to eat worms.

By the time the worms were impaled across the hook, the children's bodies were tap-dancing with excitement, and the rigs were given over to their control. Anne Marie and Grandma sat in fold-out chairs along the bank and produced a steady flow of jovial tears in their amusement with the spectacle of the children fishing. Mike stood at a distance with a smile that showed he loved sharing his land and kindness.

The intensifying hilarity, which broadly followed the spe-cific instructions of Grandpa, began when the first child screamed, "I *got* one!" Immediately following the exclamation, a fish appeared dangling from the pole and whipping itself into exhaustion. But just before Grandpa got that fish off the hook and onto a stringer, the other child would exclaim, "I got one, *too!*" And Grandpa bolted over to assist.

"I got ANOTHER one!"

"I got ANOTHER one, too!"

Back and forth went Grandpa between children until it seemed every fish in the pond must have been on that stringer!

"Off with their heads!" Cried Grandpa, back at the house. And with that, he showed the fishermen how to prep their catch for a fish fry. It was, of course, appropriate to behead a fish, so long as you eventually ate that fish.

Grandma heated up the iron skillet, and before all the scales could be washed off their hands, a mess of fried fish was waiting at the table.

The Golden Lamp Stand

Fathers—and grandfathers—love for their children to catch fish. Jesus knew this when He perceived His disciples' lack of faith. They were unsure if they deserved the Holy Spirit or if the Father would be inclined to give them the Holy Spirit.

Knowing that you belong to the Father helps with this. When you have offered yourself to Him in complete surrender at the Altar, the Holy Spirit will recognize your humility. At this, He will lift you up and bring you into the inner courts, or the Holy Place.

> I fell on my face. And the glory of the Lord came
> into the house by the way of the gate facing toward
> the east. And the Spirit lifted me up and brought

me into the inner court; and behold the glory of the
Lord filled the house. (Ezekiel 43:3-5)

In the Hebrew Temple, the Holy Place was for priests only,
people who were entirely dedicated to the Lord, who had no
other life than the one they lived exclusively for Him, and whose
sole purpose was to honor and glorify the Lord in His service.
In the New Covenant, we are all priests in the house of the
Lord (see Revelation 1:6), and Christ has called us all to the
same exclusive commitment to live only for Him. This exclu-
siveness is the essence of what it means to be consecrated and
is the means by which we may live a holy life and be useful to
our Lord.

This first room of the dual-chambered temple is illuminated
by the Golden Lamp Stand. The implication and symbolism
of this Lamp Stand are that you will not be able to see anything without the Holy Spirit. Don't forget that we are climbing
a mountain, intent on reaching a summit beyond imaginable in
beauty and awe. But, to proceed beyond this point, you must be
fully saturated in, anointed by, and filled with the Holy Spirit of
Heaven. He is the One who will guide you to the summit.

You have experienced the work of the Holy Spirit in you as
He enabled you to see your misery without Him. He demonstrated His kindness to you by helping you understand your
desperate need for maturity and sanctification. He brought you
to repentance for your rebellion, arrogance, fear, and greed.
You experienced His ministry as you surrendered to Him on
the altar and offered yourself as a living sacrifice, like a living
worship song. He brought you to these places along the mountainous trail because there was much work that needed to be
done in your heart, and He is doing it!

The Baptism of the Holy Spirit

But He didn't bring you here to send you away. He brought you here to take you further and further into the deepest places of His ministry and grace. This is what is meant by the words of the baptizer: "He will baptize you with the Holy Spirit and fire" (Mathew 3:11).

Baptism in the Holy Spirit has become a statement of doctrinal divide. But this is only because the minds of men *ponder* more than the hearts of men *hunger*. Pondering for explanation outweighs hungering for the Spirit. Imagine the lopsidedness of a person who would rather explain what his friend is like than be with his friend. When academic pursuits supplant spiritual ones, hearts grow cold and often die.

We are commanded to love the Lord our God with all our hearts *and* minds. Both. We should sharpen our minds in the study of the Word, but we should not think that we can do this without the intricate involvement of the Counselor, who leads us into all truth, and who reminds us of everything Jesus has said. Because of the Holy Spirit living in us, we can get on our knees anywhere in the universe, cry out to the Living God, and find Him there. And oh, what a discovery!

The Holy Spirit is the infinite God, unexplainable beyond certain points, but one thing is clear: Any explanation of the Holy Spirit will mean little to a dying world coming from a person who doesn't thirst for Him. *Thirst* for the Holy Spirit leads to a baptism in the Holy Spirit. He honors thirst with rivers of refreshing water, into which he will submerge your entire being for the purposes of His heart. Thirst was David's driving force (see Psalm 63:1), and thirst was Jesus' prerequisite to receiving "living water" (John 4:10).

But this thirst can not be for anything that feels tingly. You can feel tingly at an Adele concert. I'm sure someone has wept listening to the Willie Nelson song, *"You Were Always On My Mind."* You can feel emotional in a movie theatre. Hunger for the presence of—, work of—, and power of the Holy Spirit must be embanked by a discipline to the Holy Scriptures. A "holy spirit" apart from Holy Scripture is an unholy spirit.

Remember, the Holy Spirit is a "Consuming Fire" (Hebrews 12:29). If you get close to Him, you will feel the heat. You *will*. His heat will melt away the passions of your flesh and crucify your self-interest. Heat makes people even thirstier. What you feel when near Him will always benefit you but won't always feel pretty. Consider how Jeremiah felt while the Holy Spirit spoke through him to give Israel a rebuke and the world the Scriptures:

> My soul, my soul! I am in anguish! Oh, my heart! My heart is pounding in me; I cannot be silent, because you have heard, O my soul, the sound of the trumpet, the alarm of war. (Jeremiah 4:19)

You might labor over your own insufficiency or over a lost soul. You might weep for no apparent reason. You might lay flat on your face in silent reverence and awe. Whatever the case, you will feel, and you will change. You cannot do otherwise while being near a "Consuming Fire."

Hunger for the truth of Scripture for the purpose of knowing the One True God will be filled (see Matthew 5:6). Both the Holy Spirit and the Holy Scriptures are referred to as Lamps and Guides. Thus they function one and the same in bringing us to the summit. But one cannot be without the other. The

Pharisees had the Scriptures without the Messiah. Look what Jesus said to them:

> And the Father who has sent me has himself testified concerning me. You have never heard his voice nor seen his form, nor does his word dwell in you, for you do not believe the one he sent. **You diligently study the Scriptures because you think that by them you possess eternal life.** These are the Scriptures that testify about me, yet you refuse to come to me to have life. (John 5:37-40, emphasis mine)

The religious community of Jesus' time refused to come to Jesus, selecting instead an academic knowledge of the Scriptures. Jesus ascended into Heaven, and the Father sent us the Holy Spirit (see John 14:26). The religious community of *our* time refuses to come to the Holy Spirit, selecting instead an academic knowledge of the Scriptures. Many today make the same mistake for which Jesus rebuked the Pharisees. The Holy Spirit is as much a gift from the Father as the Holy Son (see John 3:16, Luke 11:13, and Acts 2:38). Don't reject Him, thirst for Him. Seek His fullness, His power, and His gifts.

A.W. Tozer put it like this:

> Sound Bible exposition is an imperative must in the Church of the Living God. Without it no church can be a New Testament church in any strict meaning of that term. But exposition may be carried on in such a way as to leave the hearers devoid of any true spiritual nourishment whatever. For it is not mere words that nourish the soul, but God Himself, and unless

and until the hearers find God in personal experience they are not the better for having heard the
truth. The Bible is not an end in itself, but a means
to bring men to an intimate and satisfying knowledge of God, that they may enter into Him, that they
may delight in His Presence, may taste and know the
inner sweetness of the very God Himself in the core
and center of their hearts.

It is imperative that you renounce fear. If you are afraid of
experiencing Him because, like those standers-by on the day
of Pentecost, you have laughed and criticized (see acts 2:13),
repent, for God has not given you a spirit of fear. Your dignity is
hay, wood, and stubble—and it must be burned up. Did Christ
cherish dignity while hanging naked and pierced on a cross (see
Isaiah 53:3-5)? You must brace yourself, trust the Word of God,
and prepare to experience the Baptism of the Holy Spirit. He
will not take you beyond the point you are *willing* to go. Your
hunger and willingness must drive you now, for that is what it
means to seek Him with all your heart.

The Holy Spirit is willing to fill us again and again. John's
use of the word in Matthew 3:11 means to dip repeatedly, or
submerge, according to Strong's Greek translation for the Greek
word "*baptizo*." It's important to note that John was not speaking
to Jesus' disciples or those present at Pentecost; he was talking
to *his* disciples and those who came to him to be baptized for
repentance.

Paul explains this in Acts 19:1-6,

> While Apollos was at Corinth, Paul took the road
> through the interior and arrived at Ephesus. There

he found some disciples and asked them, "Did you receive the Holy Spirit when you believed?" They answered, "No, we have not even heard there is a Holy Spirit." So Paul asked, "Then what baptism did you receive?" "John's baptism," they replied. Paul said, "John's baptism was a baptism of repentance. He told the people to believe in the one coming after him, that is in Jesus." On hearing this, they were baptized into the name of the Lord Jesus. When Paul placed his hands on them, the Holy Spirit came on them, and they spoke in tongues and prophesied.

What comes after the baptism in the Holy Spirit is up to the Holy Spirit. The *charismata* of the Holy Spirit are His free gifts. This Greek word has the exact origin as the word for grace, *charis*. Grace is given to the humble. Humility is demonstrated by gratitude and sincere love. If my children loved their Christmas or birthday gifts more than they loved me, I would stop giving them gifts. They must love their mother and me. It would be absurd to raise children who don't love us but only love the gifts we give them. I am confident that the Holy Spirit maintains this same priority. If you learn to thirst for Him—not His gifts, not results in ministry, not notoriety—He will give His gifts sooner than you expected!

When the matter of cherishing the person of the Holy Spirit above all else is settled, we can be assured that our hearts are full of His love. We can move from chapter 13 to chapter 14, from loving Him to loving like Him. When we love as He loves, He empowers us with His gifts—as He determines. These gifts, sometimes called "manifestations," which occurred throughout the book of Acts, such as speaking in tongues and prophesying, are strongly encouraged by the Apostle Paul in his letter to the Corinthians, with a priority placed on prophecy:

> Follow the way of love and eagerly desire the spiritual gifts, especially the gift of prophecy. For anyone who speaks in a tongue does not speak to men but to God. Indeed, no one understands him; he utters mysteries with his Spirit. But everyone who prophesies speaks to men for their strengthening, encouragement, and comfort. (1 Corinthians 14:1-3)

But what if my children rejected a gift I gave them, saying, "I don't want *THIS!*" Would someone who profoundly loves the Holy Spirit reject a gift He wants to give them? Can we follow the "way of love" while eagerly *denying* the spiritual gifts? Can we select 1 Corinthians 13 and reject 12 and 14 and not be guilty of treating prophesy with contempt? Can we subjectively approach Scripture like this and still proclaim inerrancy? No, we cannot.

By inspiration of the Holy Spirit, the Apostle writes that we are to *follow the way of love **AND** eagerly **desire** the spiritual gifts.* Of the spiritual gifts, Paul writes, "All these are the work of one and the same Spirit, and he gives them to each one, just as he determines" (1 Corinthians 12:11). It is not as important what spiritual gift you have as it is that you are hungry for the Holy Spirit. If you are hungry for the Holy Spirit—walking in obedience to His Word—and ask the Father, He will fill you with the Holy Spirit. The Holy Spirit will allow you to mature and grow, and when He determines the time is right, He will gift you with any one, or more, of His spiritual gifts.

One Sunday, Anne Marie stood worshiping in the morning church service. As the music quieted and a time of sweet adorations settled on the congregation, a woman stood up and prayed in tongues. When she sat down, another woman stood up and declared what had been prophesied. After the church service, the two women spoke to one another about the experience when a Jewish man, only visiting and unconverted, approached them and asked them where they both learned to speak Hebrew. They both contested, "we don't speak Hebrew." Astonished, he replied, pointing to one and then the other, "you spoke perfect Hebrew, and you translated it flawlessly." The Holy Spirit will give his gifts to yielded, fearless vessels, but we must eagerly desire them and abandon our love of dignity. Is this not what is meant by the Apostle when he writes,

> But if an unbeliever or an inquirer comes in while everyone is prophesying, they are convicted of sin and are brought under judgment by all, and the secrets of their hearts are laid bare. So they will fall down and worship God, exclaiming, "God is really among you!" (1 Corinthians 14:24-25)

Summiting the mountain of the Lord *can't* be done without the Holy Spirit. The Holy Spirit will decide what gifts you need; you just come hungry, and don't deny Him the space to do in you the good work the Father has determined should be done. Spiritual gifts are important, but they are also refined over time and developed as we go up the mountain and come down with fire from the Holy of Holies.

I will provide explanation of the gift of prophecy in a later chapter. What is essential to understand is this: if you are

271

immersed in the Holy Spirit, He has the right to give you His gifts as described in 1 Corinthians 12 and 14.

We are commanded to be filled with the Spirit. The Apostles and early church believers were filled with the Holy Spirit on the day of Pentecost as described in Acts 2:4, then again in Acts 4:31, and presumably on many more occasions. Don't settle for one experience with God. As often as you need to crucify the flesh, you need to be filled with the Spirit. The two should always go together in that order. When you have mortified the sinful nature, you have prepared a place for Him, and with thirst and persistence, you will be filled.

I hope for fresh baptisms in the Holy Spirit as often as I can possibly get away and be with Him. Look to find Him EVERY time you seek Him with all your heart. What must it look like to "find Him"?

The Seven-Fold Spirit of God

The Lamp Stand has three arms on each side and one central shaft. These seven little fires represent the seven-fold Spirit of God (see Zechariah 4:1-6, Revelation 4:5). Although the connection is not directly made in Scripture, it makes sense to see the Golden Lamp Stand with the central shaft representing the Spirit of the Lord and its arms representing each of the six characteristics of the Holy Spirit described in Isaiah 11:2,

> The Spirit of the Lord will rest on him (central shaft), The Spirit of Wisdom (arm one) and of Understanding (arm two), the Spirit of Counsel (arm three) and of Power (arm four), the Spirit of

Knowledge (arm five), and of the Spirit of the Fear
of the Lord (arm six). (Paraphrase)

Imagine lighting this Lamp Stand. One candle at a time,
you think of each of these characteristics of the Holy Spirit. As
you meditate on who the Holy Spirit is, you begin to pray that
the Spirit of the Lord will rest on you, too. More fire enters the
scene, and with it, more light, more heat. Then you move on
to praying for each specific characteristic, just as if you were
lighting those candles.

Perhaps it will help if you pray something like this:

Holy Spirit, I invite you to come and rest on me. I need You deeply.
Come and help me; You are the Helper. Come and guide me and
lead me in Your ways. Come to me and help me. May the Spirit
of the Lord rest on me. Rest on me, Spirit of wisdom and under-
standing, Spirit of counsel and power, Spirit of knowledge and of
the fear of the Lord. Let my delight be in the fear of the Lord. I
wait for You, Holy Spirit.

His flame moves onto you, and you begin to burn with His
holy passions. You sense the purposes and interests that glow
in the heart of God, and they burn in yours too. Evangelism,
compassion, deliverance for captives, healing for the sick, and
the preaching of the Word begin to carry more significance
in your heart as it burns with His heat. This is the work of
transformation.

It will be helpful to notice how the Spirit of Wisdom and
Understanding is so eager to share her wealth with the fool.

"Wisdom has built Her house; She has hewn out its
seven pillars. She has prepared Her meat and mixed
Her wine; She has also set Her table. She sends out
Her maids, and She calls from the highest pint of the
city. 'Let all who are simple come in here!' She says
to those who lack judgment. 'Come, eat My food and
drink the wine I have mixed. Leave your simple ways
and you will live; walk in the way of understanding'"
(Proverbs 9:1-6)

Again, it is important—for the purpose of growing our
faith—to notice how eager God is to share with you His wisdom.
He says,

"If any of you lacks wisdom, he should ask God who
gives generously to all without finding fault, and it
will be given to him. But when he asks, he should
believe and not doubt, because he who doubts is like
a wave of the sea, blown and tossed by the wind. That
man should not think he will receive anything from
the Lord" (James 1:5-7).

Believe that the Spirit of Wisdom and Understanding wants
to rest on you; ask Him to, and He will!

Pray again that the Spirit of the Lord will rest on you, the
Spirit of Counsel and of Power. It will be helpful to know that
Jesus promised you the Spirit of Counsel when He said, "It will
be given you in that hour what you are to say. For it is not you
who speak, but it is the Spirit of your Father who speaks in you."
(Matthew 10:19-20). Jesus also promised you the Spirit of Power
when He said, "But you will receive power when the Holy Spirit

has come upon you" (Acts 1:8). You must believe that the Holy Spirit will be given to you when you ask, and you must ask.

Pray again that the Spirit of Knowledge and the Fear of the Lord will rest upon you. You must pray in faith, understanding that knowledge comes easily to the discerning (see Proverbs 14:6) and that God desires you to grow in knowledge, "In your faith supply moral excellence, and in your moral excellence, knowledge..." (2 Peter 1:5). You must know that God wants you to grow in fear of the Lord as He has invited you, "Come, you children, listen to Me; I will teach you the fear of the Lord" (Psalm 34:11). Again, you must know that the Father will give you the Spirit when you ask.

Envision yourself with wisdom to discern the best, most loving actions in life, with understanding to clarify the mysteries that often crimp hope, with counsel for those who need guidance and power for those that need healing or deliverance. Imagine yourself with growing knowledge of God and a heart that fears the Lord, shunning evil and standing in awe of the Almighty. This is what the Father imagines for you. He wants to give you his Spirit, and these are the sevenfold attributes of the Spirit of the Lord. In the words of the Apostle, "Be filled with the Spirit" (Ephesians 5:18).

Fathers and Fish
August 2017
Branson, Missouri

Grandma Geyer invited the family to spend a few days at a condo situated just below the dam at Beaver Lake. When I was a kid, she would take me fishing for catfish in Osage Creek, which ran through our property in Elm Springs, Arkansas. She also took Asher on his first fishing conquest in the back bays of Orange Beach, Alabama, where he caught his first fish. So, she picked this condo because of its proximity to the fish-filled waters that flowed through its backyard.

The sun vivified the banks of the White River so that the grass glowed green, and the morning due sparkled in the light. Ice-cold water rustled by our grassy landing, quietly harboring a plenitude of trout.

Andrew, Asher, and I cast our lures into the transparent water, aiming at the trout we could see drifting along. The cool of the morning turned to the heat of the afternoon, and the hot afternoon back to a cool evening. The whole day had been spent nursing the anticipation of a catch.

Andrew went away a bit earlier to seek fishing counsel and found himself standing in a bait shop. Eventually, he returned with a little box full of mini-jigs, and we all followed his guidance. Andrew caught a fish right away and proved his journey of discovery to have been profitable. I caught one, too, but Asher's hook remained empty.

I had been praying all day long and carrying on a conversation with the Lord about whether or not Asher should be divinely assisted in catching a trout. In all his trying, he didn't catch one, and we retired much to his reluctance as the evening sun disappeared behind the lofty bluffs of the Ozark hills.

The following day at 6:00 a.m., I woke Asher and Andrew, and we descended to the tranquil banks of our trout conquest. Fog hovered over the glassy stream, obscuring its inhabitants. We surveyed the optimal locations from which to cast our temptations toward the evasive creatures. I chose a steeper bank with immediately deeper waters. Asher went back to his location from the day before, but the trout were difficult to see this time of day. Andrew waded out onto a rocky island and complained of his frozen feet, nevertheless casting his line.

I amped my conversation with the Lord up to a fully invested petition of grave importance and even documented several Scriptural promises about fathers and fish and the goodness of giving.

> Now suppose one of you fathers is asked by his son
> for a fish; he will not give him a snake instead of a
> fish, will he? Or if he is asked for an egg, he will not
> give him a scorpion, will he? If you then, being evil,
> know how to give good gifts to your children, how
> much more will your heavenly Father give the Holy
> Spirit to those who ask Him? (Luke 11:11-13)

For two quiet hours, we caught nothing. The sunlight crept up onto the bluff opposite our bank, and a familiar glow rose from the grassy bend where we stood the previous day. We migrated back toward that area from our failed "improvements."

We could see the trout better with the sun directly on the water, and we worked at tempting them with our mini jigs. They seemed to be window-shopping. Andrew commented on some of the larger specimens; perhaps they were wiser, too.

Asher moved slowly downstream, looking to improve his position. Then I noticed he was struggling to real in a trout, and I ran to help him. Over and around and up and down, the fish jerked and yanked in every direction to free itself, but Asher pulled it in!

Thank you whispers shot from my heart to heaven like harpoons as we pulled the 16" Rainbow colored fish from the river. I helped Asher put his trophy on a stringer, assuring him that it was "keeping size," and, "yes, we would eat him later." So invigorating was the satisfaction of catching a trout that Asher went immediately back to work, and not long after, he caught another one!

The sun was slipping away again, and we knew we had better get up the hill to the condo with our stringer full of fish. On the way up, Andrew congratulated Asher for his catch with some good uncle love and a few pats on the back. That evening, Grandma Geyer helped us make a trout dinner, and we laughed about everything that had happened. In those moments, I saw once again that our Father gives good gifts to his children (see James 1:17).

The Language of the Holy Spirit

The Father will give you the Holy Spirit if you ask. But you must become like an angler of His outpouring. When you see water, you must want a baptism like a fisherman wants a fish. You must be willing to cast your line when it seems unlikely, to cast your net again after a long night of nothing. By faith in His goodness, you must persist in the place of His presence until you have a catch—a catch you know came from Him, one you can't contain or even haul in.

You are destined to be anointed by the Holy Spirit and possess His power and character. Through intimacy with the Holy Spirit, everything you do is made effective and eternal. It's no coincidence that there was a Golden Lamp Stand in the Holy Place.

Listen to the Lord. Wait for Him patiently. Renew your mental focus. If you are distracted, ask the Holy Spirit to help you keep your focus on Him. Wait for Him. It is perhaps

His most used tactic to require His pursuers to wait for Him. Patience and perseverance are petals on the wildflower of sacrificial love. He requires this to weigh wholeheartedness, a condition of finding the Lord (Jeremiah 29:13).

It's important to know that the Holy Spirit will want to communicate with you, but He doesn't always use words. It's not that He doesn't *ever* use words, but He more often uses other means to communicate to us.

The Holy Spirit's primary language is revelation. He reveals glorious truths, aspects of His nature, and His purposes. In fact, this is the language of heaven. He is not dependent on words to convey His brilliant realities but simply opens the minds of believers to understand His Word (see Luke 24:45).

In the manifest presence of God on Earth, this language is employed by the Holy Spirit. For He is the Spirit of Wisdom and Revelation (see Ephesians 1:17 and compare Isaiah 11:2), and His express purpose is to reveal the glory of Jesus to men (see John 16:13-15). Because Jesus is the Incarnate Word, that which the Spirit reveals will always align with the written Word of God. He will not instruct otherwise, nor will he reveal beyond the scope of what has been revealed in Scripture.

It is in this seeing and hearing that the hard, confused, and broken heart is revived and restored with fresh inspiration and a vigorous thirst for more of the Knowledge of God. This is the heart that hears:

> Now we have received, not the spirit of the world, but
> the Spirit who is from God, so that we may know the
> things freely given to us by God, which things we
> also speak, not in words taught by human wisdom,
> but in those taught by the Spirit, combining spiritual

thoughts with spiritual words. But a natural man does not accept the things of the Spirit of God for they are foolishness to him; and he cannot understand them, because they are spiritually appraised. But he who is spiritual appraises all things, yet he himself is appraised by no one. For who has known the mind of the Lord, that he will instruct Him? But we have the mind of Christ. (1 Corinthians 2:13-16)

These "things" that come from the Spirit are not as simple as words one hears, physically vibrating the facets of the biological ear. Any fool can hear words in his own language, but these words are not commonly heard in this manner. Rather, they are discerned by the spirit of a person who has the Holy Spirit living inside them. It is of the carnal, unspiritual man that it is said, "My thoughts are not your thoughts, neither are your ways my ways" (Isaiah 55:8-9).

But if you were restored to fellowship with the Almighty by the blood of Christ, you may say, as Paul said, "We have the mind of Christ." And so, if His thoughts fill our minds, we can know that He is, in fact, revealing much to us of Himself and His purposes. Words form in our minds as we apprentice ourselves to the Holy Spirit, and He instructs us in the way that fathers instruct children: by showing. And in doing so, He will make His ways known to us, as He did to Moses (see Psalm 103:7), that we would walk in them and honor Him and teach others to do the same.

A cold, silent, sinful world produces ears that do not hear and eyes that do not see. In the silence of heaven's voice, death and despair grow and overtake human hearts as crippling ivy covers a once fruitful vine. There, in the quenched Spirit of God, the spirit of man is strangled. All consciousness of sin evaporates, and lives are lived as each person believes and does what is right in their own eyes.

Scripture is ever so clear "Where there is no revelation, the people cast off restraint" (Proverbs 29:18, NIV). Self-government never had so great a friend as the Spirit of Wisdom and Revelation! It is for this reason Paul prayed for the Ephesians, for in knowing Christ better would they also be set free from sin, empowered by grace, and charge through the world in victorious beauty (see Ephesians 1:17-19).

It is only in the manifest presence of the Holy Spirit that such clear understanding is translated from the Father's heavenly language to the distinguishable verbiage of our thoughts—regardless of our earthly language. And in His presence, with our thoughts illuminated by the revelation He brings, we will comment, "Were not our hearts burning within us while He was speaking to us on the road, while He was explaining the Scriptures to us?" (Luke 24:32)

And now, with an enthroned, resurrected Christ, the role of opening Scripture and speaking to us is passed to the Spirit of Truth. For Christ passed this baton in saying,

> But when He, the Spirit of truth, comes, He will guide you into all the truth; for He will not speak on His own initiative, but whatever He hears, He will speak; and He will disclose to you what is to come. He will glorify Me, for He will take of Mine and will disclose it to you. (John 16:13-15)

In this way, the Spirit makes known all of that which is the Father's, that which has been given to the Son, and that which will be forever ours. Thus, the role of the Holy Spirit is to guide into truth and reveal what is spoken in heaven.

"Blessed are those who hunger and thirst…for they will be satisfied" (Matthew 5:6). Labor for the Lord, seek him with all your strength, make it your primary occupation, and you will find him. Pursue the Holy Spirit at all costs of energy, time, and resources. For, "A worker's appetite works for him, for his hunger urges him on." (Proverbs 16:26). And standing by the rippling waters—passing with the minutes of the day, and nursing the urge for a catch, you will receive the Holy Spirit afresh, and all His fiery passion with Him.

All serious mountaineers must have a Guide and must listen uncompromisingly to the Guide's directions. It is easier to hear and follow when you are close; for this reason, summiting the mountain of the Lord relies exclusively on drawing near to the Lord. Draw near to him now, call on his name, and follow him deep into the mountains.

Conclusion and Contemplation

Cultivate a burning desire for the Holy Spirit. God has promised to give you the Holy Spirit when you ask Him. Are you thirsty for the Holy Spirit? Will you ask the Father for His mighty Gift?

Prayer of Commitment

Father, thank you for the promise of the Holy Spirit. I believe! I ask today to be filled with the Holy Spirit, led by the Holy Spirit, gifted by the Holy Spirit, and empowered by the Holy Spirit. I ask You to guide me in truth for Your glory and honor. Speak to me, Lord; I am listening. Open my mind to understand everything the Scriptures say concerning Jesus that I may know the good, pleasing, and perfect will of the Father. Amen.

Discussion Questions

1. Who is a priest under the New Covenant?
2. What must we do to receive the promise of the Holy Spirit?
3. What is the baptism of the Holy Spirit? Discuss what it means to eagerly desire the spiritual gifts. Do you?
4. Should I feel something when I am close to the Holy Spirit or when He fills me? Explain the role of the Scriptures in my experience of God's presence and His gifts.
5. What was the mistake of the Pharisees as it relates to studying Scripture? How do we make the same mistake today? When we study Scripture, how can we avoid this mistake? See Luke 24:45
6. Describe the seven arms of the Lamp Stand by reading Isaiah 11:2.
7. Should we always expect to hear a voice when God communicates to us directly?
8. What is the language of heaven and of the Holy Spirit?
9. What is the difference between giving directions and leading someone somewhere? Which does the Holy Spirit more often do?
10. What are the consequences of living without revelation?

Chapter XIV

RIDERS

Fellowship at the Table of God

Imperative
We must meet with Elohim at His table
and share the bread of "panim."

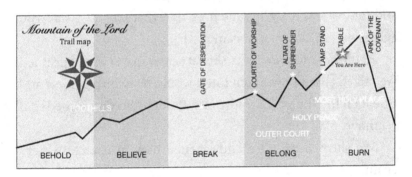

Doolies and Noodles
October 2014

A s we came around the bend, with an inclined forest to
the right and a rippling creek to the left, a massive red
barn came into view. Beyond the barn was a fescue field, short-
ened by the grazing of several paints, buckskins, and red-brown
quarter horses.

A half a dozen doolies were parked in the grass with
trailers attached to them, empty. Just outside the barn was an

oval-shaped corral of sorts, in which young ladies rode tall horses.

"Look, Dad!" Asiah pointed. "I know." I said, smug about my secrets.

"Am I gonna…?"

"Yep!"

It was daddy-daughter date night, and I was taking my little sweetheart for a surprise horseback riding expedition.

In a helmet and on the saddle, Asiah trotted proudly about the indoor riding arena. When she stopped, she leaned forward to tell the horse what a good horse it was, and it could understand English. It responded by blowing air out of several angles and contortions of its lips and nostrils. "That's right!" Asiah said agreeably, and away they sauntered.

At the noodle restaurant, she sat across from me and grinned. We talked about how much fun it would be to own a horse and ride it all the time. Not in the city, though. Maybe, someday, if we move.

We slurped noodles and learned how to use chopsticks again.

"I want to be a veterinarian," She decided.

"Really?" I queried.

"Yes, because I will be able to be around more horses," she calculated.

"You could, especially in Kentucky." I surmised.

The conversation went on to include such subjects as why grapes are purple and whether Captain Underpants was a bad guy or a good guy.

"He's a bad guy," she said.

"Yeah."

Not long after this experience, Asiah's grandfather bought her a horse, and it lives on the family farm. When she rode it for the first time, it trotted around the farm under her tender guidance. "Willow" is a beautiful black and white Tennessee Walker, one of the gentlest horses I've ever had the pleasure of riding. I remembered this conversation at the noodle table. Someone else remembered that conversation, too. How gracious is the Father at His table!

Usually, something happens between people before they meet at a table. An incredible experience, challenging or entertaining, deepens the bond between friends, brothers, sisters, or families. Then, the magic happens. Food is served, and sentences are finished between bites while excitement rises and falls, energized by the humor and sincerity between those on either side.

At the center of Hebrew social culture was always a table, where friendships grew deeper, and families grew stronger. In the place where God would share with Israel His glory, He wanted them to know that relationship was to be first. Friendship with God, intimacy with God, and Father-child bonding with God were to be central to the functionality of His temple.

The Bread of His Presence

Are you beginning to see why there was a table in the Holy Place? And it had bread on it! Not just any bread either; this was the bread of "panim," or "The Presence" (Exodus 25:30). We noted earlier in this book that *panim* means *face* or *face to face*. The Holy Place was the place of His presence, where the priests could go daily to engage Elohim in a period of deep communion and fellowship.

In his masterful work *The Temple, Its Ministries and Services*, Alfred Edersheim states,

> The 'bread' 'laid before Him' in the northern or most sacred part of the Holy Place was that of His Presence, and meant that the covenant-people owned 'His Presence' as their bread and their life. That the 'Presence' meant the special manifestation of God, as afterwards fully vouchsafed in Christ, 'the Angel of his Presence.'

When you journey deep into a time of seeking God, you must know that you are functioning as a priest in the temple of God. You cannot expect to be filled with the Holy Spirit without experiencing His presence any more than you can expect to be filled with food without experiencing *its* presence. You will know that you are full when you have eaten, whether it is the bread of the presence or the bread that makes your sandwich.

What could the apostle have meant by saying, "I press on so that I may lay hold of that for which also I was laid hold of by Christ Jesus" (Philippians 3:12)? What could Paul have taken hold of that he would not also deeply experience? For what had Christ taken hold of Paul if not to give him access to the Most Holy Place, where the manifestation of God's presence was forever available? If you are not experiencing an outpouring of the Holy Spirit, it can only mean that you are unrepentant, in a hurry, or both. Attend to both, and ensure that you come face to face with the Almighty, for this is your sustenance, your life-bread; it was for this you were created.

Let me, therefore, further elaborate to secure for you an advancement beyond wordy, dry petitions speckled about in a month's time. Let me take you into the deep, inner workings of the Holy Spirit, the Wielder of the Sword of Truth, the Baker of the Bread of Heaven. It is Him, into whose rich fellowship you will again enter, who serves you this Bread that came down from heaven in all its savor and delectable exquisiteness. As you go to this place with Him *today*, let me encourage you to make this your daily practice, and you will find Him poured out upon you. And this *will* come to pass, but not until *after* you have placed all your effort entirely toward this heavenly cause of summiting the mountain of the Lord.

The Bread of His Word

If the temple is a model for how we are to seek God today, we must know that the table wasn't there for a business lunch. Business hours are over. It's a daddy-daughter-dinner-date, and He wants to look us in the eyes. He wants us to experience His closeness, His protection, His love, and His wisdom. He wants us to know that He is near to us and has our good in mind. And with this in mind, we must approach Him by faith, accepting that as we draw near to Him, He will draw near to us. (See James 4:8)

And what occurs when we are in the presence of God? We come away illuminated like glow-in-the-dark toys, emanating brightly the glory of God, for "they looked to Him and were radiant (Psalm 34:5). We are filled with His bread, which is his Word, because he feeds it to us as he fed the 5,000. We soak up the truth of His nature by osmosis, by simple proximity, and are riveted by the potency of His eternal purposes.

It is having "been with Jesus" (Acts 4:13) that overthrows the human nature and instills the divine nature, replacing cowardice with courage. It is walking beside the living Word, the Bread of Heaven, that feeds the spirit, sanctifies the soul, and mortifies the flesh. Do not be fooled by your eyes; Jesus is alive, and you can walk beside him now. Jesus is this Living Word, the Bread of Heaven.

> "For the bread of God is that which comes down out of heaven, and gives life to the world." Then they said to Him, "Lord, always give us this bread." Jesus said to them, "I am the bread of life; he who comes to Me will not hunger, and he who believes in Me will never thirst." (John 6:33,35).

To help us remember that we cannot live on the bread of earth alone, Jesus instituted communion. We are to take the bread and wine in remembrance that the Word of the Father dwelt among us and demonstrated to us perfectly the will of the Father. Jesus, at the table with his disciples, did this:

> And when He had taken some bread and given thanks, He broke it and gave it to them, saying, "This is My body which is given for you; do this in remembrance of Me." (Luke 22:19).

Bread already had a strong symbolism in the Bible. But then Christ came and made it even stronger. Bread is broken and shared at the table and is eaten by those listening to one another, engaged in one another's lives, and enjoying one another. Jesus, the Bread of Life, was broken and is shared with the hungry, the needy, and the lost so that they may be restored to spiritual vitality and physical well-being. Jesus represents all that the Father wants to communicate to us, His meaning, His intentions, His Logos.

The Double-Edged Sword of Logos and Rhema

The Logos has always been Elohim. He was with God in the beginning. He is God. Jesus is the bread that came down from heaven, and Jesus is the Logos:

> "In the beginning was the *Logos*, and the *Logos* was
> with God, and the *Logos* was God." "And the *Logos*
> became flesh, and dwelt among us, and we saw his
> glory, glory as of the only begotten from the Father,
> full of grace and truth." (John 1:1-2, 14, italics mine)

The exchange of meaning is the essence of communication. Words are but a medium whereby meaning can be transferred from one to another. Whether spoken or written, words are not the intended result; it is meaning. If I write you a letter in a language you don't understand, my logos is not conveyed to you. The words are meaningless. This *meaning* is the essence of Logos.

According to Thayer's Greek Lexicon:

> **LOGOS**: Properly, a collecting, collection (see
> λέγω) — and that, as well of those things which are
> put together in thought, as of those which, having
> been thought i. e. gathered together in the mind, are
> expressed in words. Accordingly, a twofold use of
> the term is to be distinguished: one, which relates to
> speaking, and one which relates to thinking.

Along this train of thought, one can see that from all eternity, the Logos has been the communicative intentions of God, firmly established in His thoughts long before they ever were spoken to the prophets. The Logos was employed in the creation of all things (see John 1:3, Colossians 1:16, Hebrews 1:2), including the embodiment of eternal truths in the Holy Scriptures. The Logos of the Father was fed to the Prophets by the Holy Spirit, much in the same way that the raven brought the prophet his food (see 1 Kings 17:1-6). When the Spirit of Truth moved these prophets to speak, (see 2 Peter 1:20-21), He did so, as always: glorifying the Logos and revealing to them the thoughts of the Father—and they subsequently penned this revelation, giving us Scripture. And all Scripture is immutable and inerrant, flawless, by the breath of God, and carrying the full authority of His immeasurable power with the full intent of His Logos.

In a different manner of displaying the contents of His mind to humanity, the Father issued onto earth his Son as the embodiment of His purposes. In this way, He fulfilled His name Immanuel, God with us, and became the Bread that came down from heaven. The Logos was *with* God and *was* God before becoming flesh and dwelling among us.

To know the Logos is to walk beside Him, observing Him, becoming united with Him in his purposes. It is to feel what one feels when they walk beside someone they admire, esteem, and love—even in silence, absorbing the exquisite joy of proximity. Additionally, to know the Logos requires that one study the experiences, so delineated in Scripture, of the men of old who walked with Him. These experiences are the penned Logos given to the prophets to write down at the behest of the Holy Spirit. Every nuance and movement is to be understood as one learns to walk beside Elohim Incarnate, Jesus Christ, Immanuel.

Whether a follower of the incarnate Christ during His ministry on earth or a follower of the resurrected Christ in His ministry before the Father, one will notice His gestures, His movements, and His intentions. Followers of Christ are impacted by the life which is in Him. The words He says to us are "Spirit and are life" (John 6:63). In the living Logos is such a source of life that it was said:

> For the *Logos* of God is living and active and sharper than any two-edged sword, and piercing as far as the division of soul and spirit, of both joints and marrow, and able to judge the thoughts and intentions of the heart. (Hebrews 4:12)

John described Christ in this way: "and out of His mouth came a sharp two-edged sword" (Revelation 1:16). Christ was not just the embodiment of the Father's intentions by way of the example He set for us, He was also the Father's voice. Therefore, the living, active, and resurrected Logos was, is, and forever will be the life of God and the thoughts of God—and the singular passageway to knowing God—His ways, His thoughts, and His eternity.

Two words are used to describe the Word of God in the New Testament. It is of the *Logos* the author of Hebrews speaks, and to His *Rhema* he refers when he says:

> God, after He spoke long ago to the fathers in the prophets in many portions and in many ways, in these last days has spoken to us in His Son (The Logos), whom He appointed heir of all things; and through whom also He made the world. And He is

the radiance of His glory and the exact representation of His nature, and upholds all things by the
word of His power (The Rhema). (Hebrews 1:1-3,
parenthetical phrases mine)

The doubled edges of the Sword of Truth are the Logos
and the Rhema. Logos is word "meaning," and Rhema is word
"force." A sword may represent a tool of war, a weapon of battles, or a means to defend. You may learn that the sword is
composed of the strongest steel, is weighted perfectly, and with
an edge too sharp to touch without being wounded. However,
this weapon must be swung, it must be carried into enemy territory and utilized, and it must powerfully deliver its blow. This
delivery of meaning is the Rhema. It is the incarnation of the
meaning, the incarnation of the Word. The Spoken Word is the
that which shatters the timbers (see Psalm 29:5), moves mountains (see Mark 11:23), and proclaims liberty to the captives
(see Luke 4:18).

In this position of mind, the companion of Christ waits
eagerly to hear Him speak (Rhema) and will hang on His every
word when He does. And then they will ask, "were not our
hearts burning within us while He was speaking to us on the
road, while He was explaining the Scriptures to us?" (Luke
24:32).

Rhema is a spoken word that has proceeded from the mouth
of God.

For this reason, Rhema is the substance of faith. As the
Apostle states, "So faith comes from hearing, and hearing by
the *Rhema* of Christ" (Romans 10:17).

Peter queried, "Lord, to whom shall we go? You have the *Rhema* of eternal life" (John 6:68). Peter beheld both the living Logos, and heard His eternal-life-producing Rhema.

Philip begged, "Lord, show us the Father and it is enough for us" (John 14:8).

> Jesus said to him, "Have I been so long with you, and yet you have not come to know me, Philip? He who has seen Me has seen the Father; how can you say, 'Show us the Father'? Do you not believe that I am in the Father, and the Father is in me? The *rhema* that I say to you I do not speak on My own initiative, but the Father abiding in Me does His works. (John 14:9-10)

Knowing Christ, is therefore knowing the Logos, which is His character: the embodiment of the thoughts of the Father represented in the incarnate Immanuel, communicated to the prophets and apostles, and written into Scripture. But knowing Christ falls short if halted there, because it is the resurrected Christ that sustains all things, including the life of the believer, by His spoken Rhema, which is the life-force of truth that proceeds from His lips.

It is a dreadful mistake to believe that the risen Logos is mute. He speaks to His people now as He always has. His sheep hear His voice as they always have. To attempt now to follow Christ and to believe you cannot hear His spoken word is to lacerate any hope of ever having divine faith inspired by His Rhema.

And yet, it is an even more dreadful thing to believe that Christ would speak anything to a person which does not align with the written Logos of Scripture. There is still revelation, in the sense that Christ reveals Himself and understanding of his Word to us, and this is because we have been given the Spirit of Revelation (Ephesians 1:17). But there is no *new* revelation, in the sense that any original message could be added to the Scriptures or supplant them with any new directives. For Christ to contradict Himself in this manner would be an assassination of the immutable character of God. Thus, as hearers tune their spiritual ears to the whispers of God, they must make it a priority to know the Scripture and understand its Logos. When the Father sees that you honor His written Word, He will consider you for the privilege of hearing His spoken Word. This spoken Word will sustain you.

It is, in fact, the Rhema upon which the life of man *must* be sustained, not earthly bread. In the Rhema words of the Logos to His disciples, "Man shall not live on bread alone, but on every Rhema that proceeds out of the mouth of God." (Matthew 4:4).

Every believer will be sustained, empowered, and enjoined to the cause of Christ by standing near, abiding in, and observing the Living Logos; by listening to the Rhema He speaks. These things take place at the Table of His presence. God wants to share His table with His people and break the bread of His Word with them. The table represents what God wants for every follower of Christ: intimate communion and the impartation of His life-giving word.

The Table of His Rest

The table of the Lord represents His rest. For as much as entering heaven will be permanent rest for His children, entering His tabernacle means rest for us in the days of this earthly life. For this reason, He invites us to recline at His table and receive His rest.

> Therefore, let us fear if, while a promise remains of
> entering His rest, any one of you may seem to have
> come short of it. For indeed we have had good news
> preached to us, just as they also; but the word they
> heard did not profit them, because it was not united
> by faith in those who heard. (Hebrews 4:1-3)

This is the place where our heavy burdens slip off, and He gives us a light, easy rest in Him. This is the place of quiet waters, where He restores our souls. Jesus said,

> Come to Me, all you who are weary and heavy-laden,
> and I will give you rest. Take My yoke upon you and
> learn from Me, for I am gentle and humble in heart,
> and You will find rest for your souls. For My yoke
> is easy and My burden is light. (Matthew 11:28-30)

But you must come to Him. You must "seek the Lord while He may be found" (Isaiah 55:6). It is not a strange mishap that you carry your own burden, heavy and strenuous, when you fail to come to Christ. It is an *obvious* failure to ignore the directive of Christ to "come to" Him. All *coming to Christ*, as it were, in the pursuit of God, in the devoted time of communion with Him, leads to the table of His presence. This table is one to which He invites us to come and find rest.

Indeed, Christ waits for you to open the door so that He may join you at the table. He says, "Behold, I stand at the door and knock; if anyone hears My voice and opens the door, I will come in to him and will dine with him and he with Me" (Revelation 3:20).

David knew this table. After describing the ways the Lord leads him toward rest and restoration, He said,

> Your rod and your staff, they comfort me. You prepare a table before me in the presence of my enemies. You have anointed my head with oil; my cup overflows. Surely goodness and lovingkindness will follow me all the days of my life, and I will dwell in the house of the Lord forever. (Psalm 23:4-6)

The woman with the alabaster jar knew this table. She knew that it was about depth, intimacy, and worship:

> And there was a woman in the city who was a sinner; and when she learned that He was reclining at the table in the Pharisee's house, she brought an alabaster vial of perfume, and standing behind Him at His feet, weeping, she began to wet His feet with her tears, and kept wiping them with the hair of her head, and kissing His feet and anointing them with the perfume. (Luke 7:37-38)

Jesus, when he got up from the table and washed the feet of His disciples, demonstrated that His intentions are for mutually exchanged love and devotion (See John 13:1-5). The table is not where a man only speaks to God; it is a place where God shows man the "full extent of His love." When we pour out the pure nard of our affections upon the Lord, He is honored. As His own, He turns and washes our feet. This is the incredible love of our God! So important is this ministry of Jesus to you, His disciples, that if you refuse it, he says you have no part with Him.

Therefore, do not rush by the table; there is no fast food in the temple of the Lord. This is an opportunity to listen to the Father, wait on Him as He renews your strength, and reinforce your love for Him above all else. This is where you learn to eat the bread of life, the Logos of the Father. It is the place where

> He humbled you and let you be hungry, and fed you with manna which you did not know, nor did your fathers know, that He might make you understand that man does not live by bread alone, but man lives by everything that proceeds out of the mouth of the Lord (Deuteronomy 8:3).

It is where you answer the door at which Jesus knocks, sit down with Him and rest, and lean back against Him. (See John 13:25)

Conclusion and Contemplation

Listen to His Word, and let your hearts burn within you. Elohim has prepared a table for you. Jesus is at the door knocking. Will you let Him in to partake in the bread of His Word?

Prayer of Commitment

Father, I thank You for Your table and for inviting me to it. Thank You that Christ's body, which is the bread of life, was broken for me so that I could be reconciled to You. Speak Your word to me, Lord; I'm listening. I love You and thank You for Your nearness.

Thank You for the cup of Your promises. I receive them by faith. Thank You for the blood of Jesus, shed for me for the remission of sin. I thank You for giving me pure hands and a clean heart through the work of Jesus on the Cross. In gratitude, I pour out the pure nard of my affection for You, a fragrant offering of love and devotion. Father, I quiet myself before You. I'm waiting for You, Lord. I have come to You, Father, teach me the fear of the Lord. Amen.

Discussion Questions

1. Why do people like to sit across from each other at tables and share a meal?
2. Why did God put a table in the temple?
3. Does God want you to experience His presence? What are two reasons you may not be experiencing His presence?
4. What was the purpose of breaking bread in Hebrew culture?
5. How is the Word of God like bread?
6. What is the intention of communication? Can communication with God be non-verbal?
7. What is the difference between Logos and Rhema?
8. What role does rest have at the table of the Lord? Should we take time to rest when we are seeking the Lord diligently?
9. Which do you prefer with God: results or relationship? Can you have both?

Chapter XV

GAZERS

Intercession In God's Furnace

Imperative
We must intercede with Jesus in the Most Holy Place.

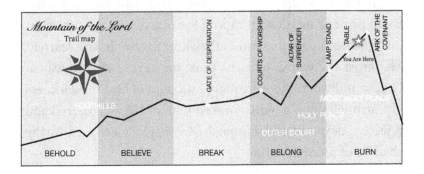

Lunar Eclipse
October 2014
Louisville, Kentucky

W e all set out on a walk through the neighborhood in hopes of locking our curious eyes on the earth-eclipsed moon. It eased upward out of the cityscape horizon amidst frothy clouds illuminated by its silvery light. Still too obscured to observe were the effects of the eclipse. So we turned our eyes to the pink and purple swaths of light that stretched across the sunsetting sky behind the grove of massive oaks in Shelby Park.

A crisp fifty-degree evening pushed a subtle breeze across our faces. Its breath carried the aroma of early autumn, filling the lungs, refreshing the soul, and making the dusky vista all the more intoxicating to behold. Our children exploded into dances and bounces and scurried six feet up the sides of trees in a celebration of beauty and family and the goodness of life.

The picturesque horizon darkened as evening turned to night, and we turned once again to the moon. Now, nearly free from the tenacious clouds which had seemingly been intent to conceal, it rose just above the spires of Sojourn Church. Earth's shadow lay upon the blood-orange orb, darkening its cause.

As I gawked upward, I supposed that humans across the Earth must be full of admiration; the marvels of creation must intrigue both Christian and atheist, both simple and learned. All across the world, humans must be staring wondrously at God's handiwork. But were they? I thought of how the darkness of Earth fell upon a blood-soaked Christ. He was marred and rejected, despised and vanquished; His glory eclipsed by the shadow of a sinful world.

Christ the Intercessor

An eclipse is an event in which three heavenly bodies interact, one going between the two others in perfect alignment. This creates an interesting sight for enthusiasts of celestial events, but also a rather poignant parallel for anyone who wishes to understand what is supposed to happen in the Most Holy Place.

Under the old covenant, the high priest would go into the Most Holy Place once a year to make *intercession* for the people of Israel. What is meant by "making intercession" is that he would literally "go between" the people and the Lord. He would sprinkle blood on the atonement cover of the Ark of the Covenant to make atonement and pray for God's mercy toward them. As the priest prayed and the incense filled the room, so did the glory and presence of Elohim.

But until Christ came, access to such a place of God's presence was limited. The Veil of the Temple, or curtain, was there to prohibit access to anyone but the high priest, and he was only able to go beyond it once a year on the Day of Atonement.

Christ's death created access to the Most Holy place for every believer. The significance of the rending of this curtain at the time of Christ's death on the cross is profound. Primarily that all believers now have access to the manifest presence of God in His throne room. This alone is a breathtaking reality. But we, like the priest, also have *authority* to go before Him on behalf of anyone in the world and pray. It is precisely this authority that gives us reason to come before His throne in confidence. (see Ephesians 3:12, Hebrews 4:16)

Christ's purpose in intercession was and is atonement; that is the justification of the sinner. When God's infinite, holy justice is stirred by the rebellion of men, He is inclined to issue punishment. But the point at which "mercy triumphs over judgment" (James 2:13) is where Christ appears on behalf of mankind to present His endurance of the Cross as the punishment our sins deserve (see Isaiah 53:5, Hebrews 12:2). In Christ's appearance, the requirement of holy justice is satisfied; thus, everyone who calls upon the name of the Lord will be saved. It's essential for clear understanding to take a look at what John had to say about Christ's work of intercessory atonement:

> My little children, I am writing these things to you
> so that you may not sin. And if anyone sins, we have
> *Parakletos* with the Father, Jesus Christ the righteous.
> (1 John 2:1, italics mine.)

Strong's Concordance offers two uses for the word "*parakletos*." In the verse above, it is translated as "advocate" in most English translations, which also means "intercessor," or one who goes between two parties as a mediator. Paul wrote to Timothy, "For there is one God, and one *Mediator* also between God and men, the man Jesus Christ" (1 Timothy 2:5). The implication is that Jesus would be defending us as would an attorney before the throne of God.

But the remission of sin is not the only function of justification. If it were, it *might* not convey the potential of relationship. The removal of offense does not guarantee the restoration of relationship in the social constructs of humanity. I will forgive you if you steal from me, but it might take a while before I trust you again. Therefore, Christ's work is broader than the remission of sin; it *also* includes the restoration of relationship.

Justification makes a person as right in God's sight as Jesus is. The work of justification renders a righteousness not of men but of God, "that which is through faith in Christ, the righteousness which comes from God on the basis of faith" (Philippians 3:9). Under the New Covenant, established by the death and resurrection of the Messiah, God will not look on us according to our iniquity, but according to the righteousness in Christ. For this reason, we have permanent, eternal access to the throne of grace, where we can confidently make our petitions before Almighty God.

And so the work of Christ before the throne of God is not just that He would hold back His wrath or even just forgive our sins. But it is that He completely removes our offense, clothes us in His righteousness, and makes us heirs with Him of His eternal blessings and favor. We now have as much a right to appear before the Father in confidence as Christ does. This is the work of Christ the Intercessor, and when we approach the throne of grace with confidence in this work, exhibiting faith in Christ in this way, He rewards us with His presence, power, and peace.

Solar Eclipse
August 2017
Paducah, Kentucky

We left Louisville early in the morning to go to Paducah to observe a total solar eclipse. Getting close to one of these happens seldom more than once in a person's life without having to execute major travel plans. Fortunately, we were very close to the optimal location to view the phenomenon.

We found a city park in Paducah with rolling grassy hills and lots of room to look upward. What we experienced was nothing short of magical. I felt as if I were receiving yet another gift of God's miraculous creation, but something I knew I would only see one time in all my life.

We used special viewing devices to observe the eclipse without injuring our eyes. Fortunately, there were no clouds in the sky; it was a totally blue-blazing August day. The moon was near the sun; it looked about an inch away. It was a typical daytime moon, white and pasty.

We made some friends as we shared the anticipation of the eclipse and noticed the moon beginning to creep into the sun's perimeter. The sky was still blue until then, but it began to turn gray. Traffic could be heard on a distant highway.

As the moon took a more significant portion of the sun's position, everything seemed to be slowing down, and it got quieter. Cars on the freeway pulled over and stopped, their engines silenced, stalled drivers gazing. The moon moved to the center of the sun.

For a moment, silence fell on the land as the light faded out. A sunset became equally visible on all points of the horizon. Birds returned to their nests and began their songs and activities. A cricket choir began its evening chorus, and cicadas initiated their dusk-time dronings. Our dog whimpered, confused.

An imposing moon had crept across the disc of the sun, gradually muting its effect, and nighttime fell upon us in the middle of the day. Time stood still and seemed to watch with us. Above us were stars innumerable and a silver ring of light bursting forth from deep in the dark sky.

Our dog blasted through the lawn, barking indirectly. Asher, Asiah, and I joined him and ran around in the grass shouting praises, leaping, and marveling at the divinely orchestrated spectacle until it took another fantastic turn.

The moon was situated ever so perfectly between the sun and the Earth, and the ring of fire became even on all sides. Then, in the 10 o'clock position, it produced a shimmering diamond!

The diamond ring effect of a solar eclipse only lasts a few seconds, but it felt like time stood still as we gazed. It was like the moment at a wedding when the groom slips a diamond ring on his bride. A quiet hush swept through the willows and across the darkened lawn. We stood in awe of our world and universe and of the gifts of a good and merciful God.

We gathered those in the park with us for prayer, and about 20 of us—strangers—stood in a circle, praying with tears and giving thanks to God for such an experience. As heartfelt prayers continued to bellow forth, my thoughts drifted. I wondered what the inhabitants of heaven must have felt when the victorious, resurrected Son of God appeared for the first time before the Throne of Glory on behalf of his bride, eclipsing wrath and placing on her hand a diamond ring to seal His covenant of love with her forever.

A Craftsman at His Side

God is working. He is a craftsman, and we are His workmanship. Access to the throne of grace is given for the meeting of our own needs, but also for the petitions we make, which will avail much in the lives of others. Christ has commanded us to go and make disciples, teaching them to obey Him. He has taught us that to do this effectively, we must pray, and He has commanded us to pray. But to fulfill commands in obedience, we must be driven by the love He has poured into our hearts through the Holy Spirit. Love makes a command an invitation as much, if not more than, an obligation. Therefore, God has extended His invitation to us to partner with Him in his work:

> Then I was the craftsman at His side. I was filled with delight day after day, always rejoicing in His presence, rejoicing in His whole world, and delighting in mankind. (Proverbs 8:30-31, NIV)

Paul was a co-laborer with Christ. He worked not only at preaching the gospel, making disciples, teaching sound doctrine, and establishing churches, but he also worked at prayer for all of these ends. He was a craftsman at the side of Christ. Consider his "struggle" for the churches:

> We proclaim Him, admonishing every man and teaching every man with all wisdom, so that we may present every man complete in Christ. For this purpose also I labor, striving according to His power, which mightily works within me. For I want you to know how great a struggle I have on your behalf and for those who are at Laodicea, and for all those who have not personally seen my face, that their hearts may be encouraged having been knit together in love, and attaining to all the wealth that comes from the full assurance of understanding, resulting in a true knowledge of God's mystery, that is, Christ Himself, in whom are hidden all the treasures of wisdom and knowledge. (Colossians 1:28-2:3)

Christ prayed for His disciples, but not only for them. He said, "I do not ask on behalf of these alone, but for those also who believe in Me through their word" (John 17:20). If Christ "always lives to make intercession" (Hebrews 7:25), and if He "interceded for the transgressors" (Isaiah 53:12), then He is interceding now as you read this. He, like Moses, is perpetually lifting up holy hands in prayer that we might be victorious, and He is delighting in the whole world and delighting in mankind. He continues to pray for those who will believe through the message we proclaim.

To engage in this ministry of intercession is a tremendous privilege, and a "serious call." William Law, in his 18th Century landmark work on devotion, *A Serious Call to a Devout and Holy Life*, describes the effects of intercession like this:

> "For a frequent intercession with God, earnestly beseeching Him to forgive the sins of all mankind, to bless them with His providence, enlighten them with His Spirit and bring them to everlasting happiness, is the divinest exercise that the heart of man can be engaged in. When therefore you have once habituated your heart to a serious performance of this holy intercession, you have done a great deal to render it incapable of spite and envy, and to make it naturally delight in the happiness of all mankind."

To partner with Christ, a craftsman at His side, and to make an impact that will have an eternal effect, we must do the vital work of intercessory prayer. But there is a benefit to leaving our comforts at the closet door, crucifying our flesh, and going down to our knees on behalf of others. That benefit is intimacy with the Holy Spirit.

The Altar of Prayer

Beyond the Veil, in the Most Holy Place, was the Altar of Incense. The incense burned on this altar represents prayer in the eternal temple of heaven. The priest would also take coals from the altar of sacrifice, carry them with incense into the Most Holy Place, and put them on the Altar of Incense. This would fill the room with aromatic smoke to protect the priest from dying. As priests of the New Covenant, every believer can take the fire of the Holy Spirit and lift up prayers before the Ark of the Covenant in the Most Holy Place, or the place of God's throne. These prayers rise like incense, filling the room with the sweet aroma of God's presence and filling the golden bowls with prayers that touch the heart of God.

> And when He had taken the book, the four living creatures and the twenty-four elders fell down before the Lamb, each one holding a harp and golden bowls full of incense, which are the prayers of the saints. (Revelation 5:8)

> Another angel came and stood at the altar, holding a golden censer; and much incense was given to him, so that he might add it to the prayers of all the saints on the golden altar which was before the throne. And the smoke of the incense, with the prayers of the saints, went up before God out of the angel's hand. Then the angel took the censer and filled it with the fire of the altar, and threw it to the Earth; and there followed peals of thunder and sounds and flashes of lightning and an earthquake. (Revelation 8:3-5)

> He shall take a firepan full of coals of fire from upon the altar before the Lord and two handfuls of finely ground sweet incense, and bring it inside the veil. He shall put the incense on the fire before the Lord, that the cloud of incense may cover the mercy seat that is on the ark of the testimony, otherwise he will die. (Leviticus 16:12-13)

Here is a lesson I would like to convey from this focus on altars, incense, and fire: we cannot effectively pray unless we carry coals of fire from the Altar of Surrender with us into the Most Holy Place and place them on the Altar of Prayer. Incense needs to burn for it to rise up and fill the room with its smokey aroma. For the Levitical priest, this incense was intercessory in nature, protecting the priest from death. This is the kind of prayer being offered by Christ, who ever lives to intercede for us. To be a craftsman at his side, we must offer this kind of prayer, too.

But if you carry only incense, it won't burn; and *you* won't burn for God. All the preceding efforts made in this mountaineering expedition were to deepen this intimacy with the Holy Spirit, kindling His fire. Rending your heart, breaking up hardened ground, surrendering every aspect of your life to Him, asking the Father to fill you with the Seven-fold Spirit, breaking bread at the table with Him, and listening to hear His voice, are every bit as much a part of effectively engaging in the work of Christ, the intercessor.

The Father does not want to listen to prayers from a cold heart. He wants heat. He wants fire on the altar! He wants you to blaze with passion for Him and for this passion to be the reason you want to be beside Him in his work of intercession. The craftsman at the side of Christ is always "delighting in his presence" (Proverbs 8:30, NIV).

For this reason, it is important to note that if you do not sense deep fellowship with the Holy Spirit, His energy working powerfully within you, you can retreat to any point in the temple model to re-engage examination & confession at the gate, thanksgiving and praise in the courts, surrender at the altar, or communion and worship in the Holy Place. But if your fire goes out, your incense will stop burning, the smoke will dissipate, and your intercessory prayer time will have become a religious exercise—producing only death.

I will often fluctuate between intensely focused worship and adoration and moments of intercessory petition for others to keep the flame burning hot in me for the Person of the Holy Spirit. We can not become so infatuated with results in the purposes of God that we lose sight of our relationship with the Person of God. This is nowhere more true than in the work of intercessory prayer.

With this critical basis for prayer locked in the mind, let us examine several essential principles of intercessory prayer. I want to be quick to say there are many principles of prayer. I will only point out a few that have been instrumental in my prayer life. I recommend much reading and studying of the lives of the people of history who best exercised the call to intercessory prayer. Ultimately, the Holy Spirit will teach you to pray as you immerse yourself in the Word of God and in His presence; you simply must make time and be hungry for Him.

Prophetic Prayer

Prophecy can be broken into two categories: general and specific. General prophecy is the use of the authority of Christ in the believer to proclaim the truth of God's word in a manner that benefits others. This can be spoken directly to people, as in preaching, teaching, and evangelism, or it can be spoken before the throne of God, as in the ministry of intercessory prayer.

Specific prophecy is to proclaim revealed truth to a person or group of people about themselves or their current or future situations. A "word of knowledge" (1 Corinthians 12:8) is a prophetic announcement by which the Holy Spirit enables a person to have knowledge of a situation that they could have by no other means. This may come in the form of past events, present circumstances, or future events. Detailed instruction on spiritual gifts is beyond the scope of this text; for such a study, I recommend *The Gifts and Ministries of the Holy Spirit* by Lester Sumrall.

For the purposes of intercessory prayer, we will focus on the use of *general prophecy*. It is wise to build a foundation and practice of proclaiming the written word of God over others and petitioning God according to His written word. Prophetic proclamation finds its roots in the fact that "Death and life are in the power of the tongue" (Proverbs 18:21). We can literally speak life into the lives and circumstances of others, "I said to you… 'Live!'" (Ezekiel 16:6). It also follows the nature of "God, who gives life to the dead and calls into being that which does not exist" (Romans 4:17), and God has acted on, and has expected His people to act on, this principle throughout Scripture. Consider this example of His expectations in the message given to Isaiah, "Saying to those who are bound, 'Go forth,' to those who are in darkness, 'show yourselves.'" (Isaiah 49:9).

Jesus demonstrates this use of faith and speech when He commands the wind and the waves to be still. His question to His disciples, "Where is your faith?" (Luke 8:25), implies His expectation that they would have implemented the same use of faith and speech. Jesus also directly tells them,

> And Jesus answered saying to them, "Have faith in God. Truly I say to you, whoever **says** to this mountain, 'be taken up and cast into the sea,' and does not

doubt in his heart, but believes that what he **says** is going to happen, it will be granted to him. Therefore I say to you, all things for which you pray and ask, believe that you have received them, and they will be granted you." (Mark 11:22-24, emphasis mine)

The use of such prophetic utterances can be seen in the lives of many of the early church believers who spoke to people's circumstances in the authority of Christ, bringing forth instant change. Such changes were quantified in physical healing (Acts 3:6), death (Acts 5:9), blindness (Acts 13:11), and deliverance (Acts 16:18).

All believers can function in general prophesy so long as their hearts are right and they are proceeding from the place of communion and intimacy with the Holy Spirit. Beyond these prerequisites, they need no more than the testimony of Jesus, for "the testimony of Jesus is the spirit of prophecy" (Revelation 19:10). The apostle Paul stated, "But one who prophesies speaks to men for edification and exhortation and consolation." (1 Corinthians 14:3). According to Paul, every believer should eagerly desire spiritual gifts, especially the gift prophesy. Because the gifts are enabled by the Holy Spirit, this furthermore establishes the importance of continual intimacy with Him. Ask Him to give you prophetic utterances in your prayers, and then begin with truths from Scripture, by faith, proclaiming them over the subjects of your prayers.

The following are some examples of how you might pray scripture over people as you intercede for them:

- Prophetic prayer for someone who is lost—
  - Psalm 34:14
    - **Proclamation:** *In the name of Jesus, I say, "turn from evil, repent, humble yourself before the mighty hand of God."*
    - **Petition:** *Father, I pray that You would help (insert name) to turn from evil, to come to repentance, and humble himself before You.*
  - Isaiah 49:9
    - **Proclamation:** *In the name of Jesus, I "Say to the captives 'come out' and to those in darkness, 'be free!'"*
    - **Petition:** *Father, I pray that You would now speak this word over (insert name) by Your Holy Spirit: "Come out, Be free!" Oh, God deliver (insert name) from the evil one, from captivity. You are the Great Deliverer.*
  - Psalm 32:4-5
    - **Proclamation:** *In the name of Jesus, I say, "Let the hand of God be heavy upon (insert name). Let his strength be sapped as in the heat of summer. Confess! Acknowledge sin!"*
    - **Petition:** *Father, please be merciful to (insert name), move Your hand upon him, and bring him under Your conviction. Help him find the desperation of heart to cry out to You and be forgiven. Reconcile him to You by Your mercy.*

- *Prophetic prayer for someone who is a believer—*
  - Ephesians 5:17
    - **Proclamation:** *In the Name of Jesus Christ, I say, "be filled with the Spirit!"*

- **Petition**: *Father, I pray that You would pour out Your Holy Spirit on (insert name), in the name of Jesus. Bring your fire into their hearts, your conviction upon their minds, and Your power into their life.*
- Ephesians 3:16, 6:10
  - **Proclamation**: *In the Name of Jesus Christ, I say, "Be strong in the Lord!"*
  - **Petition**: *Father, I pray that (insert name) will be filled with power in their inner being in order that Christ might dwell in their heart through faith. I pray that they might have power together with all the saints to grasp the height, depth, width, and breadth of the love of Christ and that they might know this love that surpasses knowledge (Ephesians 3:14-19).*
  - **Proclamation**: *In the Name of Jesus Christ, I say, "Be filled with the knowledge of God's will."*
  - **Petition**: *Father, I pray that You would reveal your will to (insert name) through all spiritual wisdom and understanding (Colossians 1:9)..*

I cannot over-emphasize the importance of engaging your entire spirit, soul, and body in the work of prophetic prayer. If you are quiet and mousy, it may reflect fear and lack of desperation. Activate your voice with confidence, boldness, and faith: *believe!* Activate your body by standing with hands heavenward or kneeling with fists pounding the floor: *believe!* Do not be timid in the use of God's word when approaching God's throne. He expects you to come boldly and with confidence, with *belief!*

Creative Prayer

In his book *Intercessory Prayer*, Dutch Sheets presents a vital principle of the work of the Holy Spirit. By looking at the original language in several passages of Scripture, the Holy Spirit is seen brooding over, bringing forth, and birthing new things. He states:

> What the Holy Spirit was doing in Genesis when He "brought forth" or "gave birth to" the Earth and the world is exactly what He wants to do through our prayers in bringing forth sons and daughters. He wants to "go forth" and "hover around" individuals, releasing His tremendous power to convict, break bondages, bring revelation and draw them to Himself to cause the new birth or new creation in them. Yes, the Holy Spirit wants to birth through us.

In prayer, I have used this many times, asking the Holy Spirit to overshadow (brood over) a lost person and give them the new birth, forming Christ in them. I have asked the Holy Spirit to bring forth His gifts, ministries, and fruit in other people by hovering or moving over them. This is an essential partnership with the Master Craftsman, for He is by nature a creator, and we can be beside Him as He creates new realities for those around us.

Strategic Prayer

One of the best strategies in prayer I've seen comes from Dr. Yonggi Cho, pastor of the largest congregation of Christians in the world. Dr. Cho has shown the importance of asking God for opened doors.

> There are doors to nations and ethnic groups that can be opened. Once the door is opened, they are able to receive faith and believe. Luke wrote, "On arriving there, they gathered the church together and reported all that God had done through them and how he had opened a door of faith to the gentiles" (Acts 14:27). Going through a door of opportunity means that we face spiritual opposition from the principalities and powers that keep nations from hearing and responding to the gospel. Paul wrote, "Because a great door for effective work has opened to me, and there are many who oppose me" (1 Corinthians 16:9). How do we get the doors of faith and opportunity opened? We have seen that Christ must open the door. However, God has made us members of His body. This means that, as the Head, He has chosen to function through His body on Earth. So it takes prayers of intercession to stand against the spiritual forces keeping the doors shut. Once the prayers break through, Christ can open the door, and an entire city, nation, or race can be saved.

I have since prayed almost daily that the Lord would open a door for me to share the love of Christ with someone in my going out. I have, as a result, had many "divine appointments" with people who needed prayer or to hear of the hope I have in Christ.

In this way, I have prayed for missionaries and ministries around the globe to have an open door to proclaim the Gospel and bring people to Christ. You also can do for your missionary and evangelist friends what Paul requested be done for him:

> Devote yourselves to prayer, keeping alert in it with an attitude of thanksgiving; praying at the same time for us as well, that God will open up to us a door for the word, so that we may speak forth the the mystery of Christ, for which I have also been imprisoned; that I may make it clear in the way that I ought to speak. (Philippians 4:2-3)

The Prayer of Faith

Much has been taught about what it means to pray in faith. I will share with you the lesson I learned from a Roman.

> When Jesus had entered Capernaum, a centurion came to him, asking for help. "Lord," he said, "my servant lies at home paralyzed and in terrible suffering." Jesus said to him, "I will go and heal him." The centurion replied, "Lord, I do not deserve to have you come under my roof. But just say the word, and my servant will be healed. For I myself am a man under authority, with soldiers under me. I tell this one, "Go," and he goes, and that one "come," and he comes.. I say to my servant, "do this," and he does it. When Jesus heard this, he was astonished and said to those following him, "I tell you to the truth,

I have not found anyone in Israel with such great faith." (Matthew 8:5-10)

I have used this Centurions words to engage my faith before the throne of God. I have prayed, "Father, if You would just say the word, it will be done as You say." At this point, I will offer the words that would accomplish His will in a specific situation. I would say, "Lord, speak *justice* over the situation in which children are being exploited, sold into slavery, and abused. Lord, speak the word *justice! Justice!*" I have also asked the Lord to speak "*healing*," "*deliverance*," or to "*Expose*" the evil deeds of the wicked. By speaking the word with the Lord, I am a craftsman at His side, participating in the work of changing realities through prayer.

A Clear Conscience

The conscience has a role in the prayer of faith. Godliness in daily living and speech provides a person with a clear conscience. In the same way a person with injured legs will not be able to run, a person with an injured conscience will not be able to pray in faith. Of course, we should always come to God, even if our conscience is injured—*especially if it is so.* And he will heal us, but we will not likely be able to climb as high with this injury until it is healed. The healing of the conscience can take days, weeks, months, or longer. This time requirement for healing remains a mystery and in the wisdom of God's sovereignty. But we must present ourselves to Him in desperation if we have a walk speckled with compromise.

This becomes one of the reasons it is so important to walk by the Spirit and remain in Christ. Jesus said, "If you abide in

Me, and My words abide in you, ask whatever you wish, and it will be done for you." (John 15:7). Honoring and obeying the words and commands of Jesus is liberating and empowering and preserves a clear conscience. Peter understood that maintaining a clear conscience before God was connected to the effectiveness of prayers when he admonished husbands to be considerate toward their wives "so that your prayers will not be hindered" (1 Peter 3:7).

A clear conscience is related to single-mindedness or an unswerving commitment to a particular manner of life. James warned that this would hinder prayer when he said,

> "But he must ask in faith without any doubting, for the one who doubts is like the surf of the sea, driven and tossed by the wind. For that man ought not to expect that he will receive anything from the Lord, being a double-minded man, unstable in all his ways." (James 1:6-8)

Thus it can be seen that, though the primary cause for obedience to the Word of the Lord is because He is Lord, a secondary—and vital—other reason is the preservation of a clean conscience for the purpose of living by and praying in faith. You will find that the more you walk in obedience to Christ, maintaining a clear conscience, the greater the clarity of your cause in prayer, and the more consistent will be your victory on behalf of those held by the forces of darkness.

Breaking for others in Travail

Jeremiah described writhing in pain over Israel (see Jeremiah 4:19). Paul stated that he was in the pains of child-birth (see Galatians 4:19). The literal translation of the word Jeremiah used "chew," which in Hebrew means to *writhe in pain*, especially as in childbirth. Weeping, burning in the core, or ago-nizing over someone for their victory or salvation is what the word travail means in the context of prayer. This is the exact translation of the term the Apostle Paul uses.

When driven by the Holy Spirit, Tears for others produce the proper attitude toward their situation. We are partnering with the Master Craftsman in His work, and part of His work is to operate from a heart of compassion. Compassion is not just a feeling of sorrow for someone; it literally means to "suffer with" someone. The situation of a person lost and without hope in Christ is absolutely dire, but we miss its gravity in our worlds of distraction, comfort, and self-interest. To take the time it requires to acquaint ourselves with the grief Christ feels over a dying world will properly situate us to join Him in His inter-cession for the transgressors:

> As a result of the anguish of His soul, He will see it
> and be satisfied; by His knowledge the Righteous
> One, My Servant, will justify the many, as He will
> bear their iniquities. (Isaiah 53:11)

I must engage my body for my soul to know I am serious. I cannot recline in my Lazy Boy and mumble some soft-spoken words to the Lord about a person on their way to eternal fire.

I must get on my knees, literally pound the floor with my fist and say to the Lord,

> *"Unless you move over me by your Holy Spirit I will not be able to pray for this person in such a way as to see them changed! Unless you move over this person to convict them of their sins they will die in them! Oh God (pounding the floor) move over them now! Bring your heavy hand of conviction upon them NOW!"*

Someone once said, "we must work as if it all depends on us and pray as if it all depends on God." I believe we must do both as if it all depends on us and do both as if it all depends on God. Here's why: intercessory prayer is work. Far from casual in His approach, listen to how Jesus prayed:

> In the days of His humanity, He offered up both prayers and pleas with loud crying and tears to the One able to save Him from death, and He was heard because of his devout behavior. (Hebrews 5:7)

As I pray in this way, the Holy Spirit will begin to stir in my heart, and I will sense a deep burning travail inside of me. I must often be willing to persist in this way for long periods before the outpouring comes, but He always comes. I will often begin to heave and weep, moved by the Holy Spirit's own feeling toward the person.

Praying from the core, or from the heart, is essential to moving the object of your prayers to their "next place" in God's plan for them. By that, I mean that sometimes we need to pray for a person to meet with circumstances that will bring them to a place of humility so that they will listen to the Gospel. The Gospel is the power of God unto salvation (see Romans 1:16). We cannot only pray for the lost. They must hear the message of truth that will set them free. For them to really hear or have "ears that hear," prayer must precede preaching. On other occasions, perhaps we are praying for a person to repent of the sin they are bound to or be set free from demonic forces which have overtaken them. Similarly, these scenarios will require diligent attention to prayer for us to engage them effectively in the ministry of the Gospel.

We must have the burning of the Holy Spirit, who prays FOR us—in our place—by praying THROUGH us—in our hearts (see Romans 8:26). Without the Holy Spirit praying from deep in our bowels, we cannot expect to move our subject toward victory. Praying without the tangible, manifest presence of the Holy Spirit is equivalent to praying with no intention of having your prayers answered. If you want prayers answered, pay the price. The price of answered prayer is time and desperation, and if you are willing to lay those on the table, He will bring you more than you expected.

Praying through to Victory

I have many times prayed this way before preaching. I was not praying any longer over what to say. That was given and organized in my notes and spirit. I was praying, interceding, for the hearers to receive the word into good soil and immediately begin to produce fruit. I have never been a church pastor, expected to preach at least weekly, if not more, and I am sure that burden is, at times, tough to carry. But when I have preached or taught, I have, at times, seen nothing short of revival as the result of praying in this way in preparation. My stomach burned with the passion of the Holy Spirit for His people, and my face felt as if it would explode off of my head under the crushing weight of His glory, manifest in the room as I prayed.

This type of praying is excellent for the crucifixion of a person's flesh. I have come from these times of prayer with a great sense of the presence of God over me, no appetite for selfish pursuits, and madness for the advancement of the Gospel.

I had once been praying for some new disciples in another country. I knew that they still were dealing with deep bondage to cultural, relational, and spiritual things. So I went before the Lord in intercessory prayer. I spent an hour in fellowship with the Holy Spirit, laying my life upon His altar and surrendering, standing before His Lamp Stand and worshipping who He is, sitting at His table in the rest He gives. With a deep sense of His presence and a burning communion with Him, I went into the Holy of Holies with fire for the altar of prayer.

What I experienced was *nothing*. Literally *nothing*. I paced back and forth in my bedroom for three-quarters of an hour, re-fixing my mind on the Lord and his purposes when it would drift onto other thoughts. Still nothing. Then I fell to the floor and cried out, "help me! I'm desperate and unable to pray!" I began to pound the floor, crying out for these new believers who needed victory. And then it came.

The power of the Holy Spirit came into the room so strongly that I thought I would die under the weight of His presence. It was as if I had laid hold of a bare 220-volt hot wire. Electrifying. From my mouth, prayers flowed and shot upward with authority and focus, making me feel like I was standing *in* heaven. It was agonizing bliss with zero influence from the flesh or the devil and pure Spirit-empowered craftsmanship. My mind was absolutely fixed on Jesus and His work. I can describe it in no other way. And so for another hour I prayed and prayed, I wept and grieved with the Lord for them, I shouted and proclaimed His will over them.

I continued in this way until out of heaven came a song into my heart that I have never heard and do not remember now. I only remember that I could not disengage from the song as it flowed out of me like the waters of a mighty river. I sang and sang and sang.

Then I heard the voice of the Holy Spirit say to me, "this is what victory sounds like." I knew that I had prayed all the way through to victory and that when we went to minister to these disciples, we would see the power of God move and bring forth fruit that glorifies the Father.

The interaction with these disciples that followed was supposed to take place over the period of one hour, but instead, it went on for four hours. God gave specific words of knowledge to my wife and me, gave authority to our message, and gave us the power to set free individuals who were still dealing with lies and bondage, from which they had the right to be free in Christ.

We were given the testimony over the following days that the freedom these disciples felt was as if they were floating, being carried by the Holy Spirit, and finally able to breathe and live with joy.

Many seasoned teachers of prayer have said that we must have the object of our prayers so fixed in our minds that we are like Jacob, wrestling with no chance of retreat until we know the blessing has been given. This is my experience with praying in faith. Persist until you know you have prayed through and laid hold of the victory.

It is precisely for this type of praying that we must be intricately united with the Holy Spirit in his ministry of intercession. You cannot know that you have prayed "through" to victory without the witness of the Holy Spirit in your heart.

Reese Howells once prayed for two hours for the provision of a certain amount of money. He told his friend, who also was praying, that he had not *prayed through* and that they should pray for another two hours. After considerable time, Howells said to his friend, "you don't need to pray anymore; I am *through*." And later that week, Howells received the donation without solicitation, except before the throne in heaven.

According to Howells' biographer and personal friend, Norman Grubb, in his book entitled *Reese Howells: Intercessor*,

> Mr. Howells would often speak of "the gained position of intercession," and its truth is evident on many occasions in his life. The price is paid, the obedience is fulfilled, the inner wrestlings and groaning take their full course, and then "the word of the Lord comes." The weak channel is clothed with authority by the Holy Spirit and can speak the word of deliverance. "Greater works" (John 14:12) are done. Not only this but a new position in grace is gained and maintained, although even then, that grace can only be appropriated and applied in each instance under the guidance of the Spirit.

In this way, you can emerge from your time of prayer with confidence that the Lord will do what He has promised to do. This is very important, not only for you to stay in the place of prayer until you have received the victory, but that you walk in an attitude of faith that God is faithful to His promises.

The Heart of the Most Holy Place

This, my friends, is the heart of the Most Holy Place. It is not the place for you to focus on your own walk with God, your own needs, or you at all. It is the place of intercession, serving Elohim on behalf of others. The upward call of God in Christ Jesus leads to this pinnacle place. It is the most remarkable manner in which anyone person can serve another, that of the role of intercessory prayer before the fiery throne of God. Every mountaineer must dream of this place of summits, this zenith of zeal, and this high altar of God—and must go there at all costs.

When you are intent upon being broken before the Lord at the Gate, in the courts, and in the Holy Place, you will come to such clarity in the Lord's heart for others and will be able to stand in the Holy of Holies. There is no place for thoughts of self there; you are only in the Holy of Holies to make intercession for others. For it is there that you delight day after day in his presence, delighting in mankind and rejoicing in his whole world.

> In the same way, the Spirit also helps our weakness; for we do not know how to pray as we should, but the Spirit himself intercedes for us with groaning too deep for words. (Romans 8:26)

Conclusion and Contemplation

Jesus burns at the core of His being for us in intercessory prayer. He stands before the Father in our defense. Will you stand before the Father, with Jesus, on behalf of another, until you burn with Him…for them?

Prayer of Commitment

Father, I want to be a craftsman at Your side, working along with the Holy Spirit of Christ in the ministry of intercessory prayer. Help me conquer my flesh and find personal victory so that I might come into the Holy of Holies on behalf of others and find public victory. I need You, Lord! I am often reluctant to pray hard, offer myself as a living sacrifice, and follow You up the mountain to this place of intercession. Help me keep my walk pure so that nothing will hinder my prayers. Amen.

Discussion Questions

1. How is an eclipse a picture of intercessory prayer?
2. What is Christ eclipsing as He stands before the Father in our defense?
3. What does it mean to be a craftsman at the side of Jesus?
4. Can we stand before the Father in defense of others? What is this called?
5. What does it mean to carry coals into the Most Holy Place? Why is this important?
6. Describe general and specific prophecy. Will Holy Spirit-inspired prophesy ever contradict Scripture?
7. How can we engage in prophetic prayer?
8. Why did the centurion say, "If You will but say the word, my servant will be healed." How can we use this as a model for praying in faith?
9. Why is it important to engage my physical body in prayer?

Chapter XVI

BLAZERS
Burning with the Fire of God

Imperative
We must burn for God on his fiery mountain.

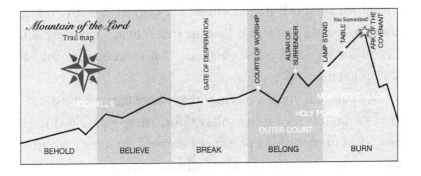

Mountain of the Lord
Trail map

GATE OF DESPERATION — COURTS OF WORSHIP — ALTAR OF SURRENDER — LAMP STAND — TABLE — You Summited! — ARK OF THE COVENANT

FOOTHILLS — MOST HOLY PLACE — HOLY PLACE — OUTER COURT

BEHOLD — BELIEVE — BREAK — BELONG — BURN

Campfire in the Gorge
November 2019

The gathering of the gear and subsequent distribution into backpacks was a challenge. I would need everyone to carry some weight as we conveyed our food and housing into the wilderness. Dads get to carry the most weight. And after a stop at the grocery, we packed it all up and drove to Red River Gorge.

The Subaru crawled along a narrow road, following the contour of the steep slope that spilled into the valley. It was exhilarating to drive a quarter-mile in a one-way tunnel through one of the mountains. I worked at keeping my eyes on the treacherous turns, but nature's allure was magnetizing. Eventually, we arrived at a parking lot that served access to the Sheltowee Trace, a 330-mile trail that courses through Kentucky and Tennessee.

The trail was parallel to a river full of giant rocks, from which people hopped into the water during the warmer months. By a narrow suspension-style walk bridge, we crossed the river and went back in the other direction until we could see our car again.

We ventured up the side of a mountain and away from the river, back down again, and around toward the north along a smaller creek. We crossed that creek several times as the trail continued alongside it, deeper into the canyon. The nice thing about following a stream is that the trail remains relatively flat, except for logs and other obstacles that sometimes must be shimmied over.

We passed incredibly scenic areas where massive moss-covered monoliths lay on the valley floor. These giants had long ago fallen from the lofty precipices above us. In some instances, trees grew from atop the giant stones, having sprouted in a sandy crevice and then sent their roots ten to twelve feet down around the stone surface to the soil below. The trail wove its way between these rock-top trees, forming a crooked hallway and a vivid picture of determination.

We found what we believed would be the perfect place to set up camp. It was by the creek, well off the path, and in a grove of sycamores whose trunks were white with patches of beige bark peeling away. We dropped our packs and breathed. The brisk autumn air with its aroma was familiar and surged into our vessels with meaning. It was almost nighttime when the fire was crackling and the tent was pitched.

Sweet potatoes wrapped in foil grew hot beneath the glowing coals. I could smell them and couldn't wait to eat one. While they cooked, we roasted brats and munched on snacks. The fire grew warm as the night grew colder, and we eventually broke out some S'mores. The hilarity of the ensuing moments escalated in direct proportion to the sugar intake and caused everyone to become slap-happy. It turns out that "dad jokes" are funny after all.

The fire flickered on the faces of my children. They smiled and waited for the next thing I would say, and then they laughed and laughed and laughed. Joy seemed to emanate more than heat from the flames around which we sat. I thought of the many times I had stood before the Lord and His fire, my heart warmed by His immeasurable love, my soul aflame with His purposes. I was glad to be in the mountains.

It was a frigid night and difficult to sleep, but the person with Charly in their sleeping bag was the warmest. Charly is our wiry-haired Terrier that made sure no squirrels, raccoons, or opossums came near our tent.

In the morning crisp, I renewed the smoldering fire ring with fresh wood, and the flame burned again. It's easy to start a fire when the coals are hot. We made coffee and oatmeal while red potatoes softened under the heat.

Hiking around the camp area, we found that the sky behind the sycamores was even bluer. Sunlight angled through the shifting branches, and as they swayed, it bounced on and off our faces. Leaves blew off their limbs, fluttering and wisping down past our faces and onto the ground.

I held Anne Marie's hand and was happy.

The Purposes of Fire

Why does the Bible speak so much of fire? Fire fell from heaven, burned in a bush without consuming it, and would eventually be that by which Christ would baptize his followers. Fire purges, purifies and empowers. God is a Consuming Fire. Fire is His nature, and fire is to be ours, too.

One of the primary intentions of this book is to drive home the idea that you *must* carry fire from the altar with you *all the time*. You can burn hot for God and stay hot (see Revelation 3:15). When your coals are hot, fires spread. You are the temple of the Holy Spirit (see 1 Corinthians 3:16 and 6:19), and you are that temple's priest (see 1 Peter 2:9, Revelation 1:6). You are a priest with a commission:

> The fire on the altar shall be kept burning on it. It shall not go out, but the priest shall burn wood on it every morning; and he shall lay out the burnt offering on it, and offer up in smoke the fat portions of the peace offerings on it. Fire shall be kept burning continually on the altar; it is not to go out. (Leviticus 6:12-13)

God wishes that we would be hot (see Revelation 3:15). What could He mean except that the fire of His Holy Spirit would burn on the altar of our hearts—and not go out?

Sometimes when we say someone is "on fire" for God, we mean they are very excited, deeply moved, and can't stop telling what God has done for them. Peter and John had this fire before the rulers and elders of the people, who called them into account for speaking about Jesus. They said, "Whether it is right in the eyes of God to give heed to you rather than to God, you be the judge; for we cannot stop speaking about what we have seen and heard" (Acts 4:19-20). Flames had recently been visible above their heads. They were quite literally "on fire" for Jesus.

The demoniac who had a legion of demons in him was delivered, healed, and restored to his right mind. "And he went away and began to proclaim in Decapolis what great things Jesus had done for him; and everyone was amazed" (Mark 5:20). He was aflame for Christ.

We want that fire of the early church. This lost and dying world wants it, too. God's use of fire is multifaceted. It both purges and empowers. Indeed, fire awaits everyone. Those who are aflame now will be at home with the Consuming Fire. But where is this fire now? In his classic, *Why Revival Tarries,* Leonard Ravenhill says this about fire,

> The prophet Moses was called by fire. Elijah called down fire. Elisha made fire. Micah prophesied fire. John the Baptist cried, "He shall baptize you with the Holy Ghost and with fire." Jesus said, "I am come to send fire on the earth." If we were as scared to miss fire baptism as we were to miss water baptism, we would have a flaming Church and another Pentecost. The "old nature" may dodge the water baptism, but it is destroyed in the fire baptism, for he shall "burn up the chaff with unquenchable fire." Until they were fire-purged, the miracle-working disciples who beheld His resurrection glory, were held back from ministering the Cross.

Let us fear this life without fire, that we may not fear eternal death in fire. Let us know this flame, yearning for its work in and through us. Let us be driven by an intense want for the roaring inferno of holy fire burning on the altars of our hearts. A baptism of fire is waiting for each of us. It must be kindled and then kindled again—morning after morning, night after night. Dr. John Henry Jowitt knew how to kindle this fire:

> Let us muse upon the King in His beauty, let us commune more with His loveliness, let us dwell more in the secret place, and the unspeakable glory of His countenance shall create within us that enthusiastic passion which shall be to us our baptism of fire, a fire in which everything un-Christian shall be utterly consumed away. (Kennedy, *The Best of John Henry Jowett*)

We have much to do: a great war to wage—and win, souls to snatch from hellfire and fill with holy fire, and we cannot do it without fire on the altar.

Fire Empowers the Work of the Lord

When you set out to share the gospel, people will rain on your parade. For this reason, you need fire. You need to be like a forest fire, immune to even the most torrential downpours of discouragement. But you need fire, not just to mitigate the enemy's work against you; you need it to light up the people with whom you are sharing the gospel. They must also be baptized in the Holy Spirit and in His fire.

Consider the constant imprisonments, persecutions, and spiritual resistance faced by the early church. How could they endure so much? Why were they impossible to dissuade, even shedding their own blood and losing their lives for Christ?

In his book *Fire on the Horizon*, Winkey Pratney brought us a picture of God's additional purposes in setting his people ablaze.

> There is one fire that God will never forbid you—the fire of His presence in your innermost being to tell a cold and dying world that His truth and His mercy are still available and that Jesus is alive.

To speak to demonized, demon-controlled, or otherwise demon-deceived people, you need fire. You need a fire that will instantly consume the cords of bondage and deceit, setting men free. You need the fire that makes the hills melt like wax, and this fire comes through the presence of the Lord (See Psalm 97:3-4).

When you share the gospel, you are not trying to communicate concepts to win a person's affirmation that you are a skilled orator. If you do that, they will put their faith in you, not Jesus. As a result, this kind of gospel preaching leaves men in chains and on a collision course with judgment fire. You need the breath of God in you so that when you speak, you are a fire-breathing furnace of fury unleashing the wrath of God on the demonic hordes that hold people hostage. Paul presented the gospel with the fire of the Holy Spirit:

> And my message and my preaching were not in persuasive words of wisdom, but in demonstration of

the Spirit and of power, so that your faith would not
rest on the wisdom of men, but on the power of God.
(1 Corinthians 2:4-5)

Again, he states, "For our gospel did not come to you in word only, but also in power and in the Holy Spirit and with full conviction" (1 Thessalonians 1:5). What was Paul's recipe for this kind of living and preaching? "Do not *"sbennumi"* the Spirit (1 Thessalonians 5:19). This Greek word means to extinguish. Think Fire extinguisher, only Holy Spirit fire.

To do the work of the Father as the Son did, you need the *gift* of the Holy Spirit, promised to those who obey (see Acts 5:32). You also need the *gifts* of the Holy Spirit, given to those who believe as the Spirit determines (see 1 Corinthians 12:11), in conjunction with our eager desire and pursuit (see 1 Corinthians 14:1). And these gifts are maintained and developed by the flame of the Holy Spirit (see 2 Timothy 1:6), which is cultivated and fanned by you and me. Get your fan out and make flames in your soul, and "Do not grieve the Holy Spirit of God, by who you were sealed for the day of redemption" (Ephesians 4:30).

This fire, however, is not your emotions. It is not your shouting and dancing to emphasize the 5 points of your sermon. Preachers who shout and dance may have a fire, or they may have a farce. Fire burns deeply within and presents outwardly in different ways. This fire can come in the monotone reading of a sermon, as with Jonathan Edwards. It can come in inexplicable loudness, preaching to 50,000 people in the open fields of England, as with George Whitfield. It can also come without words at all—in the unsettling, conviction-filled eye contact of Charles Finney—bringing people to tears and repentance before the Lord. But neither volume nor vigor can be substitutes for the fire of the Most High God which *you* bring down from *His* holy mountain.

This fire can be delivered in the break room or the boardroom, from the street corner, or from the seat corner. This fire is for every Christian because every Christian is called to preach the gospel. If you carry the fire of God down His mountain, you will lay it against the combustible debris of the Devil, and his kingdom will be conquered in the wake of holy fury.

I have found that to really get the fire of God, we mustn't just *ask* for fire. We must go into the fiery furnace of the Holy of Holies and work beside the Master Craftsman in forging Christ into the lives of His precious people through intercessory prayer. When we go beside Him in this great work, our passion for the gospel grows, our ability to communicate the gospel in the power and authority of the Holy Spirit grows, and our fears burn away in His holy flames. There is nowhere else to get *this* fire but from the Fire Himself, and He dwells high on a smoldering mountain, deep in the furnace of His temple.

Many who've taught on prayer have asserted that prayer doesn't change the immutable God; it changes us. Yes, it changes us from flesh-bound, self-interested, autocratic, traitorous sinners into co-laborers with Christ. Being near the Consuming Fire lights us on fire and gets us moving with Him. He isn't waiting for sinful people to talk Him into doing something. He's always working. He is waiting for us to get close enough to Him that we are changed by fire, made capable of carrying fire, and able to walk through the fires of earth because we have stood before Fire in heaven.

This fire fans our gifts into flame and outfits us for works of ministry. This fire cripples demons and melts iron shackles, setting men free from captivity. It is this fire that lights upon our heads just before we go out to tell the world:

> Repent and be baptized, every one of you, in the name of Jesus Christ for the forgiveness of your sins. And you will receive the gift of the Holy Spirit. The promise is for you and your children and for all who are far off—for all whom the Lord our God will call. (Acts 2:38-39)

Fire Tests Our Work for the Lord

When our work is born in the fire of God, it will endure the testing of the fire of God. One day each of us will arrive before the fiery throne of Elohim, and the work we did for the gospel will be tested. If we did none, we will have no reward. If we did poorly, we will have no reward. If this sounds like works, it is. You are called to do good works that were prepared in advance for you to *do* (see Ephesians 2:10). Don't let someone's freedom fantasy free you from the truth and imprison you in laziness.

The fiery throne of the Holy God will reveal whether our work was born in the fiery furnace of the Holy of Holies. Work born in the fiery furnace of the throne room will endure the fiery test of the throne room. It will reveal if our work was the fruit of our own imaginations and ambitions, or if it was driven by the fear of the Lord found in the temple of the Lord. It will reveal whether our work was empowered by the Holy Spirit of God and His fire or the unholy spirit of man and his fraud. The Apostle Paul put it like this:

Now he who plants and he who waters are one, but each will receive his own reward according to his own labor. For we are God's fellow workers; you are God's field, God's building. According to the grace of God which was given to me, like a wise master builder I laid a foundation and another building on it. But each man must be careful how he builds on it. For no man can lay a foundation other than the one which is laid, which is Jesus Christ. Now, if any man builds on the foundation with gold, silver, precious stones, wood, hay, or straw, each man's work will become evident; for the day will show it because it is to be revealed with fire, and the fire itself will test the quality of each man's work. If any man's work which he has built on it remains, he will receive a reward. If any man's work is burned up, he will suffer loss; but he himself will be saved, yet so as though fire. (1 Corinthians 3:8-15)

Jesus is after quality. He is not interested in lowering standards and making the narrow path wider. He wants the truth to pierce our souls, sanctify us, and empower us. He does not guarantee that we will do excellent work simply because *He* did excellent work. We are not promised that we will bear fruit because *He* bore fruit. We are not promised that we will endure hardship and *not* fall away. Many *will* fall away. Fire now will cost much, but fire in the end will cost all. We must pay this price and be engulfed in heavenly fire.

Jesus has called us into the furnace to be transformed by His divine flame, but we must answer the call. This call leads us to deny ourselves and be crucified. This call leads us to be hated by the world, persecuted by our families, and abandoned by our friends. This call leads us to give all we possess, leave all we love, and live all we are for Him. We are not among those who believe a materialistic, wealth-loving, comfort-cradled culture is the blessing of God, no—these things are circumstantial and foreign to the culture of heaven. These things are temporal, but we are fixed on what is eternal (see 2 Corinthians 4:18). God's blessing is fire, and His fire will consume all things that are not forged in His furnace.

Fire Enhances the Fear of the Lord

When you draw near to a campfire, it doesn't matter if you are Lutheran or Catholic, Baptist or Pentecostal; you will feel the heat. The variation in your doctrinal marginality will become even more marginal, and you will feel the fire when you get close to the Consuming Fire. His promise is for all believers, "draw near to God, and He will draw near to you" (James 4:8). What must it feel like to be near this fire? Some burn hot and quietly, while others dance like David did, but no one near the Consuming Fire can escape His heat.

Fire for God is not to end with only excitement or euphoria. It may produce excitement and euphoria, but fire from God is much deeper than this. The fire of God has as its primary function the production and increase of the fear of the Lord in the heart of the believer. The fear of the Lord is the revelation of God *to* us by the Holy Spirit, resulting in a transformation *in* us. We can see with our hearts, God, high and exalted, and we fall in love with Him. This love has as its counterpart hatred for evil. Jesus delighted in this and maintained it (see Isaiah 11:2).

When you have come into the Holy of Holies, you have also come through the gate in humility, into the courts in praise, over the altar in surrender, and into the Holy Place in pursuit of deep communion with the Holy Spirit. These things get the fire burning, but the Holy of Holies is the furnace seven times hotter. It is where gold is refined, where iron becomes steel, and where dross is taken from silver.

By interacting with the Holy Spirit in His fundamental operation of intercession with Christ, you will change. You will come away from this place hot for God and cold to the world, alive in Christ and dead to yourself, burning for the Kingdom of Light and shining in the kingdom of darkness.

It is no doubt that God's primary objective is for His people to fear him. However, until you get near to the Consuming Fire, you might strut around claiming to be His buddy. You might state with a brazen face the words of Luke Skywalker, "I'm not afraid." But when you get near Fire on the Mountain, you will undoubtedly remember Yoda's reply to arrogant Luke, "You will be, You will be!"

This is not fear of judgment. People who fear judgment do not fear the Judge. We have no need to fear the day of judgment if we live our days in the fear of the Judge. This is because we understand and have experienced the Love of God. The method for understanding God's love for us is not to embrace sinful living as an unavoidable factor in our nature, justifying our folly with, "well, God loves me anyway." This only breeds cold distance, a sense of abandonment, and fear of judgment.

The means whereby one may be absolutely consumed by the Love of God is to be engulfed in His flames. Heavenly fire and heavenly love are inseparable because they are the constitution of God's nature. We humans are combustible. Get near the Fire, and it will catch on, burning up any misconstrued ideas of love and filling your soul with the Love of God.

> God is love; whoever lives in love lives in God, and God in him. In this way, love is made complete among us so that we will have confidence on the day of judgment because, in this world, we are like him. There is no fear in love. But perfect love drives out fear because fear has to do with punishment. The one who fears is not made perfect in love. 1 John 4:16-18

The fear of the Lord begins with an accurate vision of the Lord. If one's only view of God is that He is a friend, they may think of patting him on the back as they offer a smug thank you, like when a friend picks up the tab at Taco Bell. But, though Christ has a vision of friendship—under the priority of Lordship—we must realize that He is God, seated on the throne. When we have a vision as Isaiah had when he saw the Lord high and lifted up, we will come to fear Him. This can be no better described than in the word of Henry Scougal:

> And when we have framed unto ourselves the clearest notion that we can of a Being, infinite in power, in wisdom, and goodness, the author and fountain of all perfections, let us fix the eyes of our souls upon it, that our eyes may affect our hearts, and while we are musing, the fire will burn. (Scougal, The Life of God in the Soul of Man)

The fear of the Lord is broad in its definition, and although it is often positioned as something other than terror or fright, it's unlikely that anyone who is near to the Lord would find these completely absent. "It is a dreadful thing to fall into the hands of the Living God" (Hebrews 10:31). The fear of the Lord begins with acknowledging who God is, which is frightening in many respects. For this reason, humility makes a lot of sense. Bowing low before Him and crying out for mercy are simply byproducts of the fear of the Lord. We need to get near to the fire of God for many reasons, but none is more critical than for the fear of the Lord. If we do not take this away with us, our work will not stand.

For this reason, the fear of the Lord is best described with two functional dynamics. First, awe and reverence for who God is. Don't underestimate awe and reverence; you are not looking at a lofty 200-year-old cathedral. Awe and reverence for God may have you weeping and trembling. It is impossible to imagine to any accurate extent what God is like, but to the extent that we draw near to Him, we will find ourselves baffled by His immensity and beauty.

The second dynamic of the Fear of the Lord is to hate what is evil. This is essential to the nature of God, and it is passed into our nature by His fire. We don't only decide to hate evil; we become hatred for evil by His transforming power. Although the will is engaged in turning away from evil, it is a change in our constitution that brings forth the hatred of evil—a literal sickness at the thought of it. Fire does this work.

Many have failed to discern between good and evil, choosing corrupt ways and justifying them by their own reasoning. Blindness and self-love persist amidst will-powered morality, and failure is inevitable. When the will is engaged in the singular objective to position the heart before the Flame of heaven, it has done its duty. Here, in the furnace of His holiness, iron-ore is transformed into sharpened steel.

Some people embrace sin due to a failure in the interpretation of Scripture, but all people embrace sin due to a failure to possess the fear of the Lord. Interpretation of Scripture is given to man as a duty before God, who wants us to be diligent and unashamed, "accurately handling the Word of Truth" (2 Timothy 2:15). It is an ignorant and unstable people who distort the Scriptures, and this to their own destruction, according to Peter (See 2 Peter 3:16). But the fear of the Lord does not produce ignorance nor instability; in fact, "The fear of the Lord is the beginning of wisdom, and the knowledge of the Holy One is understanding" (Proverbs 9:10).

People who do not burn with God's holy fire will invariably interpret Scripture loosely enough to afford themselves a moral latitude that suits their appetites. This is the behavior of those who are foreigners to the Holy of Holies, a people who are distant from God, who know nothing of His table, whose lamp is extinguished, whose altar is bare, whose courts are silent, and whose gate lies in ruins.

If you come away from time spent in God's presence and don't have a greater sense of awe for His nature and a greater hatred for evil, you might not have been interacting with Him at all. If you don't sense a struggle in your flesh, you are not near enough to the flame; if you do not feel your human nature crumpling under the weight of His fiery, fierce glory, you are not near enough to the heat of His power. A part of you will hate burning for God; this part of you should always be traveling toward Golgotha, if not already suspended on a cross. Your flesh is at war with God; in fact, the thoughts of the sinful mind are hostile toward God. But the weapon that will crucify it is His holy flame.

This is why it is important to offer your worship and prayers in an attitude that reflects the Majesty and Glory of God. Fear and trembling are befitting to the beholder of the Burning God. Humility is hope when facing a Fire that would consume us if not for borrowed merit. We don't deserve to be clothed in the righteousness of Christ, yet He extends this to us if we would place our faith in Him.

Our Blazing Mountain

Moses climbed a mountain in the physical world that we must climb in the heavenly. He saw but a glimpse and experienced but a fraction of what is available to us through Christ, and look at how it impacted him:

> For you have not come to a mountain that can be touched and to a blazing fire, and to darkness and gloom and whirlwind, and the blast of a trumpet and the sound of words which sound was such that those who heard begged that no further word be spoken to them. For they could not bear the command, "If even a beast touches the mountain it will be stoned." And so terrible was the sight that Moses said, "I am full of fear and trembling." (Hebrews 12:18-21)

Again, we are not climbing Moses' mountain. Ours is a much better climb, one that burns with a fire not of this world—a hotter, holier, heavenly fire, shut up in the bones of God Himself. Ours is a mountain where mercy triumphs over judgment, one where wrath is satisfied by the blood of Christ, a mountain on which God is approachable, where worship is the weather and joy is the climate, where Jesus is the resurrected and enthroned Lamb of God:

> But you have come to Mount Zion and to the city of the living God, the heavenly Jerusalem, and to myriads of angels, to the general assembly and church of the firstborn who are enrolled in heaven, and to God, the Judge of all, and to the spirits of the righteous made perfect, and to Jesus the mediator of a new covenant, and to the sprinkled blood, which speaks better than the blood of Abel. (Hebrews 12:22-24)

And thus mountaineering in the Kingdom of Heaven is for the exact same purpose: *to find a revealed God and learn to know, obey, and worship Him in trembling and fear.* But for us a veil has been removed and a curtain has been torn open. By passing beyond that veil, we can now, while on earth—and hereafter glowing into eternity—fearlessly facilitate, by the covenant of Christ, a voracious appetite for intimate and infinite connectedness to the very Person who is fire.

> Therefore, since we are receiving a kingdom that cannot be shaken, let us be thankful and so worship God acceptably with reverence and awe, for our God is a consuming fire. (Hebrews 12:28-29)

Conclusion and Contemplation

God is a fire, and we must burn with Him. Fellowship with Fire is fundamentally and elementally transformative. Will you draw near to the Flame of God and burn for Him?

Prayer of Commitment

Father, I want to be baptized in fire. Lead me into Your furnace and set me ablaze! Burn away the chaff in my soul and bring me into a more suitable commitment and maturity in my faith and love for You. Purify my heart, O Lord, with Your holy heat. Fill my heart with Your fire as I pray, as I share my faith, and as I serve my community and church. Let me live in a state of burning passion for the gospel and for the Savior who died for me. Take me up Your mountain and into Your furnace and fit me to carry Your flame to the nations. Amen.

Study Questions

1. What is the primary function of the fire of God? What other purposes does the fire of God serve in the believer?
2. Some have said that the fear of the Lord is not being "afraid" of God. Do you agree with this? Are there reasons we should tremble before God?
3. Describe the fear of the Lord? What else does it mean other than to be afraid?
4. Will our works be judged? Is it important how we work for the Lord?
5. What can ensure that our works will endure the testing of God's fire?

6. Is the fire of God emotions and demonstrative behavior? Does it sometimes produce these things?
7. How can the fire of God help you in your life and ministry?

BIBLIOGRAPHY

1. Bain, Ryan. *Anthem of Awakening.* Bain Management Group, 2015.

2. Bayly, Alfred F. *Fire of God Thou Sacred Flame.* Oxford University Press, 1988.

3. www.history.com "Germany Surrenders Unconditionally to the Allies At Reims." History. A&E Television Networks. November 5, 2009.

4. Bonhoeffer, Dietrich. *The Cost of Discipleship.* Touchstone. New York, 1959.

5. Bounds, E.M. *The Essentials of Prayer.* Whitaker House. New Kensington, 1994.

6. Bounds, E. M. *Power Through Prayer.* Whitaker House. New Kensington, 2005.

7. Brennan, Pat. "Our Milky Way Galaxy: How Big is Space?" *Exoplanet Exploration: Planets Beyond Our Solar System.* April 2, 2019. exoplanets.nasa.gov/blog/1563/our-milky-way-galaxy-how-big-is-space/

8. Bunyon, John. *The Pilgrim's Progress: From This World to That Which Is to Come.* Philadelphia; Chicago: S.I., 1891.

9. Cawein, Madison. *The Poetry of Madison Cawein: Volume 3.* N.p., Outlook Verlag, 2019.

10. Cho, Dr. Yonggi. Goodall, Wayne. *Prayer: Key to Revival.* Broadstreet Publishing Group. Savage, 2019.

11. Crane, Stephen. Katz, Joseph. *The Poems of Stephen Crane.* Cooper Square Publishers. New York, 1966.

12. Dallimore, Arnold A. *George Whitefield: God's Anointed Servant in the Great Revival of the Eighteenth Century.* Crossway. Wheaton, 1990.

13. Edersheim, Alfred. *The Temple: Its Ministries and Services.* Hendrickson Publishers. Peabody, 1994.

14. Finney, Charles. *Lectures on Revivals of Religion: The Prayer of Faith.* Oberlin College, 1868.

15. Finney, Charles. *The Autobiography of Charles G. Finney.* Bethany House. Minneapolis, 1977.

16. Foster, Richard. *The Celebration of Discipline.* Harper & Row. New York. 1988.

17. Frangipane, Francis. *Holiness, Truth, and the Presence of God.* Morning Star Publications. Charlotte, 1993.

18. Graham, Billy. *Just As I Am: The Autobiography of Billy Graham.* Harper Collins. New York, 1997.

19. Grubb, Norman. *Rees Howells: Intercessor.* Lutterworth Publishing. Fort Washington, 1952.

20. Gould, Hannah Flagg. *The Mother's Dream and Other Poems.* The United States. Crosby, Nichols & Company, 1853.

21. International Bible Society. *The Holy Bible New International Version.* Zondervan. Grand Rapids, 1996.

22. Jobe, Kari. "First Love." *The Blessing Live.* Sparrow, 2020.

23. Kennedy, Gerald. *The Best of John Henry Jowett*. New York. Harper & Brothers, 1948.

24. Law, William. *A Serious Call to a Devout and Holy Life*. Macmillan and Co. London, 1898.

25. Lewis, Meriwether. *The Journals of Lewis and Clark*. National Geographic. Washington, 2002.

26. Longfellow, Henry Wadsworth. *Poems and Other Writings*. Literary Classics of the United States, Inc. New York, 2000.

27. MacArthur, John. Thomas, Derek W. H. *The Inerrant Word: Biblical, Historical, Theological and Pastoral Perspectives*. Crossway. Wheaton, 2016.

28. Maslow, A.H. *Motivation and Personality*. The United States. Harper & Row, 1954.

29. Martinez, Gabriel. "Home." *Circleslide, Uncommon Days*. Centricity Music, 2006.

30. McDowell, Josh. *The New Evidence That Demands a Verdict*. Thomas Nelson Publishing, Nashville, 1999.

31. McFadden, Christopher. "The Gargantuan Antonov AN-225: The World's Largest Cargo Plane." www.interestingengineering.com. March 1, 2021

32. Murray, Andrew. *Absolute Surrender*. Martino Publishing. Mansfield Center, 2011.

33. New American Standard Bible®, Copyright © 1960, 1971, 1977, 1995, 2020 by The Lockman Foundation.

34. Powell, Doug. *Holman Quicksource Guide to Christian Apologetics*. Holman Reference. Nashville, 2006.

35. Pratney, Winkie. *Fire on the Horizon*. Renew Books. Ventura, 1999.

36. Pratney, Winkie. *The Nature and Character of God*. Bethany House. Minneapolis, 1988

37. Ravenhill, Leonard. *Why Revival Tarries*. Bethany House. Bloomington, 1987

38. Ryle, J. C. *Holiness: It's Nature, Hindrances, Difficulties, and Roots*. Moody. Chicago, 2010.

39. Ryan, Sally. "Marx to Lasalle in Berlin." www.marxists.org

40. Schaeffer, Francis. *The Great Evangelical Disaster*. Crossway. Wheaton, 1995.

41. Scougal, Henry. *The Life of God in the Soul of Man*. Martino Publishing. Mansfield Center, 2010

42. Sheets, Dutch. *Intercessory Prayer*. Regal Books. Ventura, 1996.

43. Sterling, George. "Night On the Mountain." *The Complete Poetry of George Sterling*. Hippocampus Press, New York, 2013.

44. Strong, James. Strong's *Exhaustive Concordance of the Bible*. Thomas Nelson Publishing. Nashville, 1996.

45. Stuart Gets Lost. *MADtv*. Stuart Larkin. Season 4, Episode 3. September 19, 1998

46. Tozer, A. W. 1897-1963. *The Pursuit of God*. Harrisburg, Pa., Christian Publications, 1948

47. Thayer, Joseph H. *The New Thayer's Greek-English Lexicon of the New Testament*. Hendrickson. Peabody, 1981.

48. Walker-Smith, Kim. "Show Me Your Glory." *Come Away*. Jesus Culture, 2010.

ABOUT THE AUTHOR

Chris Wedin has been engaged in the ministries of worship, evangelism, and discipleship for over 30 years. He has travelled all over the world sharing the love of Christ, helping the poor, smuggling Bibles, and making disciples. During these quests, he delivered the Gospel to some of the most remote places on Earth.

Whether to the mountainous villages of Asia and Africa, or the distant indigenous communities of the Amazon, Chris has spent many hours trekking, climbing, and canoeing to share the love of Christ with those who've never heard.

He has spoken in conferences, colleges, and churches through out the United States, challenging believers toward a greater depth of love for Christ and His Great Commission.

Chris has a B.S. in Business Administration from Troy University and has years of experience in sales, retail management, and business leadership. He is enthusiastic and supportive of Christian entrepreneurship, because of the doors of opportunity to both share the Gospel in our own country and support the work of missions around the world.

Chris is an avid outdoor adventurer, mountain biker, snow-boarder, triathlete, and extreme sports enthusiast. He and his wife, Anne Marie, reside in Louisville Kentucky, from where they embark upon many adventures with their children, Asher and Asiah.

CONFERENCE

The Mountaineer Conference is a 9-15 hour conference (2-3 days) and covers the material in this book. Our hope is that by placing a high emphasis on the practical application of these truths, your community of believers will move into profound intimacy with Jesus and a high level of impact in your spheres of influence, both local and global.

To schedule Chris Wedin for *The Mountaineer Conference* or to come to speak to your church or group or you may use the contact information below:

chriswedin@gmail.com

STREAMS
OF MERCY

Bringing hope
to the hopeless.

We are caring for the most needy
around the world.

By purchasing *The Mountaineer: An Explorer's Guide to Summiting the Mountain of the Lord*, you have helped to feed, clothe, house, educate, and demonstrate the love of God to orphans all over the world. **100% of profits from this book will go to this cause: rescuing orphans.** If you would like to know more about how we are helping the helpless, please visit www.streamsofmercy.org. You can be an ongoing participant in one of the worlds greatest rescue operations!

Thanks again!

Chris

CPSIA information can be obtained
at www.ICGtesting.com
Printed in the USA
LVHW011639060822
725289LV00002B/3

9 781662 853234